Third Edition

TEACHER'S GUIDE

Betty Schrampfer Azar
Barbara F. Matthies
Shelley Hartle

Fundamentals of English Grammar, Third Edition
Teacher's Guide

Azar Associates
Shelley Hartle, Editor
Susan Van Etten, Manager

Pearson Education, 10 Bank Street, White Plains, NY 10606

Vice president of instructional design: Allen Ascher
Editorial manager: Pam Fishman
Project manager: Margo Grant
Development editor: Janet Johnston
Vice president, director of design and production: Rhea Banker
Director of electronic production: Aliza Greenblatt
Executive managing editor: Linda Moser
Production manager: Ray Keating
Production editor: Robert Ruvo
Director of manufacturing: Patrice Fraccio
Senior manufacturing buyer: Edie Pullman
Cover design: Monika Popowitz
Text composition: Carlisle Communications, Ltd.
Text font: 10.5/12 Plantin

ISBN: 0-13-013634-4

Printed in the United States of America
2 3 4 5 6 7 8 9 10–CRK–06 05 04 03

Contents

Preface

This *Teacher's Guide* is intended as a practical aid to teachers. You can turn to it for notes on the content of a unit and how to approach the exercises, for suggestions for classroom activities, and for answers to the exercises.

General teaching information can be found in the *Introduction*. It includes:

- the rationale and general aims of *Fundamentals of English Grammar*
- the classroom techniques for presenting charts and using exercises
- suggestions on the use of the *Workbook* in connection with the main text
- supplementary resource texts
- comments on differences between American and British English
- a key to the pronunciation symbols used in this *Guide*

The rest of the *Guide* contains notes on charts and exercises. The notes about the charts may include:

- suggestions for presenting the information to students
- points to emphasize
- common problems to anticipate
- assumptions underlying the contents
- additional background notes on grammar and usage

The notes that accompany the exercises may include:

- the focus of the exercise
- suggested techniques as outlined in the introduction
- possible specialized techniques for particular exercises
- points to emphasize
- problems to anticipate
- assumptions
- answers
- expansion activities
- item notes on cultural content, vocabulary, and idiomatic usage (Some of these item notes are specifically intended to aid any teachers who are non-native speakers of English.)

General Aims of *Fundamentals of English Grammar*

The principal aims of *Fundamentals of English Grammar* are to present clear, cogent information about English grammar and usage, to provide extensive and varied practice that encourages growth in all areas of language use, and to be interesting, useful, and fun for student and teacher alike. The approach is eclectic, seeking to balance form-focused language-learning activities with abundant opportunities for engaged and purposeful communicative interaction.

Most students find it helpful to have special time set aside in their English curriculum to focus on grammar. Students generally have many questions about English grammar and appreciate the opportunity to work with a text and teacher to make some sense out of the bewildering array of forms and usages in this strange language. This understanding provides the basis for advances in usage ability in a relaxed, accepting classroom that encourages risk-taking as the students experiment, both in speaking and writing, with ways to communicate their ideas in a new language.

Teaching grammar does not mean lecturing on grammatical patterns and terminology. It does not mean bestowing knowledge and being an arbiter of correctness. Teaching grammar is the art of helping students make sense, little by little, of a huge, puzzling construct, and engaging them in various activities that enhance usage abilities in all skill areas and promote easy, confident communication.

The text depends upon a partnership with a teacher; it is the teacher who animates and directs the students' language-learning experiences. In practical terms, the aim of the text is to support you, the teacher, by providing a wealth and variety of material for you to adapt to your individual teaching situation. Using grammar as a base to promote overall English usage ability, teacher and text can engage the students in interesting discourse, challenge their minds and skills, and intrigue them with the power of language as well as the need for accuracy to create understanding among people.

Classroom Techniques

Following are some techniques that have proven useful.

- *Suggestions for Presenting the Grammar Charts* are discussed first.
- Next are some notes on interactivity: *Degrees of Teacher and Student Involvement.*
- Then *Techniques for Exercise Types* are outlined.

• Suggestions for Presenting the Grammar Charts

A chart is a concise visual presentation of the structures to be learned in one section of a chapter. Some charts may require particular methods of presentation, but generally any of the following techniques are viable.

Presentation techniques often depend upon the content of the chart, the level of the class, and the students' learning styles. Not all students react to the charts in the same way. Some students need the security of thoroughly understanding a chart before trying to use the structure. Others like to experiment more freely with using new structures; they refer to the charts only incidentally, if at all.

Given these different learning strategies, you should vary your presentation techniques and not expect students to "learn" or memorize the charts. The charts are just a starting point for class activities and a point of reference.

Technique #1: Use the examples in the chart, add your own examples to explain the grammar in your own words, and answer any questions about the chart. Elicit other examples of the target structure from the learners. Then go to the accompanying exercise immediately following the chart.

Technique #2: Elicit oral examples from the students before they look at the chart in the textbook. To elicit examples, ask leading questions whose answers will include the target structure. (For example, for the present progressive, ask: "What are you doing right now?") You may want to write the elicited answers on the board and relate them to the examples in the chart. Then proceed to the exercises.

Technique #3: Assign the chart and accompanying exercise(s) for out-of-class study. In class the next day, ask for and answer any questions about the chart, and then immediately proceed to the exercises. (With advanced students, you might not need to deal thoroughly with every chart and exercise in class. With intermediate students, it is generally advisable to clarify charts and do most of the exercises.)

Technique #4: Lead the students through the first accompanying exercise PRIOR to discussing the chart. Use the material in the exercise to discuss the focus of the chart as you go along. At the end of the exercise, call attention to the examples in the chart and summarize what was discussed during the exercise.

Technique #5: Before presenting the chart in class, give the students a short written quiz on its content. Have the students correct their own papers as you review the answers. The quiz should not be given a score; it is a learning tool, not an examination. Use the items from the quiz as examples for discussing the grammar in the chart.

The here-and-now classroom context: For every chart, try to relate the target structure to an immediate classroom or "real-life" context. Make up or elicit examples that use the students' names, activities, and interests. The here-and-now classroom context is, of course, one of the grammar teacher's best aids.

Demonstration techniques: Demonstration can be very helpful to explain the meaning of structures. You and the students can act out situations that demonstrate the target structure. Of course, not all grammar lends itself to this technique. For example, the present progressive can easily be demonstrated (e.g., "I *am writing* on the board right now"). However, using gerunds as the objects of prepositions (e.g., "instead *of writing*" or "thank you *for writing*") is not especially well suited to demonstration techniques.

Using the chalkboard: In discussing the target structure of a chart, use the chalkboard whenever possible. Not all students have adequate listening skills for "teacher talk," and not all students can visualize and understand the various relationships within, between, and among structures. Draw boxes and circles and arrows to illustrate connections between the elements of a structure. A visual presentation helps many students.

Oral exercises in conjunction with chart presentations: Oral exercises usually follow a chart, but sometimes they precede it so that you can elicit student-generated examples of the target structure as a springboard to the discussion of the grammar. If you prefer to introduce any particular structure to your students orally, you can always use an oral exercise prior to the presentation of a chart and written exercises, no matter what the given order is in the textbook.

The role of terminology: The students need to understand the terminology, but don't require or expect detailed definitions of terms, either in class discussion or on tests. Terminology is just a tool, a useful label for the moment, so that you and the students can talk to each other about English grammar.

• Degrees of Teacher and Student Involvement

The goal of all language learning is to understand and communicate. The teacher's main task is to direct and facilitate that process. The learner is an active participant, not merely a passive receiver of rules to be memorized. Therefore, many of the exercises in the text are designed to promote interaction between learners as a bridge to real communication.

The teacher has a crucial leadership role, with "teacher talk" a valuable and necessary part of a grammar classroom. Sometimes you will need to spend time clarifying the information in a chart, leading an exercise, answering questions about exercise items, or explaining an assignment. These periods of "teacher talk" should always be balanced by longer periods of productive learning activity when the students are doing most of the talking. It is important for the teacher to know when to step back and let the students lead. Interactive group and pair work play an important role in the language classroom.

INTERACTIVE GROUP AND PAIR WORK

Many of the exercises in this text are formatted for group or pair work. The third edition of *FEG* has many more exercises explicitly set up for interactive work than the previous edition had. Interactive exercises may take more class time than would teacher-led exercises, but it is time well spent, for there are many advantages to student–student practice.

When the students are working in groups or pairs, their opportunities to use what they are learning are greatly increased. In interactive work, the time they spend actually using English is many times greater than in a teacher-centered activity. Obviously, the students in group or pair work are often much more active and involved than in teacher-led exercises.

Group and pair work also expand the students' opportunities to practice many communication skills at the same time that they are practicing target structures. In peer interaction in the classroom, the students have to agree, disagree, continue a conversation, make suggestions, promote cooperation, make requests, be sensitive to each other's needs and personalities — the kinds of exchanges that are characteristic of any group communication in the classroom or elsewhere.

Students will often help and explain things to each other during pair work, in which case both students benefit greatly. Ideally, students in interactive activities are "partners in exploration." Together they go into new areas and discover things about English usage, supporting each other as they proceed.

Group and pair work help to produce a comfortable learning environment. In teacher-centered activities, students may sometimes feel shy and inhibited or even experience stress. They may feel that they have to respond quickly and accurately and that *what* they say is not as important as *how* they say it — even though you strive to convince them to the contrary. When you set up groups or pairs that are non-competitive and cooperative, the students usually tend to help, encourage, and even joke with each other. This encourages them to experiment with the language and speak more.

MONITORING ERRORS IN INTERACTIVE WORK

Students should be encouraged to monitor each other to some extent in interactive work, especially when monitoring activities are specifically assigned. (Perhaps you should remind them to give some *positive* as well as corrective comments to each other.) You shouldn't worry about "losing control" of the students' language production; not every mistake needs to be corrected. Mistakes are a natural part of learning a new language. As students gain experience and familiarity with a structure, their mistakes in using it begin to diminish.

And the students shouldn't worry that they will learn each other's mistakes. Being exposed to imperfect English in this kind of interactive work in the classroom is not going to impede their progress in the slightest. In today's world, with so many people using English as a second language, students will likely be exposed to all levels of proficiency in people with whom they interact in English, from airline reservation clerks to new neighbors from a different land to a co-worker whose native language is not English. Encountering imperfect English is not going to diminish their own English language abilities, either now in the classroom or later in different English-speaking situations.

Make yourself available to answer questions about correct answers during group and pair work. If you wish, you can take some time at the end of an exercise to call attention to mistakes that you heard as you monitored the groups. Another possible way of correcting errors is to have copies of the *Answer Key* available in the classroom so that students can look up their own answers when they need to.

• Techniques for Exercise Types

The majority of the exercises in the text require some sort of completion, transformation, combination, discussion of meaning, or a combination of such activities. They range from those that are tightly controlled and manipulative to those that encourage free responses and require creative, independent language use. The techniques vary according to the exercise type.

FILL-IN-THE-BLANKS AND CONTROLLED COMPLETION EXERCISES

The term "fill-in-the-blanks" describes exercises in which the students complete the sentences by using words given in parentheses. The term "controlled completion" describes exercises in which the students complete sentences using the words in a given list. Both types of exercises call for similar techniques.

Technique A: Ask a student to read an item aloud. You can say whether the student's answer is correct or not, or you can open up discussion by asking the rest of the class if the answer is correct. For example:

TEACHER: Juan, would you please read Number 3?
STUDENT: Ali *speaks* Arabic.
TEACHER (to the class): Do the rest of you agree with Juan's answer?

The slow-moving pace of this method is beneficial for discussion not only of grammar items but also of vocabulary and content. The students have time to digest information and ask questions. You have the opportunity to judge how well they understand the grammar.

However, this time-consuming technique doesn't always, or even usually, need to be used, especially with more advanced classes.

Technique B: You, the teacher, read the first part of the item, then pause for the students to call out the answer in unison. For example:

> TEXT entry: "Ali *(speak)* _____ Arabic."
> TEACHER (with the students looking at their texts): Ali . . . .
> STUDENTS (in unison): speaks (plus possibly a few incorrect responses scattered about)
> TEACHER: . . . speaks Arabic. *Speaks.* Do you have any questions?

This technique saves a lot of time in class, but is also slow-paced enough to allow for questions and discussion of grammar, vocabulary, and content. It is essential that the students have prepared the exercise by writing in their books, so it must be assigned ahead of time as homework.

Technique C: With a more advanced class for whom a particular exercise is little more than a quick review, you can simply give the answers so the students can correct their own previously prepared work in their textbooks. You can either read the whole sentence ("Number 2: Ali speaks Arabic.") or just give the answer ("Number 2: speaks"). You can give the answers to the items one at a time, taking questions as they arise, or give the answers to the whole exercise before opening it up for questions. As an alternative, you can have one of the students read his/her answers and have the other students ask him/her questions if they disagree.

Technique D: Divide the class into groups (or pairs) and have each group prepare one set of answers that they all agree is correct prior to class discussion. The leader of each group can present their answers.

Another option is to have the groups (or pairs) hand in their set of answers for correction and possibly a grade.

It's also possible to turn these exercises into games wherein the group with the best set of answers gets some sort of reward (perhaps applause from the rest of the class).

Of course, you can always mix Techniques A, B, C, and D — with the students reading some aloud, with you prompting unison response for some, with you simply giving the answers for others, with the students collaborating on the answers for others. Much depends on the level of the class, their familiarity and skill with the grammar at hand, their oral-aural skills in general, and the flexibility or limitations of class time.

Technique E: When an exercise item has a dialogue between two speakers, A and B, ask one student to be A and another B and have them read the entry aloud. Occasionally, say to A and B: "Without looking at your text, what did you just say to each other?" (If necessary, let them glance briefly at their texts before they repeat what they've just said in the exercise item.) The students may be pleasantly surprised by their own fluency.

OPEN COMPLETION EXERCISES

The term "open completion" describes exercises in which the students use their own words to complete the sentences.

Technique A: Exercises where the students must supply their own words to complete a sentence should usually be assigned for out-of-class preparation. Then in class, one, two, or several students can read their sentences aloud; the class can discuss the correctness and appropriateness of the completions. Perhaps you can suggest possible ways of rephrasing to make a sentence more idiomatic. Students who don't read their sentences aloud can revise their own completions based on what is being discussed in class.

At the end of the exercise discussion, you can tell the students to hand in their sentences for you to look at, or simply ask if anyone has questions about the exercise and not have the students submit anything to you.

Technique B: If you wish to use an open completion exercise in class without having previously assigned it, you can turn the exercise into a brainstorming session in which students try out several completions to see if they work. As another possibility, you may wish to divide the students into small groups and have each group come up with completions that they all agree are correct and appropriate. Then use only these completions for class discussion or as written work to be handed in.

Technique C: Some open completion exercises are designated WRITTEN, which usually means the students need to use their own paper, as not enough space has been left in the textbook. It is often beneficial to use the following progression: (1) assign the exercise for out-of-class preparation; (2) discuss it in class the next day, having the students make corrections on their own papers based on what they are learning from discussing other students' completions; (3) then ask the students to submit their papers to you, either as a requirement or on a volunteer basis.

TRANSFORMATION AND COMBINATION EXERCISES

In transformation exercises, the students are asked to change form but not substance (e.g., to change the active to the passive, a clause to a phrase, a question to a noun clause, etc.).

In combination exercises, the students are asked to combine two or more sentences or ideas into one sentence that contains a particular structure (e.g., an adjective clause, a parallel structure, a gerund phrase, etc.).

In general, these exercises, which require manipulation of a form, are intended for class discussion of the form and meaning of a structure. The initial stages of such exercises are a good opportunity to use the chalkboard to draw circles and arrows to illustrate the characteristics and relationships of a structure. Students can read their answers aloud to initiate the class discussion, and you can write on the board as problems arise. Another possibility is to have the students write their sentences on the board. Also possible is to have them work in small groups to agree upon their answers prior to class discussion.

ORAL EXERCISES

The text has many interactive speaking–listening exercises. Often the directions will say "Work in pairs, in groups, or as a class."

For pair work exercises, tell the student whose book is open that s/he is the teacher and needs to listen carefully to the other's responses. Vary the ways in which the students are paired up, ranging from having them choose their own partners to drawing names or numbers from a hat. Roam the room and answer questions as needed.

For group work exercises, the students can take turns being group leader, or one student can lead the entire exercise. The group can answer individually or chorally, depending on the type of exercise. Vary the ways in which you divide the students into groups and choose leaders.

If you use an oral exercise as a teacher-led exercise:

a. You, the teacher, take the role of Speaker A. (You can always choose to lead an oral exercise, even when the directions specifically call for pair work; treat exercise directions calling for pair or group work as suggestions, not as iron-clad instructions for teaching techniques.)

b. You need not read the items aloud as if they were a script from which you should not deviate. Modify or add items spontaneously as they occur to you. Change the items in any way you can to make them more relevant for your students. (For example, if you know that some students plan to watch the World Cup soccer match on TV soon, include a sentence about that.) Omit irrelevant items.
c. Sometimes an item will start a spontaneous discussion of, for example, local restaurants or current movies or certain experiences the students have had. These spur-of-the-moment dialogues are very beneficial to the students. Being able to create and encourage such interactions is one of the chief advantages of a teacher-led oral exercise.

WRITING EXERCISES

Some writing exercises require sentence completion, but most are designed to produce short, informal compositions. In general, the topics or tasks concern aspects of the students' lives in order to encourage free and relatively effortless communication as they practice their writing skills. While a course in English rhetoric is beyond the scope of this text, many of the basic elements are included and may be developed and emphasized according to your purposes.

For best results, whenever you give a writing assignment, let your students know what you expect: "This is what I suggest as content. This is how you might organize it. This is how long I expect it to be." If at all possible, give your students composition models, perhaps taken from good compositions written by previous classes, perhaps written by you, perhaps composed as a group activity by the class as a whole (e.g., you write on the board what the students tell you to write, and then you and the students revise it together).

In general, writing exercises should be done outside of class. All of us need time to consider and revise when we write. And if we get a little help here and there, that's not unusual. The topics in the exercises are structured so that plagiarism should not be a problem. Use in-class writing if you want to appraise the students' unaided, spontaneous writing skills. Tell your students that these writing exercises are simply for practice and that — even though they should always try to do their best — any mistakes they make should be viewed simply as tools for learning.

Encourage the students to use their dictionaries whenever they write. Point out that you yourself never write seriously without a dictionary at hand. Discuss the use of margins, indentation of paragraphs, and other aspects of the format of a well-written paper.

ERROR-ANALYSIS EXERCISES

For the most part, the sentences in this type of exercise have been adapted from actual student writing and contain typical errors. Error-analysis exercises focus on the target structures of a chapter but may also contain miscellaneous errors that are common in student writing at this level, e.g., final *-s* on plural nouns or capitalization of proper nouns. The purpose of including them is to sharpen the students' self-monitoring skills.

Error-analysis exercises are challenging and fun, a good way to summarize the grammar in a unit. If you wish, tell the students they are either newspaper editors or English teachers; their task is to locate all mistakes and write corrections. Point out that even native speakers — including you yourself — have to scrutinize, correct, and revise what they write. This is a natural part of the writing process.

The recommended technique is to assign an error-analysis exercise for in-class discussion the next day. The students benefit most from having the opportunity to find the errors themselves prior to class discussion. These exercises can, of course, be handled in other ways: as seatwork, written homework, group work, or pair work.

PREVIEW EXERCISES

The purpose of these exercises is to let the students discover what they do and do not know about the target structure in order to get them interested in a chart. Essentially, PREVIEW exercises illustrate a possible teaching technique: quiz the students first as a springboard for presenting the grammar in a chart.

Any exercise can be used as a preview. You do not need to follow the order of material in the text. Adapt the material to your own needs and techniques.

DISCUSSION-OF-MEANING EXERCISES

Some exercises consist primarily of you and the students discussing the meaning of given sentences. Most of these exercises ask the students to compare the meaning of two or more sentences (e.g., *Jack is talking on the phone* vs. *Jack talks on the phone a lot)*. One of the main purposes of discussion-of-meaning exercises is to provide an opportunity for summary comparison of the structures in a particular unit.

Basically, the technique in these exercises is for you to pose questions about the given sentences, then let the students explain what a structure means to them (which allows you to get input about what they do and do not understand). Then you summarize the salient points as necessary. Students have their own inventive, creative way of explaining differences in meaning. They shouldn't be expected to sound like grammar teachers. Often, all you need to do is listen very carefully and patiently to a student's explanation, and then clarify and reinforce it by rephrasing it somewhat.

GAMES AND ACTIVITIES

Games and activities are important parts of the grammar classroom. The study of grammar is and should be fun and engaging. Some exercises in the text and in this *Guide* are designated as "expansion" or "activity." They are meant to promote independent, active use of target structures.

When playing a game, the atmosphere should be relaxed, not competitive. The goal is clearly related to the chapter's content, and the reward is the students' satisfaction in using English to achieve the goal. (For additional class material, see *Fun with Grammar: Communicative Activities for the Azar Grammar Series,* by Suzanne W. Woodward, available as a photocopiable book from Longman [877-202-4572] or as downloads from **www.longman.com**).

PRONUNCIATION EXERCISES

A few exercises focus on pronunciation of grammatical features, such as endings on nouns or verbs and contracted or reduced forms.

Some phonetic symbols are used in these exercises to point out sounds that should not be pronounced identically; for example, /s/, /əz/, and /z/ represent the three predictable pronunciations of the grammatical suffix spelled *-s* or *-es.* It is not necessary for students to learn a complete phonetic alphabet; they should merely associate each symbol in an exercise with a sound that is different from all others. The purpose is to help students become more aware of these final sounds in the English they hear in order to promote proficiency in their own speaking and writing.

In the exercises on spoken contractions, the primary emphasis should be on the students' hearing and becoming familiar with spoken forms rather than on their production of these forms. The students need to understand that what they see in writing is not exactly what they should expect to hear in normal, rapidly spoken English. The most important part of most of these exercises is for the students to listen to your oral production and become familiar with the reduced forms.

Language learners are naturally conscious that their pronunciation is not like that of native speakers of the language. Therefore, some of them are embarrassed or shy about speaking. In a pronunciation exercise, they may be more comfortable if you ask groups or the whole class to say a sentence in unison. After that, individuals may volunteer to speak the same sentence. The learners' production does not need to be "perfect," just understandable. You can encourage the students to be less inhibited by having them teach you how to pronounce words in their languages (unless, of course, you're a native speaker of the students' language in a monolingual class). It's fun — and instructive — for the students to teach the teacher.

SEATWORK

It is generally preferable to assign exercises for out-of-class preparation, but sometimes it's necessary to cover an exercise in class that you haven't been able to assign previously. In "seatwork," you have the students do an unassigned exercise in class immediately before discussing it. Seatwork allows the students to try an exercise themselves before the answers are discussed so that they can discover what problems they may be having with a particular structure. Seatwork may be done individually, in pairs, or in groups.

HOMEWORK

The textbook assumes that the students will have the opportunity to prepare most of the exercises by writing in their books prior to class discussion. Students should be assigned this homework as a matter of course.

The term "written homework" in this *Guide* suggests that the students write out an exercise on their own paper and hand it in to you. How much written homework you assign is up to you. The amount generally depends upon such variables as class size, class level, available class time, your available paper-correcting time, not to mention your preferences in teaching techniques. Most of the exercises in the text can be handled through class discussion instead of the students' handing in written homework. Most of the written homework specified in the text and in the chapter notes in this *Guide* consists of activities that will produce original, independent writing.

Using the *Workbook*

The *Workbook* contains selfstudy exercises for independent study, with a perforated answer key found at the end of the book. Encourage your students to remove this answer key and put it in a folder. It's much easier for them to correct their own answers if they make their own answer key booklet.

If you prefer that the students not have the answers to the exercises, ask them to hand in the answer key at the beginning of the term. Some teachers may prefer to use the *Workbook* for in-class teaching rather than for independent study.

The *Workbook* mirrors the main text. Exercises are called "exercises" in the main text and "practices" in the *Workbook* to minimize confusion when you make assignments. Each practice in the *Workbook* has a contents title and a reference to appropriate charts in the main text and in the *Chartbook*.

You may assign the *Workbook* practices or, depending upon the level of maturity or sense of purpose of the class, leave them for the students to use as they wish. You may assign them to the entire class, or only to those students who need further practice with a particular structure. You may use them as reinforcement after you have covered a chart and exercises in class, or as introductory material prior to discussing a chart in class.

In addition, the students can use the *Workbook* to acquaint themselves with the grammar of any units not covered in class. Earnest students can use the *Workbook* to teach themselves.

Supplementary Resource Texts

Two teacher resource texts are available. One is *Fun with Grammar: Communicative Activities for the Azar Grammar Series* by Suzanne W. Woodward, available as a photocopiable book from Longman (877-202-4572) or as downloads from **www.longman.com**. The text contains games and other language-learning activities compiled by the author from her and other teachers' experience in using the Azar texts in their classrooms.

The other is *Test Bank for Fundamentals of English Grammar, Third Edition,* written by Stacy Hagen. The tests are keyed to charts or chapters in the student text. They can be reproduced as is, or items can be excerpted for tests that teachers prepare themselves. The *Test Bank* will be available in August 2003.

As another resource, the Grammar Exchange at the Azar Web site (**www.longman.com/grammarexchange**) is a place to ask questions about grammar (sometimes our students ask real stumpers). It is also a place to communicate with the author about the text and to offer suggestions you might have.

Notes on American vs. British English

Students are often curious about differences between American and British English. They should know that the differences are minor. Any student who has studied British English (BrE) should have no trouble adapting to American English (AmE), and vice versa.

Teachers need to be careful not to inadvertently mark differences between AmE and BrE as errors; rather, they should simply point out to the students that a difference in usage exists.

DIFFERENCES IN GRAMMAR

Many of the differences in grammar are either footnoted in the main text or mentioned in the chart notes in this *Guide*. For example, the footnote on page 55 compares the British phrase "in future" with the American phrase "in the future."

Differences in article and preposition usage in certain common expressions follow. These differences are not noted in the text; they are given here for the teacher's information.

AmE	BrE
be in ***the*** *hospital*	*be in* **Ø** *hospital*
be at ***the*** *university (be in college)*	*be at* **Ø** *university*
go to ***a*** *university (go to college)*	*go to* **Ø** *university*
go to **Ø** *class/be in* **Ø** *class*	*go to* ***a*** *class/be in* ***a*** *class*
in ***the*** *future*	*in* **Ø** *future* (OR *in* ***the*** *future)*
did it ***the next*** *day*	*did it* **Ø** *next day* (OR ***the*** *next day)*
haven't done something ***for/in*** *weeks*	*haven't done something* ***for*** *weeks*
ten minutes ***past/after*** *six o'clock*	*ten minutes* ***past*** *six o'clock*
five minutes ***to/of/till*** *seven o'clock*	*five minutes* ***to*** *seven o'clock*

In addition, a few verbs have irregular forms ending in *-t* in the simple past and past participle, with use of the *-t* endings more common in BrE than AmE, especially in the verbs *dreamt, leant, smelt, spelt,* and *spoilt.* Both the *-ed* and *-t* forms are given in Chart 2-7 (Irregular Verbs) since the two forms are used in both BrE and AmE to varying degrees.

DIFFERENCES IN SPELLING

Variant spellings can be noted but should not be marked as incorrect in the students' writing. Spelling differences in some common words follow.

AmE	**BrE**
jewelry, traveler, woolen	*jewellry, traveller, woollen*
skillful, fulfill, installment	*skilful, fulfil, instalment*
color, honor, labor, odor	*colour, honour, labour, odour*
-ize (realize, apologize)	*-ise/ize (realise/realize, apologise/apologize)*
analyze	*analyse*
defense, offense, license	*defence, offence, licence* (n.)
theater, center, liter	*theatre, centre, litre*
check	*cheque (bank note)*
curb	*kerb*
forever	*for ever/forever*
focused	*focused/focussed*
fueled	*fuelled/fueled*
jail	*gaol*
practice (n. and v.)	*practise* (v.); *practice* (n. only)
program	*programme*
specialty	*speciality*
story	*storey (of a building)*
tire	*tyre*

DIFFERENCES IN VOCABULARY

Differences in vocabulary usage between AmE and BrE usually do not significantly interfere with communication, but some misunderstandings may develop. For example, a BrE speaker is referring to underpants or panties when using the word "pants," whereas an AmE speaker is referring to slacks or trousers. Students should know that when American and British speakers read each other's literature, they encounter very few differences in vocabulary usage. Similarly, Southerners in the United States and New Englanders have differences in vocabulary, but not so much as to interfere with communication. Some differences between AmE and BrE follow:

AmE	**BrE**
attorney, lawyer	*barrister, solicitor*
bathrobe	*dressing gown*
can (of beans)	*tin (of beans)*
cookie, cracker	*biscuit*
corn	*maize*
diaper	*nappy*
driver's license	*driving licence*
drug store	*chemist's*
elevator	*lift*
eraser	*rubber*
flashlight	*torch*
gas, gasoline	*petrol*
hood of a car	*bonnet of a car*
living room	*sitting room, drawing room*
math	*maths* (e.g., *a maths teacher)*
raise in salary	*rise in salary*
rest room	*public toilet, loo, WC (water closet)*
schedule	*timetable*

AmE	**BrE**
sidewalk	*pavement, footpath*
sink	*basin*
soccer	*football*
stove	*cooker, Aga*
truck	*lorry, van*
trunk of a car	*boot of a car*
be on vacation	*be on holiday*

Key to Pronunciation Symbols

THE PHONETIC ALPHABET (Symbols for American English)

CONSONANTS

Phonetic symbols for most consonants use the same letters as in conventional English spelling: /b, d, f, g, h, k, l, m, n, o, p, r, s, t, v, w, y, z/.*

Spelling consonants that are not used phonetically in English: c, q, x.

A few additional symbols are needed for other consonant sounds.

/ θ / (Greek theta) = voiceless *th* as in ***th**in, **th**ank*
/ ð / (Greek delta) = voiced *th* as in ***th**en, **th**ose*
/ ŋ / = *ng* as in *si**ng**, thi**n**k* (but not in *danger)*
/ š / = *sh* as in ***sh**irt, mi**ss**ion, na**t**ion*
/ ž / = *s* or *z* in a few words like *plea**s**ure, a**z**ure*
/ č / = *ch* or *tch* as in *wa**tch**, **ch**ur**ch***
/ ǰ / = *j* or *dge* as in ***j**ump, le**dge***

VOWELS

The five vowels in the spelling alphabet are inadequate to represent the 12–15 vowel sounds of American speech. Therefore, new symbols and new sound associations for familiar letters must be adopted.

Front	**Central**	**Back** (lips rounded)
/i/ or /iy/ as in *b**ea**t*		/u/, /u:/, or /uw/ as in *b**oo**t*
/ɪ/ as in *b**i**t*		/ʊ/ as in *b**oo**k*
/e/ or /ey/ as in *b**ai**t*		/o/ or /ow/ as in *b**oa**t*
		/ɔ/ as in *b**ough**t*
/ɛ/ as in *b**e**t*	/ə/ as in *b**u**t*	
/æ/ as in *b**a**t*	/a/ as in *b**o**ther*	

Glides: /ai/ or /ay/ as in b**i**te
/ɔi/ or /ɔy/ as in b**oy**
/au/ or /aw/ as in ab**ou**t

British English has a somewhat different set of vowel sounds and symbols. You might want to consult a standard pronunciation text or BrE dictionary for that system.

*Slanted lines indicate phonetic symbols.

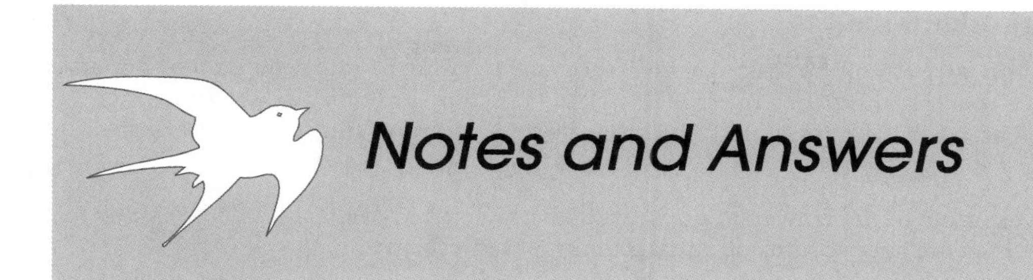

Chapter 1: PRESENT TIME

ORDER OF CHAPTER	CHARTS	EXERCISES	WORKBOOK
First day of class: talking/writing		Ex. 1 → 3	Pr. 1
Simple present and present progressive	1-1 → 1-2	Ex. 4 → 8	Pr. 2 → 10
Frequency adverbs	1-3	Ex. 9 → 13	Pr. 11 → 15
Final *-s*	1-4	Ex. 14 → 18	Pr. 16 → 20
Non-action verbs	1-6	Ex. 19	Pr. 21
Present verbs: short answers to yes/no questions	1-7	Ex. 20 → 21	Pr. 25
Cumulative review		Ex. 22 → 23	Pr. 22 → 24, 26

General Notes on Chapter 1

• This chapter includes some of the most fundamental and useful structures in everyday English. Students learn to ask and answer questions that are useful in getting and giving information, describing, and keeping a conversation moving along.

The book emphasizes everyday English, a style and register acceptable in most situations. The first exercise models a simple dialogue for an interview to help classmates get acquainted. Then the charts and exercises focus on important details of a few fundamental verb structures.

• TERMINOLOGY: The text does not differentiate between verb "tenses" and "aspects." The usual student understanding of the term "tense" is a verb form that expresses time relationships; most students are comfortable with the term. The goal is always to present and explain structures with a minimum of technical terminology. The hope is that the students will leave their formal study of English one day with good control of its structures; terminology can and probably will be soon forgotten.

The present progressive is also called the present continuous in some texts.

☐ EXERCISE 1, p 1. Introductions.

First explain the purpose of the task: pairs of students are going to interview each other and then introduce their partners to the rest of the class. (If your students already know each other, you might ask them to pretend to be other people—famous film stars, historical figures, etc.)

PART I. The example of the conversation between Kunio and Maria is intended to show the learners what they are supposed to do during their own interviews.

SUGGESTIONS:

• Have two students read the dialogue aloud.

• Model some parts of the dialogue yourself. For example, you could model various ways a native speaker might say "Hi. My name's (. . .)" and have the students try to imitate your intonation. You could model any of the sentences and have the whole class repeat.

• Model everyday contracted speech. For example: *Where are* becomes "*Where're.*"

• Point out phrases that keep a conversation moving along. Discuss their meanings and functions: *And you?* (meaning "And where are you living now?" which refers to the immediately preceding question) and *How about you?* (meaning the speaker is asking the other person the same question that immediately preceded).

PART II. The students can complete the paragraph as seatwork prior to class discussion.

EXPECTED COMPLETIONS: . . . Maria is from Mexico. Right now, she's living on Fifth Avenue in an apartment (OR: in an apartment on Fifth Avenue). She has been here for three days. She came here to study English at this school before she goes to another school to study computer programming. In her free time, she likes to get on the Internet.

PART III. The students are to use information from the dialogue to create an introduction, as practice for creating their own introductions later. Have the students, working individually or in small groups, write Maria's introduction of Kunio. Then, the students can read their introductions aloud as you write their words on the board as a basis for discussion.

POSSIBLE INTRODUCTION:

I would like to introduce Kunio to you. He's from Japan. Right now, he's living in a dorm. He has been here for two months. Right now he's studying English. Later, he's going to study engineering at this school. In his free time, he reads a lot. He also likes to get on the Internet.

PART IV. Elicit questions from the class on the given topics. Write the questions on the chalkboard, then call attention to the same or similar questions in the dialogue between Kunio and Maria.

EXPECTED QUESTIONS:

What is your name?
Where are you from? / What country are you from? / What's your hometown?
Where are you living now? / Where do you live?*
How long have you been in (this city)?
Why did you come here?
What do you like to do in your free time? / Do you have any hobbies? / What do you enjoy doing in your spare time?

---

* *Where are you living now?* (present progressive) is usually the form of a question about a current but probably temporary residence: a dormitory, an apartment, etc. *Where do you live?* (simple present) is more often the question about the resident's permanent home. In addition to a street address, the question *Where do you live?* can elicit a response of a city or state/province (e.g., *I live in Kansas City, Kansas.)*. The distinction between these forms is subtle. In this interview, either question is appropriate and will elicit the desired information.

The next step is to divide the students into pairs, mixing language groups in a multilingual class or mixing proficiency levels in a monolingual class. Give the pairs ten minutes or so to do the interviews and prepare their introductions. Allow the students to read from their notes during the introductions.

PART V: Encourage the class to write down the names of their classmates as a way of getting to know each other.

As a follow-up to the in-class activity, you could ask the students to write the information from their interviews in a short composition (in class or out of class) and hand it in.

☐ EXERCISE 2, p. 2. Introducing yourself in writing.

This practice is intended to reinforce the first exercise. It allows you to get to know your students and evaluate their proficiency.

The suggestions in the text for ways in which to handle the compositions resulting from this assignment can be used for any writing assignments throughout the term. You may wish to keep this first writing sample for now and return it to the students after several months so that they can see how much their English has improved since the first day of class.

☐ EXERCISE 3, p. 3. Pretest (error analysis): present verbs. (Charts 1-1 → 1-6)

This exercise previews some common problems in using present verb forms.

Students should be given time in class to solve the exercise prior to class discussion. You might want to ask the students to write out and hand in the corrected sentences in order to evaluate their level of understanding and usage ability. Group or pair work would be another possibility. For example, a pair or group could write out all the corrected sentences and then give that paper to another pair or group to read and correct again if necessary. As another possibility, students could be asked to write the corrected sentences on the board for class discussion. (It's probably wise to ask for volunteers rather than assigning students to boardwork, especially the first day of class.)

ANSWERS: **1.** **I am a** student at this school. (OR: **We are** students at this school.) **2.** I **am not** living at home right now. **3.** I **am** living in this city. **4.** **I'm studying** English. **5.** I **don't know** my teacher's name. **6.** *(Teacher's name)* teach**es** our English class. **7.** She/He expect**s** us to be in class on time. **8.** We always **come** to class on time. **9.** **Does Omar go** to school? / **Is Omar** going to school? **10.** Tom **doesn't** go to school. **11.** My sister **doesn't** have a job. **12.** **Does** Anna **have** a job?

CHARTS 1-1 AND 1-2: SIMPLE PRESENT vs. PRESENT PROGRESSIVE

• It is assumed that the students are already acquainted with these two present tenses, their negative and question forms, and contractions with *am, are, is,* and *not*. It is not assumed that the students have full control of these forms and their uses, however.

• The time-line diagram below is used to demonstrate tenses throughout the text, with the vertical crossbar representing "now" or the "moment of speaking."

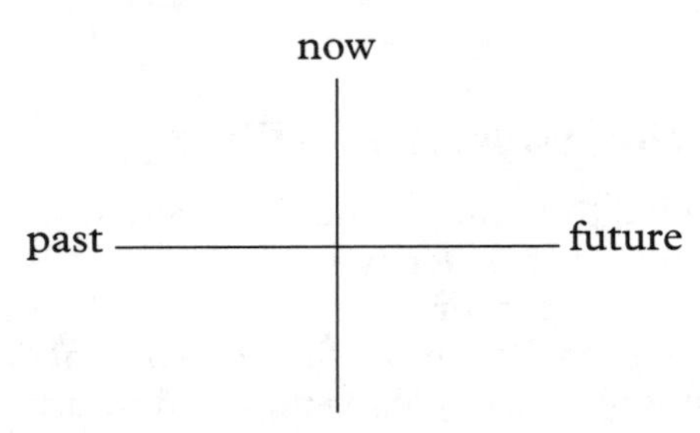

• The other tenses in the text are presented with the same time-line diagram. For example, see Chart 2-8 for the diagrams for the simple past and past progressive.

NOTES on presenting the grammar in Charts 1-1 and 1-2.*

• One option for presenting Chart 1-1 is to draw the diagrams on the board, discuss the examples briefly, then proceed immediately to the exercises.

• As another option, you could review all the grammar points in Charts 1-1 and 1-2 before turning to the exercises. Elicit examples from the class, write them on the board, discuss differences in meaning, manipulate forms, and orally model the contractions. You might, for example, use the verb *sit* and have the students make sentences about themselves and their classmates in statements, negatives, and questions such as these:

(Pedro) sits in class every day. (Pedro) is sitting (in that seat) right now. He doesn't sit in the back row every day. He isn't sitting in the back row right now. Does he usually sit in the center row? Is he sitting in the center row?

Ask leading questions so that the students will answer variously with *I, s/he,* and *they* as the subjects. Ask other questions so that students give short answers. For example: *Is (Talal) sitting next to (Janko)? Who is sitting in front of (Somchart)?*

• To get across the idea that the simple present expresses daily habits, ask the class to give you examples of their daily habits. To contrast with the present progressive, ask them if they are doing these things right now. An example of a daily habit: *I eat breakfast every day.* Contrast: *Are you eating breakfast right now?* Just a few examples should suffice to help the students understand the chart. The exercises that follow give them many opportunities to use the target structures.

• To emphasize that one use of the simple present is to express general statements of fact, ask the class to give you examples: *Rain falls. Birds fly. The earth is round.* Try to elicit eternal truths that exist in the past, present, and future.

• To emphasize the meaning of the present progressive, have students perform a few actions such as standing up or holding a pen for other students to describe. (Exercise 6 that follows has a list of actions that students can perform.)

*See the *Introduction:* Classroom Techniques (p. ix) for suggestions for presenting grammar charts.

☐ EXERCISE 4, p. 5. Simple present vs. present progressive. (Charts 1-1 and 1-2)

Give the students a few moments to become acquainted with the illustration. Perhaps ask some students to describe what they see going on in the picture. Do items 1, 2, and 3 with the class to show them what they are supposed to do, then let them finish the exercise on their own prior to class discussion.

ANSWERS:

1. right now	**6.** habit	**11.** right now
2. right now	**7.** right now	**12.** habit
3. habit	**8.** right now	**13.** habit
4. right now	**9.** habit	
5. habit	**10.** right now	

As a follow-up, you could ask the students to cover the written text, but not the illustration, and write a paragraph about the picture, using their own words and what they remember from the class discussion.

☐ EXERCISE 5, p. 5. Simple present vs. present progressive. (Charts 1-1 and 1-2)

Students need to prepare the exercise prior to class discussion; they can do it as seatwork, or this exercise could be assigned as homework for the next day as you proceed to Exercise 6 in class. See the *Introduction,* p. xii, for suggestions on a variety of ways to handle fill-in-the-blanks exercises in the classroom.

Assign practices in the *Workbook* to reinforce the students' classwork. The *Workbook* contains only self-study practices; all answers are given in an answer key at the back of the book.

ANSWERS: **2.** am sitting . . . sit **3.** speaks . . . is speaking **4.** Does it rain . . . is **5.** Is it raining . . . is starting [*sprinkle* = to rain lightly] **6.** is walking **7.** walks . . . Do you walk . . . Does Oscar walk **8.** am buying . . . buy

☐ EXERCISE 6, p. 7. Using the present progressive. (Charts 1-1 and 1-2)

You might want to ask the class to close their books during this exercise; the teacher is the only one who needs to have his or her book open. Unfamiliar vocabulary can be written on the board. If, however, the vocabulary is difficult for your class, let them keep their books open.

Try to elicit definitions or demonstrations of meaning from the class before you supply them. Vocabulary that may be difficult: *whistle, hum, bite, fingernails, rub, palms, kick, knock, shake, scratch.* (NOTE: In India and some other cultures, whistling may be considered rude.)

The words in the text in an oral exercise such as this are not intended as a script for the teacher. They are prompts. For the first item, for example, the teacher would probably say to a student, "Would you please stand up? Thank you," and then elicit the present progressive from another student.

The complete sentence responses are designed to provide practice with the target structures. You might mention that short answers [e.g., *Maria (is).*] are more natural than complete sentences in response to conversational questions (e.g., *Who is standing there?*).

The directions for activities in this exercise could be written on slips of paper and handed to pairs of students, who could then perform the actions as a pair while the rest of the class describes the action using the present progressive. This would encourage the use of plural pronouns *(they, their, them)* and plural verb forms.

EXPANSION: Suggest to the learners that they talk to themselves during the day, either silently or aloud. For example, if they are entering their apartment: *I'm turning the doorknob.*

I'm opening the door. I'm walking into my apartment. I'm closing the door. They can get a lot of valuable practice with English by talking to themselves. Ask them if they ever talk to themselves in their own language. They may or may not admit it. Assure them that most people do talk to themselves and that it's a good language-learning technique.

EXPANSION: Here are some other ideas for eliciting present verbs:
(1) Ask a student to pretend to be a television reporter. S/he is covering an event live. The event is an exciting ESL or EFL English class at *(name of your school)*. The TV audience doesn't know much about this kind of class. The reporter needs to tell the audience the nature of the class and describe what is happening at the moment during the live broadcast. The reporter could also interview some of the class members. Students can take turns being the reporter. You should demonstrate being the reporter first, then ask for a volunteer to continue.
(2) Use a video camera to make a movie of the class. Perhaps you could videotape pantomimes or some other predetermined activity. Show the movie in class and ask the students to describe what is happening on the screen.
(3) Show a videotape in class without the sound. Have the students describe the actions, using present verbs. They will need to guess what is going on in addition to describing the physical activities.
(4) Set up a pretend microphone. Ask one student at a time (preferably volunteers) to pretend to be a radio news reporter. The audience needs to be informed about important events in the world today. (The reporters will probably need to use past verbs as well. This role play could be postponed until Chapter 2.)

☐ EXERCISE 7, p. 7. Using the present progressive. (Charts 1-1 and 1-2)

Ask half the class to perform activities. Each member of the group can perform a different action; several students can perform the same action if they wish. Then ask students in the other half of the class to identify a person or persons in the activity group and describe the activity, using the present progressive.

EXPANSION: After the groups have performed their activities, ask individual students to perform an activity of their choice while the rest of the class describes it in writing, using their classmates' names and the present progressive.

☐ EXERCISE 8, p. 8. Using the present progressive. (Charts 1-1 and 1-2)

NOTE: In a pantomime, one pretends to do something, using no words, only actions. You yourself should demonstrate the art of pantomime for the class before breaking the students into groups. Pretend to comb your hair, blow up a balloon, be asleep, etc. Your relaxed manner and willingness to perform publicly will encourage shy students to at least try a pantomime themselves. You might want to put suggestions for actions to pantomime on note cards and hand them out. If not, help the class brainstorm some ideas in addition to the suggestions in the text. Additional suggestions: brushing your hair, typing, talking on the phone, swimming, laughing, drinking through a straw, erasing something, shaking hands with someone, reading a newspaper.

CHART 1-3: FREQUENCY ADVERBS

• Discuss the meanings of frequency adverbs. Perhaps present to the students the specific frequency of some activity and ask them which adverb would be best. Examples:

I drink coffee every morning of the week. = ***always***
I drink coffee six mornings a week. = ***usually***
I drink coffee four or five mornings a week. = ***often***
I drink coffee two, three, or four mornings a week. = ***sometimes***
I drink coffee once every two weeks. = ***seldom***
I drink coffee once or twice a year. = ***rarely***

• Other possible points to discuss:

(1) *Usually* and *often* are close in meaning. If any students want to pursue a distinction, you might say that *usually* is 95% of the time, and *often* is 90% of the time. Or you might say that *usually* means "most of the time, regularly" and *often* means "many times, repeated times, frequently."

(2) *Often* can be pronounced /ɔfən/ or /ɔftən/.

(3) In discussing the difference between *seldom* and *rarely*, you might describe *seldom* as 5% of the time and *rarely* as 1% of the time.

☐ EXERCISE 9, p. 9. The meaning of frequency adverbs. (Chart 1-3)

Elicit more than one response to the items to create various contexts for the frequency adverbs. Keep the focus on the meaning of the frequency adverbs. If a student says, "I seldom watch TV," ask him or her exactly how often he watches TV in order to review the meaning of *seldom*.

☐ EXERCISE 10, p. 10. Position of frequency adverbs. (Chart 1-3)

This is an exercise on usual midsentence word order of frequency adverbs.

ANSWERS: **2.** Tom is always at **3.** The mail usually comes **4.** The mail is usually here **5.** I generally eat **6.** Tom is generally in **7.** . . . do you generally eat **8.** Are you usually in

☐ EXERCISE 11, p. 10. Frequency adverbs in negative sentences. (Chart 1-3)

Emphasize that *seldom, rarely, hardly ever,* and *never* are negative adverbs; they already carry a negative meaning, so *not* is not used with them. INCORRECT: *He doesn't rarely shave.* (The double negative, *doesn't rarely*, would give the meaning that he shaves a lot.)

ANSWERS:

1. c. Jack frequently doesn't shave
d. Jack occasionally doesn't shave
e. Jack sometimes doesn't shave
f. Jack always shaves
g. Jack doesn't ever shave
h. Jack never shaves
i. Jack hardly ever shaves
j. Jack rarely shaves
k. Jack seldom shaves

2. a. I usually don't eat breakfast.
b. I don't always eat breakfast.
c. I seldom eat breakfast.
d. I don't ever eat breakfast.

3. a. My roommate generally isn't home
b. My roommate sometimes isn't home
c. My roommate isn't always home
d. My roommate is hardly ever home

☐ EXERCISE 12, p. 10. Using the simple present with frequency adverbs. (Charts 1-1 → 1-3)

In this exercise the students talk about themselves, sharing "real" information while using the target structures.

See the *Introduction,* p. xiv, for suggestions about handling oral pairwork in the classroom.

☐ EXERCISE 13, p. 11. Topics for discussion or writing. (Charts 1-1 → 1-3)

If you use small groups for this exercise, appoint a leader or have each group elect their leader. (See the *Introduction,* p. xi, for suggestions on setting up group work.) The leader can change for Parts I and II. The questioner should choose only one of the frequency adverbs for each question. With luck, you'll soon have a room full of students enjoying conversations with each other and using the target structures.

CHART 1-4: FINAL -*S*

- You might mention to your students that final -*s* causes ESL/EFL students a lot of trouble, usually in omitting it erroneously, although sometimes also by adding it when it's not needed. Students need to pay special attention to their usage of final -*s,* from beginning through advanced levels of study.
- It is important for students to understand that added to a noun, final -*s* indicates plural number. Added to a verb, it indicates singular. (Students might rightfully object that this is a less-than-ideal way to indicate number!) Review with your students the terms "noun" and "verb." Refer them to Chart 6-3, "Subjects, Verbs, and Objects," p. 159, for information about nouns and verbs.
- Spelling rules for adding final -*s* are in Chart 1-5 on p. 13 of the textbook.
- It is a good idea for you to inform the class of the three pronunciations of final -*s* at this point: /s/, /z/, and /əz/. Students need to become aware of and begin to work with the pronunciations even though the text itself delays concentrated work on this area until Chapter 6, "Nouns and Pronouns" (Chart 6-1, p. 157).

☐ EXERCISE 14, p. 12. Using final -S. (Chart 1-4)

Emphasize that final -*s* indicates singular on verbs (simple present) and indicates plural when added to nouns.

ANSWERS: **3.** listens = *a singular verb* **4.** students = *a plural noun* **5.** helps = *a singular verb* **6.** Planets = *a plural noun* **7.** lists = *a singular verb* **8.** likes, takes, sits, feeds = *singular verbs;* bus = *a singular noun* [Make the point that some words simply end in -*s* as their regular spelling: *bus, guess, always, politics, business, gas, address.*]; birds, Ducks, pigeons = *plural nouns*

☐ EXERCISE 15, p. 12. Preview: spelling of final -S/-ES. (Chart 1-5)

Ask the students to quickly complete this exercise without looking at Chart 1-5. Perhaps you could tell them to cover page 13 with a sheet of paper. One of the points in using previews is for students to discover what parts of a chart they do and do not already know.

All of the spelling rules in Chart 1-5 are represented in the items in this exercise. As you discuss the correct answers in class (perhaps written on the board by volunteers), iterate the spelling rule each item illustrates.

During class discussion, give the students the pronunciations of the endings and have them practice saying them themselves.

If your students seem to be having difficulty with the spellings and need more practice adding *-s*, write some verbs on the board and ask students to add final *-s/-es* to them. The *Workbook* provides additional practice.

ANSWERS:

1. talks /s/
2. wishes /əz/
3. hopes /s/
4. reaches /əz/
5. moves /z/
6. kisses /əz/
7. pushes /əz/
8. waits /s/
9. mixes /əz/
10. blows /z/
11. studies /z/
12. buys /z/
13. enjoys /z/
14. flies /z/
15. carries /z/

CHART 1-5: SPELLING OF FINAL *-S/-ES*

• Give additional examples of the points made in the chart and have students supply the correct endings. Suggestions of verbs to use:

(a) *begin → begins;* (b) *come → comes;* (c) *watch → watches, push → pushes, guess → guesses, mix → mixes, fizz → fizzes* [very few verbs end in *-z*]; (d) *worry → worries;* (e) *play → plays;* (f) *goes* and *does* are oddities.

• A common error is adding *-es* when only *-s* is needed (INCORRECT: *visites, growes*). Emphasize when *-es* is and is not added.

• In connection with example (e), *pays,* you may wish to point out that *pays* is pronounced /peyz/, but that when final *-s* is added to *say,* the pronunciation of the vowel changes: *says* is pronounced /səz/.

• Discuss the pronunciation of *does* /dəz/ and *goes* /gowz/. Tell them you know that they look like they should be pronounced similarly, but that English has some funny little oddities, just as any other language. In fact, some of the most common short words in English are the most unusual in spelling and pronunciation (e.g., *their, says, was, has*). As with most things, frequent use has caused them to change shape.

• In conjunction with discussing spelling, present the pronunciation of final *-s/-es* (which is presented in Chapter 6, Chart 6-1, p. 157). A summary of the pronunciation of final *-s/-es* follows:

It is pronounced /s/ after voiceless sounds, e.g., *meets.*
It is pronounced /z/ after voiced sounds, e.g., *needs.*
It is pronounced /əz/ after *-sh, -ch, -s* [including *-ks*], *-z,* and *-ge/-dge* sounds (e.g., *wishes, watches, passes, mixes, sizes, judges*).

☐ EXERCISE 16, p. 13. Simple present verbs: using final -S/-ES. (Charts 1-4 and 1-5)

The focus of this exercise is on (1) identification of subjects and verbs in simple sentences; (2) the use of final *-s/-es* in the simple present; and finally (3) the spelling of final *-s/-es.* Ask the students to find the subjects and verbs in the sentences. The ability to recognize subjects and verbs is essential to their successful use of this textbook. If necessary, refer the students to Charts 6-3 (Subjects, Verbs, and Objects) and 6-4 (Objects of Prepositions) on pp. 159 and 161, respectively.

Include a discussion of pronunciation; the goal at this point is for students to become aware of the three different pronunciations of *-s/-es*. Further and more concentrated work on the pronunciation of final *-s/-es* follows in Chapter 6.

EXPANSION: Give a spelling test. Give the simple form of a verb and ask students to write the correct *-s/-es* form. They can grade each other's papers or correct each other's boardwork. Possible verbs to use (some of which students will be unfamiliar with, but should still be able to figure out how to spell with final *-s/-es*): *stay, supply, hiss, flash, taste, disappear, break, match, cry, enter, explain, finish, exist, occur, marry, rely, relay.*

ANSWERS: **1.** barks /s/ **2.** bark *(no change)* **3.** floats /s/ **4.** flow *(no change)* **5.** worries /z/ **6.** buys /z/ **7.** fly *(no change)* **8.** teaches /əz/ **9.** asks /s/ **10.** watches /əz/ [*game shows* = programs where contestants play games in order to win prizes] **11.** consists /s/ **12.** sleep *(no change)* **13.** contains /z/ **14.** freezes /əz/ . . . boils /z/ [F = Fahrenheit; C = Centigrade or Celsius] **15.** crosses /əz/ . . . walks /s/ . . . uses /əz/ **16.** [Note that the subject is *parts; of the world* is a prepositional phrase, not the subject of the sentence. The subject here can also be called the "head of the noun phrase."] enjoy *(no change)* . . . [The subject is *each season.* Note that *each* is always grammatically singular; it is immediately followed by a singular noun.] . . . lasts /s/ . . . brings /z/ [Point out the parallel verbs: one subject *(each season)* has two verbs connected by *and.* The second verb also needs to agree with the singular subject.]

□ EXERCISE 17, p. 14. Simple present verbs: using final -S/-ES. (Charts 1-4 and 1-5)

The principal purpose of this exercise is to get students up, moving, and talking to each other while they are focusing on the correct use of the target structures.

The vocabulary in this practice will be difficult for many of the students; vocabulary development is one of the intentions. You could ask for and answer questions about the meanings of words prior to the students doing the practice, or you could leave them on their own as they explain to each other the meanings of the words with the aid of their dictionaries. Both approaches to vocabulary discussion have their own advantages. A teacher can give quick and accurate information; in peer teaching, the students have the chance to practice various communication skills.

An alternative way of handling this exercise is to write out the items yourself on slips of paper and simply pass them out. This approach shortens the time needed to explain the directions.

If you have more than 24 students in your class, you will need to add more items of your own. If you have fewer than 24 students, some students will have two slips of paper that they will need to find matches to.

You may wish to add to the directions that the student whose slip has the subject of the sentence should do the writing on the board.

Once all the sentences are written on the board, you may wish to ask students to underline the subjects and verbs. The sentences can also be used for pronunciation practice.

If class time is limited, this exercise can be assigned for out-of-class written homework.

ANSWERS:

1. (+8) A star shines in the sky at night.
2. (+23) Automobiles cause air pollution.
3. (+19) A rubber band stretches when you pull it.
4. (+18) A hotel supplies its guests with clean towels.
5. (+22) Newspaper ink stains my hands when I read the paper.
6. (+15) Oceans support a huge variety of marine life.
7. (+20) A bee gathers nectar from flowers.
9. (+13) A hurricane causes great destruction when it reaches land.
10. (+21) A river flows downhill.

12. (+24) Does physical exercise improve your circulation and general health?
12. (+16) An elephant uses its long trunk like a hand to pick things up.
14. (+17) Brazil produces one-fourth of the world's coffee.

☐ EXERCISE 18, p. 15. The simple present and the present progressive. (Charts 1-1 → 1-5)

The term *progressive* comes from the idea of an activity being "in progress." The emphasis in this exercise is on connecting the use of the progressive with the idea of an activity in progress (all of the pictures show activities in progress) and then to contrast that with the use of the simple present for habitual activities and generalizations.

Encourage the students to use their imaginations and make free associations in interpreting what is going on in the pictures—whatever comes into their minds that is related to the pictures. The answers given below are only samples; the students will create different responses.

The illustrations are intended as a spur to spontaneous talk in which the target structures are practiced. If working in pairs or small groups, the students do not need to be closely monitored to make sure the directions for the exercise are being followed exactly. Almost any conversation involving the pictures and the target tenses is good.

EXPANSION: Ask students to come up with miscellaneous vocabulary suggested by the pictures. For example, in the example for Exercise 18: *palm tree, tropical island, drops of water, splash, kick, elbow.*

SAMPLE RESPONSES: **1.** The girl **is kicking** a soccer ball. She probably **plays** soccer frequently. Soccer **is** a sport that both boys and girls enjoy. *(foot, shirt, soccer shoes, shorts, fist, ponytail, socks)* **2.** The man **is cooking** something. He probably **doesn't cook** very often. Cooking **requires** skill and experience. *(frying pan, burn, stove, burner, chef's hat, spatula, apron)* **3.** The man **is whistling**. He **is driving** a taxi. He probably **drives** a taxi every day. He probably **whistles** only when he doesn't have a passenger. Taxi drivers **don't** usually **whistle** when they have passengers. *(musical notes, steering wheel, button, blow)* **4.** The man **is kissing** the baby on the top of his/her/its head. He**'s carrying** a briefcase. The baby **is sitting** in a high chair. The man probably **kisses** the baby every day before he **goes** to work. Parents **show** affection to their children by kissing them. *(high chair, bowl, briefcase, suit, tie)* **5.** The woman **is pouring** a glass of juice. She probably **pours** a glass of juice every morning for breakfast. Juice **is** part of a healthy breakfast. *(blouse, short sleeves, polka dots, carton)* **6.** The little boy **is crying** because his ice cream fell out of the cone. He probably **cries** a lot when things happen that make him unhappy. Children **cry** when bad things happen. *(ice cream cone, stripes, tears, shorts, melt)* **7.** The woman **is dreaming** about herself. In her dream, she **is smelling** flowers. She **is smiling**, both in the dream and in real life. She probably **dreams** a lot. Most people **dream** every night, but not all dreams **are** happy like this one. *(pillow, mattress, covers, blanket, bedstead)* **8.** The woman **is tying** her shoe. She **looks** like a runner. She probably **runs** often. Running **is** good exercise. *(stripes, shoe laces)* **9.** The man **is climbing** a mountain. He probably **climbs** mountains frequently. He **looks** like he's an expert. Mountain climbing **requires** a lot of skill and equipment. *(steep, boots, rope, hammer, spike or piton)* **10.** The men **are running**. They probably **run** for exercise. Running **is** good exercise. *(sweat, V-neck shirt)* **11.** The woman **is riding** a motorcycle/motorbike. She **looks** comfortable on it; she probably **rides** a motorcycle often. Motorcycles **are** fun to ride. *(engine, wheels, shorts, helmet, goggles, handlebars)* **12.** The man **is hitting** a golf ball. He probably **doesn't** play golf a lot. Golf **is** a difficult game to play well. *(golf club, swing)*

CHART 1-6: NON-ACTION VERBS

- The key point is the difference between "states" and "activities." No verb is inherently nonprogressive. The intention of this chart and its terminology is simply to inform the students that certain common verbs are usually not used in the progressive form.
- The list of non-action (i.e., stative or nonprogressive) verbs is by no means complete. It presents only a few common verbs.
- Remind students about negative verb forms:

Progressive:	*I'm studying English now.*	***I'm not** studying French.*
Nonprogressive:	*I like tea.*	***I don't like** coffee.*

- Vocabulary:

  look at = focus attention on sights vs. *see* = notice, become aware of
  listen to = pay attention to sounds vs. *hear* = notice, be aware of

☐ EXERCISE 19, p. 17. Progressive verbs vs. non-action verbs. (Chart 1-6)

This exercise emphasizes non-action (i.e., stative) verbs, which describe a state that exists now, not an activity that is in progress now.

ANSWERS: **1.** am looking . . . see **2.** Do you need . . . Do you want **3.** think . . . know . . . forget . . . remember **4.** Do you believe . . . are you talking . . . exist **5.** are . . . are having . . . have . . . are playing . . . like . . . are sunbathing [Note the correct spelling with no "e."] . . . are trying . . . are listening . . . hear **6.** are you thinking . . . am thinking . . . Do you like . . . think **7.** do you prefer . . . like . . . am reading . . . prefer . . . are . . . value . . . means . . . is . . . loves . . . sounds **8.** spins . . . is spinning . . . Are you trying . . . Do you really think . . . Do you believe . . . are growing . . . are getting . . . are taking . . . are speaking

CHART 1-7: PRESENT VERBS: SHORT ANSWERS TO YES/NO QUESTIONS

- Students need to understand that auxiliary verbs can substitute for verb phrases. For example, in the first short answer in the chart *(Yes, he does), does* means "likes tea."

☐ EXERCISE 20, p. 20. Short answers to yes/no questions. (Chart 1-7)

Discuss the meaning of the short answers. For example, in item 1: *Yes, she does* means "Yes, she has a bicycle."

Note that it may seem impolite to give only a short answer and then stop talking. A short answer is often followed by more detailed information or another question that keeps the conversation open. A short answer might cut off the dialogue and appear a bit rude in everyday conversational situations.

Refer students to Chart 5-1, p. 121, if they need more information about the forms of yes/no questions.

ANSWERS: **2.** Is it raining . . . it isn't . . . don't think **3.** Do your friends write . . . they do . . . get **4.** Are the students taking . . . they aren't . . . are doing **5.** Does the weather affect . . . it does . . . get **6.** Is Jean studying . . . she isn't . . . is . . . is playing . . . Does Jean play . . . she doesn't . . . studies . . . Is she . . . she is . . . plays . . . Do you play . . . I do . . . am not

☐ **EXERCISE 21, p. 21. Short answers to yes/no questions. (Chart 1-7)**

This exercise can be led by you, with the students' books closed, or the students can work in pairs, one with book open and the other with book closed. It is good practice for students to listen and reply without reading from the text.

EXPECTED ANSWERS: **1.** Yes, I do. OR No, I don't. **2.** Yes, s/he is. OR No, s/he isn't / No s/he's not. **3.** Yes, s/he does. OR No, s/he doesn't. **4.** Yes, they are. [No contraction possible.] OR No, they're not / No, they aren't. **5.** Yes, I am. [No contraction possible.] OR No, I'm not. **6.** No, it's not / No, it isn't. **7.** No, they don't. **8.** Yes, it does. OR No, it doesn't. **9.** Yes, they are. [No contraction possible.] OR No, they aren't / No, they're not. [The preferred answer is a matter of opinion or of the definition of "intelligent."] **10.** Yes, s/he is. [No contraction possible.] OR No, s/he isn't / No s/he's not. **11.** Yes, it is. [No contraction possible.] **12.** No, they don't.

☐ **EXERCISE 22, p. 21. Review: present verbs. (Chapter 1)**

See the *Introduction,* p. xii, for suggestions on ways of handling fill-in-the-blanks exercises.

All of the items in this exercise are dialogues. Two students can be asked to read the two roles.

You may wish to model normal contracted speech for questions: *Do you* = "*D'you*"; *Where are* = "*Where're*"; *What are* = "*What're*"; etc.

ANSWERS: **2.** Are they watching . . . aren't . . . are playing **3.** hear . . . Do you hear . . . do **4.** are you listening . . . want **5.** am . . . are you doing . . . am trying . . . is resting **6.** do you think . . . think . . . don't think **7.** ["A penny for your thoughts" is an idiom meaning roughly "You look like you're thinking seriously. What are you thinking about? I'd like to know."] ["Huh?" is an informal and possibly impolite way of saying "What?" or "Excuse me?"] are you thinking . . . am thinking . . . am not thinking . . . don't believe **8.** Do you see . . . am talking . . . is wearing . . . Do you know . . . don't think [*So* means "I know him."] **9.** Do you know . . . do . . . is . . . doesn't make . . . know [Students may have fun playing around with the tongue-twisters. Ask them to see how fast they can say "She sells seashells down by the sea shore," an old and familiar English tongue-twister. The second one is simply made up and contains sounds that many ESL/EFL students have difficulty distinguishing between /s/ vs. /sh/; /s/ vs. /z/; /č/ vs. /š/. This item is intended as a fun pronunciation activity.]

☐ **EXERCISE 23, p. 23. Error analysis: present verbs. (Chapter 1)**

Students can benefit from rewriting the entire passage and incorporating the corrections. The corrected passage can be written on the board by volunteers. Students can read over each other's papers to make sure all the corrections were properly made. (See the *Introduction,* p. xv, for suggestions on various ways of handling error analysis exercises.)

ANSWERS:

(1) My friend Omar **owns** his own car now. It's brand new. Today he **is** driving to a small town north of the city to visit his aunt. He **loves** to listen to music, so the CD player is **playing** one of his favorite CDs—loudly. Omar is very happy: he is **driving** his own car and **listening** to loud music. He's **looking** forward to his visit with his aunt.

(2) Omar **visits** his aunt once a week. She's elderly and **lives** alone. She **thinks** Omar **is** a wonderful nephew. She **loves** his visits. He **tries** to be helpful and considerate in every way. His aunt **doesn't hear** well, so Omar ~~is~~ speaks loudly and clearly when he's with her.

(3) When he's there, he **fixes** things for her around her apartment and **helps** her with her shopping. He **doesn't stay** with her overnight. He usually **stays** for a few hours and then **heads** back to the city. He **kisses** his aunt good-bye and **gives** her a hug before he **leaves**. Omar is a very good nephew.

Chapter 2: PAST TIME

ORDER OF CHAPTER	CHARTS	EXERCISES	WORKBOOK
Review and preview		Ex. 1	
Simple past	2-1 → 2-3	Ex. 2 → 4	Pr. 1 → 6
Pronunciation of *-ed*	2-4	Ex. 5 → 6	Pr. 8 → 9, 11
Spelling: *-ing* and *-ed* forms	2-5	Ex. 7 → 9	Pr. 10, 12 → 15
Principal parts of verbs	2-6		
Irregular verbs	2-7	Ex. 10 → 15	Pr. 7, 16 → 18
Simple past and past progressive	2-8 → 2-9	Ex. 16 → 18	Pr. 23 → 25
Review: present and past verbs		Ex. 19 → 21	Pr. 19 → 22
Past time clauses	2-10	Ex. 22 → 23	Pr. 26
Past habit *(used to)*	2-11	Ex. 24 → 28	Pr. 28
Cumulative review			Pr. 27, 29 → 30

General Notes on Chapter 2

• In Chapter 2, students learn to use the simple past and the past progressive. They learn to associate the simple past with actions that were completed at a specific time before the present, and the past progressive with actions that co-occurred with other actions at some time before the present. They also practice some of the irregular forms and the spellings that arise in these verb tenses. The "time clause" (a subordinate or adverbial clause) is introduced. This greatly expands the learner's ability to express fairly complex ideas in English.

• TERMINOLOGY: The term "verb tense" is used more broadly here than in some other grammar books. A progressive verb form is elsewhere often called an "aspect" instead of a tense, but that distinction is not made here in order to keep terminology to a minimum.

An "irregular" verb form is one that does not follow the common pattern of adding *-ed* to the simple form to signal the past form or past participle.

☐ EXERCISE 1, p 24. Review of present verbs and preview of past verbs. (Chapters 1 and 2)

Exercise 1, an introduction to Chapter 2 and a review of Chapter 1,

a. describes the use and meaning of the present progressive.
b. describes the two main uses and meanings of the simple present.
c. describes the simple past.
d. describes the past progressive.

Identify the names of the tenses used in the items and iterate for your students the meanings (or ask them to explain what the verb tense means in the particular sentences). All of the sentences are connected to a single context; they are numbered for ease of class discussion.

The point of time in the context is the time in the illustration (9:05 = right now = the moment of speaking). Jennifer is sitting at her desk right now (present progressive), and the speaker/writer is telling us what happened to her yesterday (simple past and past progressive) as well as giving us general factual information (simple present) about this and that.

ANSWERS:

1. b	**6.** d, c	**11.** c, c, c, c
2. b, b	**7.** c, c	**12.** c
3. a	**8.** c, b, b	**13.** b, b, b
4. c	**9.** d, b, c	**14.** c, c
5. c, c	**10.** c, c, d	**15.** c, b

CHARTS 2-1 → 2-3: THE SIMPLE PAST

• Chart 2-1 is basic introductory information about the simple past. Charts 2-2 and 2-3 present the forms. Charts 2-4 and 2-5 present the pronunciation and spelling of *-ed,* as well as the spelling of *-ing* forms.

• It is assumed that most students at this level are already familiar with the basic use and forms of the simple past (but still need a lot of practice and clarification).

You may wish to work out your own presentation of the information in these charts using your own examples written on the chalkboard, leaving the charts solely for reference for the students.

You may wish to proceed quickly or even directly to Exercise 2, emphasizing the points presented in Charts 2-1 through 2-3 during the course of the exercise, referring to the charts only if necessary.

• Learners often have trouble with *did* in questions. They may neglect to change the main verb form, so they produce incorrect sentences like these:

INCORRECT: *Did he worked yesterday?*
INCORRECT: *Did you ate breakfast?*

On the chalkboard, you might show a statement and a question:

He worked yesterday.
Did he work yesterday?

Then make a circle around *-ed* and draw an arrow from *-ed* to *did.* Point out that *-ed* has moved away from *work* and has now become the word *did* in a new position. (The same change can be illustrated for the simple present, where the *-s* moves away from the main verb and joins *do* to become *does* at the beginning of a question. You could use the sentence *He works every day* to show this.)

• Assign *Workbook* practices for reinforcement and additional practice with the form and meaning of the simple past.

☐ EXERCISE 2, p. 26. Present and past time: statements and negatives. (Chapter 1 and Charts 2-1 → 2-3)

This is a review of the negative and statement (i.e., affirmative) forms of the simple present, present progressive, and simple past. It is also intended to prepare the students for the oral work in the next exercise.

Students can do this exercise as seatwork (individually, in pairs, or in groups) prior to class discussion. Before they begin, you might preview the vocabulary in this exercise: *a sofa* = a kind of furniture for two to four people to sit on; *a cruise ship* = a ship where tourists can sleep and eat as they travel from place to place; *float* = stay on the surface of water; *sink* = fall below the surface of water.

You might ask the students to name the tenses in each item. In this textbook, terminology is not intended to be memorized or tested. But it does help teacher–student communication considerably if the students learn such basic terminology as the names of these three tenses.

Students should, by this time, be clear on the use of *do/don't, does/doesn't,* and *did/didn't.* See the *Workbook,* Practices 3–6, for concentrated work on these forms.

POSSIBLE RESPONSES:

2. I don't live in a tree. I live in (an apartment).
3. I didn't take a taxi to school today. I (walked) to school today.
4. I'm not sitting on a . . . sofa. I'm sitting (on a wooden desk seat).
5. Our teacher didn't write *Romeo and Juliet.* Shakespeare wrote *Romeo and Juliet.*
6. Our teacher's name isn't William Shakespeare. Our teacher's name is . . . .
7. I wasn't on a cruise ship . . . yesterday. I was (in class) yesterday.
8. Rocks don't float, and wood doesn't sink. Rocks sink, and wood floats. [A miscellaneous note: There is one kind of wood that sinks (lignum vitae, from tropical American guaiacum trees), and certain volcanic rocks actually float. Sometimes a knowledgeable student with a scientific bent might challenge the statements in the text about wood floating and rocks sinking; it is possible to explain that the simple present often gives the idea of "as a rule or generally speaking."]
9. The teacher didn't fly into the classroom yesterday. The teacher (walked) into the classroom yesterday.
10. Spiders don't have six legs. Spiders have eight legs.

☐ EXERCISE 3, p. 27. Present and past time: statements and negatives. (Chapter 1 and Charts 2-1 → 2-3)

This exercise is intended for teacher–student communicative interaction with tense forms as the target structures. Pair work is also possible, especially in a large class.

Be sure to present only inaccurate information.

This exercise is not a drill. Get the students talking and enjoying themselves without their having to rely on the written text to understand the speaker. Repeat the cue sentences as often and as slowly as necessary. While some students find aural cues easy and exercises like this fun, others want to hang on to the written text with all their might. Gently demonstrate to them that they can indeed learn to understand spoken English and will be understood when they respond.

For a more natural-sounding discourse, begin some of the cues with something like: "I think that . . ." or "Someone told me that . . ." and then add "Is that right?" or "Is that true?"

Items 2, 3, and 4 are intended for a review of forms as necessary.

PARTIAL ANSWERS (only the negative verbs):

1. didn't get up
2. isn't standing
3. doesn't stand
4. didn't stand
5. doesn't have
6. didn't write
7. doesn't flow
8. don't cook
9. didn't teach
10. don't have
11. didn't drive
12. doesn't take
13. don't speak
14. doesn't have
15. didn't study
16. didn't go

☐ EXERCISE 4, p. 27. Present and past time: statements and negatives. (Chapter 1 and Charts 2-1 → 2-3)

Make sure students understand that the dots indicate that the speaker is to supply words to complete the sentence.

CHART 2-4: REGULAR VERBS: PRONUNCIATION OF *-ED* ENDINGS

- Explain voiceless vs. voiced sounds by having the students touch their throats to feel whether their voice box vibrates. Model the sounds and ask the class to repeat them. Encourage the students to exaggerate the final sounds during the exercises.
- As with final *-s* sounds, a student's correct use of these endings in his or her speech has a positive correlation in their correct use in writing. Paying attention to the spoken sounds of these endings greatly benefits students in their written English.
- The pronunciation symbol that looks like an upside down "e" in /əd/ is called a "schwa."

☐ EXERCISE 5, p. 28. Pronunciation of -ED endings. (Chart 2-4)

Students need an opportunity to come up with their own answers. They could do the entire exercise as seatwork first, or you could simply give them time to write the answer to each item before it is discussed. Be sure students practice the items aloud.

ANSWERS:

4. ask/t/
5. start/əd/
6. drop/t/
7. pull/d/
8. push/t/
9. add/əd/
10. pass/t/
11. return/d/
12. touch/t/
13. wave/d/
14. point/əd/
15. agree/d/

☐ EXERCISE 6, p. 29. Pronunciation of -ED endings. (Chart 2-4)

In this exercise, one student could be asked to say the word and another to write on the board the symbol for the ending he or she heard. The rest of the class could judge the correctness of the pronunciation and the written symbol. Rather than the teacher affirming the correct pronunciations in this exercise, that responsibility can be given to the students.

When the students are pronouncing sentences with these words, you might point out to them that *-ed* sounds are unstressed and can be difficult for the unalert or unaware ear to hear. It's helpful for students to purposely spend some time in the next few days listening for *-ed* endings and consciously paying attention to pronouncing them in their own utterances.

At the end of the exercise, you could ask one student to read the entire list and have the rest of the class monitor his or her pronunciation. Also, you can model the sounds for the students to repeat one more time.

ANSWERS: **1.** answer/d/ **2.** arrive/d/ **3.** continue/d/ **4.** end/əd/ **5.** explain/d/ **6.** finish/t/ **7.** fix/t/ **8.** help/t/ **9.** look/t/ **10.** plan/d/ **11.** work/t/ **12.** invite/əd/ **13.** suggest/əd/ **14.** smell/d/ **15.** cross/t/ [Idiom note: Crossing one's fingers is a gesture that represents a person's hope for good luck. In North America, when children want something to come true, they cross their fingers and make a wish. If a person says "I'm crossing my fingers for you," it expresses a wish for good luck. Ask your students if the gesture of crossing one's fingers has any meaning in their cultures.]

CHART 2-5: SPELLING OF *-ING* AND *-ED* FORMS

• The students will need your assistance in understanding this chart. Demonstrate the rules on the board and relate them to the examples in the text. Suggestions for additional examples: (a) *use, phone;* (b) *count, turn;* (c) *join, shout, need;* (d) *drop, grab;* (e) *open, order;* (f) *refer, permit;* (g) *stay, annoy;* (h) *marry, pity;* (i) *lie* [*Die, tie, lie,* and *belie* are the only common verbs that end in *-ie.*].

• Two-syllable verbs that end in *-l* (e.g., *control, cancel, travel)* are not dealt with in the chart. *Control* follows rule (f): the second syllable is stressed, so the consonant is doubled: *controlled, controlling. Cancel* and *travel* follow rule (e) in American English: the first syllable is stressed, so the consonant is not doubled: *canceled, canceling* and *traveled, traveling.* But the *-l* is doubled in British spelling: *cancelled, cancelling* and *travelled, travelling.* Another similar spelling variation is *worshiped, worshiping* in American English and *worshipped, worshipping* in British English. You can tell the students that they are correct whether they double the consonant or not in these particular words. Always consult a dictionary when necessary!

☐ EXERCISES 7 → 9, pp. 30–32. Spelling of -ING and -ED. (Chart 2-5)

Immediately follow the discussion of the chart with individual seatwork, taking small groups of items at a time (e.g., 1 through 7, then 8 through 14, etc.).

Discussion of the correct answers can be done in groups or pairs, or can be teacher-led. One or two students might work at the chalkboard, then everyone can check the correct spelling.

The students will not know the meaning of some of the words. Tell them they can figure out the spelling without knowing the meaning. Discuss the meanings only after discussing the spelling.

Exercise 7 includes the rules illustrated by examples (a) through (d) in the chart.
Exercise 8 covers the rules illustrated by examples (e) through (i) of the chart.
Exercise 9 is a summary.

EX. 7 ANSWERS:

2. waiting, waited
3. hitting, (hit)
4. writing, (wrote/written)
5. shouting, shouted
6. cutting, (cut)
7. meeting, (met)
8. hoping, hoped
9. hopping, hopped
10. helping, helped
11. sleeping, (slept)
12. stepping, stepped
13. taping, taped
14. tapping, tapped
15. raining, rained
16. running, (ran/run)
17. whining, whined
18. winning, (won)
19. explaining, explained
20. burning, burned/burnt

EX. 8 ANSWERS:

1. opening, opened
2. beginning, (began/begun)
3. occurring, occurred
4. happening, happened
5. referring, referred
6. offering, offered
7. listening, listened
8. admitting, admitted
9. visiting, visited
10. omitting, omitted
11. hurrying, hurried
12. studying, studied
13. enjoying, enjoyed
14. replying, replied
15. staying, stayed
16. buying, (bought)
17. trying, tried
18. tying, tied
19. dying, died
20. lying, lied

EX. 9 ANSWERS:

2. promising, promised
3. slapping, slapped
4. wiping, wiped
5. carrying, carried
6. crying, cried
7. praying, prayed
8. smiling, smiled
9. failing, failed
10. filing, filed
11. dragging, dragged
12. using, used
13. preferring, preferred
14. signing, signed
15. pointing, pointed
16. appearing, appeared
17. relaxing, relaxed
18. borrowing, borrowed
19. aiming, aimed
20. cramming, crammed

CHART 2-6: THE PRINCIPAL PARTS OF A VERB

• The "simple form" is also called the "base form" or "infinitive form."

• Point out that the present participle is always regular, even for irregular verbs: the simple form + *ing.* (See Chart 2-5 for spelling rules.)

• Point out the variations in patterns of irregular verbs in the simple form, simple past, and past participle:

All three parts may be different *(see, saw, seen).*
Two parts may be the same *(make, made, made).*
All three parts may be the same *(put, put, put).**

• Students may question why *see,* presented as a non-action verb in Chapter 1, has an *-ing* form. Explain that *see* has more than one meaning. When it means "visit" or "consult," it can be used in the progressive: *Bob is seeing his doctor this afternoon.* You might also mention that the *-ing* form has another use, i.e., as a gerund: *Seeing our grandchildren is always a pleasure.*

* See the *Understanding and Using English Grammar Workbook* (Chapter 1, Practice 5, p. 9) for the subcategories of vowel and consonant changes within these three categories of irregular verb patterns.

CHART 2-7: IRREGULAR VERBS: A REFERENCE LIST

• There are about 250 irregular verbs in English. Many of them are high frequency. Chart 2-7 contains 100 common irregular verbs. (For a longer list that includes more of the less frequently used verbs, consult *Understanding and Using English Grammar,* Chart 2-7, p. 22.)

Should or shouldn't the students be encouraged to memorize irregular verbs? The text tries to provide ample practice opportunities, but it seems beneficial to the ESL/EFL student and the native speaker equally to simply know these forms by memory. Most educated speakers of English can recite the principal parts of most of the irregular verbs. It's like a memory checklist they have to call on when needed.

The students at this level should already know many of the more common irregular verbs. It would be profitable for the students to memorize a few new ones every day. And of course practice is essential. Verbs used less often than others come less readily to mind (just as a native speaker may have to pause and rummage through her/his memory for the correct forms for *slay, forebear,* or *stride*). You might take three minutes a day to conduct a quick drill: say the simple form and have the class say the other forms from memory, developing a kind of rhythmic chant. Choose new verbs each day and include a few that were difficult from earlier days. Answer questions about meanings as necessary.

The irregular verb emphasis in this chapter is on the simple past form. In memory work, the students should start learning the past participles, too, even though they won't need to use them until Chapter 4, where particular exercises help students learn and practice them.

• *Burnt* and *dreamt* are principally BrE, but also occur in AmE and are included in the chart. Some other verbs (not included in the chart) that are regular in AmE but have variant spellings with *-t* in BrE are *leant, leapt, learnt, spelt, spilt, spoilt.*

☐ EXERCISES 10 and 11, pp. 34–35. Simple past: irregular verbs. (Chart 2-7)

These two exercises should be assigned as homework before class discussion, or they could be done as seatwork prior to discussion. In this kind of controlled cloze, the students need to read for meaning, then supply the appropriate word and form. Preparation is important; remind them that it's not helpful if they simply write down what other students say.

After class discussion of each of these, you might conduct an oral review, books open or closed. For example: *How did Olga get to school?* Response: *She rode her bicycle.* Other examples of questions for an oral review: *What did Frank do because he was thirsty? Do you remember that Alex had an accident while he was fixing dinner? He hurt his finger. What happened?* Etc. (Obviously, an oral review is not a normal conversation, but it does require students to get their noses out of their books and engage in listening and speaking practice.)

Exercises 10 and 11 have the same format but different verbs. The text divides this practice activity into two sections to allow for variation in ways the teacher chooses to handle them. Perhaps Exercise 10 could be done as seatwork or pair work followed by an entire class discussion, then Exercise 11 used for group work or homework.

EX. 10 EXPECTED ANSWERS:

1. drove . . . rode . . . took/rode
2. slept
3. wore
4. froze
5. drank
6. chose/took
7. hung/put
8. rang, woke
9. rose/came up
10. sent/wrote
11. taught
12. caught
13. stole/took
14. wore
15. sang, put
16. shook
17. swept
18. flew
19. held
20. fed
21. dug
22. left . . . forgot

EX. 11 EXPECTED ANSWERS:

1. cut
2. spent
3. kept
4. read
5. lost . . . went . . . found
6. held
7. met
8. forgave
9. broke
10. bought
11. fought
12. sold
13. hid
14. tore . . . threw
15. drew
16. felt
17. heard, got
18. won
19. bit
20. blew
21. caught . . . swam
22. told . . . knew

☐ EXERCISE 12, p. 37. Simple past. (Charts 2-1 → 2-7)

The goal is for the performance of the action to prompt immediate and spontaneous production of the target structure. Encourage your students to respond in a relaxed, fluent manner, taking risks and not worrying about making mistakes. Mistakes in language learning are natural and normal, and should be viewed only as opportunities for learning.

In terms of keeping the pace lively, this exercise works best if teacher-led. Group work, however, allows more students more opportunity for interactive speaking and listening practice.

ANSWERS (verbs only):

1. gave
2. opened
3. shut
4. stood
5. held
6. put
7. bent
8. touched
9. spelled [BrE: spelt]
10. shook
11. bit
12. hid
13. left
14. spoke
15. tore
16. told
17. threw
18. drew
19. turned
20. chose

☐ EXERCISE 13, p. 37. Simple past: questions and short answers. (Charts 2-1 → 2-7)

This exercise covers the simple past forms for statements, negatives, questions, and short answers.

ANSWERS: **2.** Did Tom's plane arrive . . . it did . . . got **3.** Did you go . . . I didn't . . . stayed . . . didn't feel **4.** Did Mark Twain write . . . he did . . . wrote **5.** Did you eat . . . I didn't . . . didn't have . . . didn't ring

☐ EXERCISE 14, p. 38. Simple past: questions and short answers; irregular verbs. (Charts 2-1 → 2-7)

This exercise can be like a game for the students. They should just relax and get in the conversational rhythm of question, short answer, full answer. The purpose is to provide comfortable practice using the simple past of irregular verbs. The students should understand that they can get valuable experience using target structures in exercises such as this, even with other learners who sometimes make mistakes. Their goal of fluency in English comes closer every time they use the language.

ANSWERS (verbs only):

1. slept
2. woke up
3. came
4. brought
5. put
6. lost
7. found
8. took
9. rode
10. drove
11. heard
12. read [pronounced "red"]
13. caught
14. felt
15. saw
16. went
17. had
18. thought
19. met
20. shook
21. bought
22. began
23. flew
24. ran
25. wrote
26. sent
27. lent
28. wore
29. went
30. fed
31. made
32. left
33. drank
34. fell
35. hurt
36. broke
37. understood
38. spoke
39. told
40. meant

☐ EXERCISE 15, p. 39. Past time. (Charts 2-1 → 2-7)

Sometimes a talkative Speaker A can overwhelm a somewhat timid Speaker B, so it's a good idea to have exact time limits. A few minutes is sufficient to describe a few things one did or didn't do yesterday. The students don't have to describe exactly five things they did and two or three things they didn't do. The purpose of the directions is to get them to think about various things they did.

When you correct the compositions, you might want to reproduce some of the errors the students made in use of simple past verbs and use them for discussion. Students should be told not to identify themselves when their sentences with errors are presented to the rest of the class for discussion.

Prior to handing the compositions in to you, the pairs may enjoy exchanging compositions so they can see what the other student wrote about them.

CHARTS 2-8 AND 2-9: SIMPLE PAST AND PAST PROGRESSIVE

- Relate the past progressive to the present progressive: e.g., *I am sitting in this chair right now. At this same time yesterday, I was sitting in this chair.* Show that both tenses give the idea of "in progress at a particular time."

- The distinction between *when* and *while* is not always as clear as the chart indicates. Sometimes, in fact, *when* can mean *while: When I was living in Nepal, I ate rice every day.* Still, making a sharp distinction between *when* and *while* can help students at this level learn the differences in meaning between the simple past and the past progressive. The text uses *when* as a cue for the simple past in an adverb clause and *while* as a cue for the past progressive in an adverb clause.

- Adverb clauses of time are presented in Chart 2-10. You can refer the students to that chart if you want to use the term "time clause," or you can simply use terms such as "the *when* part of the sentence" and "the *while* part of the sentence." The text doesn't focus attention on the term "clause" until Chart 2-10. Prior to that chart, time clauses used in the exercises begin with either *when* or *while.*

☐ EXERCISE 16, p. 40. Simple past and past progressive. (Charts 2-8 and 2-9)

This exercise is intended as an extension of Chart 2-8. It provides further examples for discussion of the form and meaning of the past progressive compared to the simple past.

SUGGESTION: Draw the diagrams for the two tenses on the board and point to them frequently during class discussion of this exercise to give visual reinforcement to the tense meanings.

ANSWERS:

2. was eating . . . came
3. came . . . was eating
4. was sleeping
5. was sleeping . . . rang
6. rang . . . was sleeping
7. began
8. was walking . . . saw
9. saw . . . was standing . . . was holding
10. waved . . . saw

☐ EXERCISE 17, p. 41. Using the past progressive. (Charts 2-8 and 2-9)

This exercise requires a teacher to organize and conduct it. You need to get two students doing two things at the same time. One has to begin an activity and continue it as the other begins and ends an activity. When they both finish, other students describe these activities, using the simple past and the past progressive.

EXPECTED RESPONSES: **1.** While (A) was writing a note to (. . .), (B) knocked on the door. **2.** While (A) was walking around the room, (B) clapped her/his hands once. **3.** While (A) was talking to (. . .), (B) came into the room. **4.** While (A) was reading a book, (B) tapped (A)'s shoulder. **5.** While (A) was looking out the window, (B) asked (A) a question. **6.** While (A) was whistling, (B) left the room. **7.** While (A) was looking at her/his watch, (B) asked (A) a question. **8.** [NOTE: Explain that *pantomime* / pântəmaym/ means to pretend to be doing something, using no words, only actions.] While (A) was eating, (B) sat down next to (A). **9.** While (A) was sleeping, (B) took (A)'s grammar book. **10.** While (A) was drinking a glass of water, (B) came in the room.

☐ EXERCISE 18, p. 41. Present progressive and past progressive. (Charts 1-1, 2-8, and 2-9)

Point out the similarity between the two progressives: they both describe events in progress in relation to another time or event. The only difference is the time frame, present or past.

ANSWERS: **3.** was . . . talking . . . were describing **4.** is . . . talking . . . is describing **5.** am walking **6.** was walking

☐ EXERCISE 19, p. 42. Present and past verbs. (Chapters 1 and 2)

The principal purpose of this practice is for the students to see the relationships between present and past verbs. Part I is told from a present-time perspective; the students are given a present-time setting and a dialogue. Part II reports the same events from a past perspective.

Reminder: See the *Introduction,* p. xii, for various ways of handling fill-in-the-blanks exercises.

PART I ANSWERS:

2. is studying
3. is sitting
4. isn't studying
5. is staring
6. wants
7. is looking
8. are you looking
9. am watching
10. don't know
11. admire
12. is steering
13. is drinking
14. is weaving
15. seems
16. isn't
17. looks
18. never had
19. was
20. was
21. tried
22. laughed
23. tried
24. was

PART II ANSWERS:

26. (was) studying
27. was sitting
28. wasn't studying
29. was staring
30. was watching
31. walked
32. pointed
33. was steering
34. was drinking
35. was weaving
36. seemed
37. never learned (*also possible:* had never learned)
38. was
39. offered
40. accepted

☐ EXERCISE 20, p. 43. Verb tense and irregular verb review. (Chapters 1 and 2)

This exercise concentrates on past verbs (with an emphasis on irregular verbs), but also includes present verbs.

In a long cloze exercise such as this, it is important that the students prepare their completions prior to class discussion and that the review of the correct answers in class proceeds apace.

Discuss the correct spelling of words that might cause problems: *dropped, spotted, hopped, sobbed, swimming,* etc.

EXPANSION: Following class discussion, ask the students to summarize the story of Princess Tina and the Frog Prince in their own words.

EXPANSION: Another possibility is to have the class retell the story in a chain: one student begins the story with a sentence or two, then the next student says what happens next, then a third continues the story, etc.

ANSWERS:

(3) chose . . . took . . . held . . . walked . . . dropped . . . picked . . . spotted . . . bent . . . was
(4) hopped . . . picked . . . brought . . . am . . . claim
(5) told . . . refused . . . heard . . . laughed . . . laughed . . . said
(6) felt . . . am . . . fell . . . sobbed . . . loved . . . believed . . . didn't understand . . . hid . . . kept . . . grew . . . had . . . rang
(7) left . . . ran . . . went . . . ate . . . drank . . . cut . . . washed . . . swept . . . made . . . took . . . was
(8) went . . . was . . . swam . . . became . . . was swimming . . . lost . . . quit . . . was drowning . . . appeared . . . pushed . . . saved
(9) did you save . . . are . . . have . . . do not . . . am
(10) said . . . began . . . sat . . . listened . . . understood . . . told . . . shared . . . spent . . . talked . . . laughed . . . played . . . worked
(11) were sitting . . . bent . . . kissed . . . turned . . . took . . . saved . . . looked . . . saw . . . found . . . am . . . saw . . . found
(12) returned . . . got . . . were . . . ignored . . . didn't talk . . . made . . . gave . . . lived

☐ EXERCISE 21, p. 48. Past time. (Chapter 2)

You may wish to take time in class to explain how to write quoted speech if you would like your students to try to write a story similar to "Tina and the Frog Prince."

Item 2: A fable is a story that teaches a lesson. Often animals are characters.

Item 3: The story-writing can take place over several days as the paper makes its way through the class. Its principal purpose is fun and involvement. Students should be encouraged to be humorous.

Small classes (twelve or less) can all work on the same story. Larger classes should be divided into groups of eight to ten.

When the story is completed, you can make various uses of it to encourage editing and revising skills. (1) Photocopy it and have each student proof and rewrite it, being very careful about spelling and punctuation. (If possible, put the story on a computer all the class has access to.) (2) Photocopy it and proof it together with the class. (3) Give the story to groups to put into good written shape. (4) Tell the students to rewrite the story the way <u>they</u> want it to happen.

CHART 2-10: EXPRESSING PAST TIME: USING TIME CLAUSES

• Be sure to emphasize that examples (a) and (b) have no difference in meaning. Discuss punctuation. Point out that a time clause is not a complete sentence. It cannot stand alone. It must be connected to a main or independent clause. *I went to bed* is a complete sentence. *After I finished my work* is not a complete sentence.

• In speaking, the voice drops low at the end of a sentence, but it tends to drop a little then rise a little at the end of a time clause before a main clause. You might want to demonstrate this.

• *When, after, before, until, as soon as,* and *while* are subordinating conjunctions, but the text does not use that terminology. They can be called "words that introduce time clauses" or "time clause words."

After, before, and *until* are also used as prepositions, so do not always introduce a time clause; they may be followed by a (pro)noun object rather than a subject and a verb: *I walked home* ***after class****. I'll call you* ***before dinner****. We stayed there* ***until six o'clock****.* The other conjunctions in this chart *(as soon as, while,* and *when)* are not used as prepositions.

• Most students could benefit from your discussing additional examples with *as soon as* and *until.* Develop examples from the classroom context if possible, or from the students' lives. For example (after the students perform these actions): *Maria raised her hand as soon as Po raised his hand. She didn't raise her hand until he raised his hand.* OR: *Marco didn't sit down until Anna sat down. As soon as Anna sat down, Marco sat down.*

☐ EXERCISE 22, p. 49. Past time clauses. (Chart 2-10)

This is an exercise on complex sentence structure and punctuation. It is intended to provide further examples for discussion of the grammar in Chart 2-10. It can be done as seatwork leading to board work.

ANSWERS:

2. Before I left my apartment this morning, I unplugged the coffee pot.
   OR I unplugged the coffee pot before I left my apartment this morning.
3. Until I was seven years old, I lived on a farm.
   OR I lived on a farm until I was seven years old.
4. As soon as I heard the doorbell, I opened the door.
   OR I opened the door as soon as I heard the doorbell.
5. While the rabbit was sleeping, the fox climbed through the window.
   OR The fox climbed through the window while the rabbit was sleeping.
   When the fox climbed through the window, the rabbit was sleeping.
   OR The rabbit was sleeping when the fox climbed through the window.
6. When it began to rain, I stood under a tree.
   OR I stood under a tree when it began to rain.
7. While I was lying in bed with the flu, my friends were swimming at the beach.
   OR I was lying in bed with the flu while my friends were swimming at the beach.
   While my friends were swimming at the beach, I was lying in bed with the flu.
   OR I was lying in bed with the flu while my friends were swimming at the beach.

☐ EXERCISE 23, p. 50. Past time clauses. (Charts 2-1 → 2-10)

Each item contains adverb clauses to be identified. Point out how useful adverb clauses are to show time relationships between activities. Using complex structures, in this case time clauses, allows students to expand their repertoire in expressing relationships between ideas in their writing and speaking.

ANSWERS:

2. bought . . . went
adv cl = [before I went to the hospital yesterday to visit my friend]

3. went . . . got . . . was . . . was planting . . . was . . . was working . . . was changing . . . were playing . . . was changing . . . were playing
adv cl = [When I got there around two o'clock] and [while Mr. Smith was changing the oil in the car]

4. hit . . . was using . . . hurt
adv cl = [while I was using the hammer]

5. heard . . . began
adv cl = [As soon as we heard the news of the approaching hurricane]

6. walked . . . got . . . stopped . . . rested . . . was
adv cl = [until he got tired] and [until he was strong enough to continue]

7. was lying . . . heard . . . heard . . . turned . . . held . . . listened . . . was chewing
adv cl = [While I was lying in bed last night] and [When I heard this strange noise]

8. was looking . . . started . . . took . . . was taking . . . (was) enjoying . . . came . . . asked . . . told . . . thanked . . . went . . . stayed . . . came . . . covered . . . went . . . returned . . . noticed . . . was making . . . was humming . . . thought . . . shut . . . got . . . left . . . spent
adv cl = [while I was looking] and [while I was taking a short break outdoors and . . . on my face] and [After I told him how to get there] and [until a big cloud came and covered the sun] and [As soon as I returned to my desk]

CHART 2-11: EXPRESSING PAST HABIT: *USED TO*

• It is interesting that investigation into the question and negative forms of *used to* showed that there is no consensus on which forms are correct: *did you* ***used*** *to* vs. *did you* ***use*** *to* and *didn't* ***used*** *to* vs. *didn't* ***use*** *to.*

Some references say one is correct but not the other (and they don't agree on which of the two forms is the correct one); other texts (especially dictionaries) say that both are correct.

With one exception, the ESL grammar texts we investigated (including the first two editions of this grammar text) uniformly choose *did you* ***use*** *to* and *didn't* ***use*** *to;* only *Collins COBUILD English Grammar* (HarperCollins Publishers Ltd, 1994, p. 243) presents *did you* ***used*** *to* and *didn't* ***used*** *to* as the correct forms.

It is also interesting that references based on corpus findings present only *did you* ***used*** *to* and *didn't* ***used*** *to.* They do not cite the forms of *did you* ***use*** *to* and *didn't* ***use*** *to* at all. (See *Longman Grammar of Spoken and Written English,* Biber et al; Longman, 1999, p. 218, pp. 164–165, and *Collins COBUILD English Usage,* HarperCollins Publishers Ltd, 1992, p. 746.)

This appears to be an area of English grammar still in flux. Given the lack of agreement on this matter, this text presents both forms as possible and correct, with the edge given to the one cited in the most recent corpus-based reference works.

Questions and negatives using *used to* are of low frequency.

• *Past habit* is also termed the "habitual past."

• The usual pronunciation of *used to* is /yustə/ or /yustuw/. The /s/ is lengthened slightly, and there is only one /t/ sound. Some students want to pronounce both the *-ed* and the *t,* but this is not done.

By way of comparison, when *used* is the simple past of the verb *use* (meaning "to employ"), the "s" is pronounced /z/: *I used an axe to cut down the tree.*

• *Be used to* is presented in Chapter 10 and compared to *used to. Be used to* doesn't need to be mentioned here although questions about it may arise in Exercise 24.

☐ EXERCISE 24, p. 52. Past habit with USED TO. (Chart 2-11)

Some of the mistakes in form represented in this exercise may derive from confusions between *be used to* and *used to.* The intention is for the students to focus solely on *used to* as the habitual past and not confuse it (at this point) with a comparison to *be used to.* It may not, however, be possible (and perhaps not even desirable, depending on the level of the students) to avoid a discussion of the two similar structures during this exercise.

ANSWERS: **2.** . . . used to **work** **3.** Margo ~~was~~ used to teach **4.** Where **did** you use(d) to live? **5.** I didn't ~~was~~ use(d) to **6.** **Did** you use(d) to **7.** . . . used to **go** to the beach

☐ EXERCISE 25, p. 52. Past habit with USED TO. (Chart 2-11)

Again, this exercise is an extension of the chart, intended to provide further examples for discussion. Statement, question, and negative forms are practiced.

Relate the items in the exercise to the students' own experiences by asking leading questions: *Did you ever used to be shy? Where did you used to live? Where did you used to work?* Etc.

ANSWERS: **2.** used to think **3.** did you use(d) to live **4.** Did you use(d) to work **5.** never used to wake up / didn't use(d) to wake up . . . used to sleep **6.** used to watch . . . didn't use(d) to watch . . . did you use(d) to watch

☐ EXERCISE 26, p. 53. Past habit with USED TO. (Chart 2-11)

Students have to read for meaning and think some of these items through, so they need time to prepare before class discussion. See the *Introduction,* p. xiii, for notes on conducting open-completion exercises.

EXPECTED RESPONSES: **4.** used to play **5.** didn't use(d) to eat **6.** didn't use(d) to be . . . (politics) **7.** did you use(d) to do . . . used to *(free response)*

☐ EXERCISE 27, p. 54. Past habit with USED TO. (Chart 2-11)

The intention is that the topics be springboards to open conversations that include spontaneous use of the target structure.

☐ EXERCISE 28, p. 54. Past habit with USED TO. (Chart 2-11)

This exercise requires independent, creative use of *used to* and some thought and insight on the part of the students. They might come up with ideas more easily in groups than in individual writing.

Chapter 3: FUTURE TIME

ORDER OF CHAPTER	CHARTS	EXERCISES	WORKBOOK
Preview: future time	3-1 → 3-6	Ex. 1	
Forms: *be going to* and *will*	3-1 → 3-3	Ex. 2 → 7	Pr. 1 → 6
Sureness about the future	3-4	Ex. 8 → 12	Pr. 7 → 10
Be going to vs. *will*	3-5	Ex. 13 → 14	Pr. 11 → 13
Future time clauses and *if*-clauses	3-6	Ex. 15 → 20	Pr. 14 → 17
Review: past and future time		Ex. 21	Pr. 18
Present progressive and simple present to express future time	3-7 → 3-8	Ex. 22 → 25	Pr. 19 → 21
Be about to	3-9	Ex. 26 → 28	Pr. 22
Parallel verbs	3-10	Ex. 29 → 30	Pr. 23
Review: verb forms	Chapters 1 → 3	Ex. 31 → 36	Pr. 24 → 25

General Notes on Chapter 3

• Students learn common spoken and written forms of expressing plans, predictions, and hypotheses. They also practice expressing future time in adverb clauses of time and condition, plus reviewing present and past verb forms.

• TERMINOLOGY: English has no verb ending that signals future time. Instead, it relies on verb phrases (with modal auxiliaries and periphrastic modals) and/or time expressions to refer to the future. Since there are various ways of expressing future time, this textbook generally just uses the phrase "expressing future time" instead of referring specifically to ***will*** + *a simple form of the verb* as "the future tense." For pedagogical ease and convenience, however, the traditional term "future tense" can be used in the classroom for verb phrases that include *will* or *be going to.* The students' understanding of the term "tense" is generally a verb form that expresses time relationships; most students are comfortable with the term. The goal as always is to present and explain structures with a minimum of terminology. The hope is that the students will leave their formal study of English one day with good control of its structures; most terminology can and probably will be soon forgotten.

☐ **EXERCISE 1, p. 55. Preview: future time. (Charts 3-1 → 3-6)**

This exercise is intended as a quick introduction to the principal grammar in this chapter: *be going to, will, will probably,* and *may,* plus future time words and future time clauses. Much of this will probably be review for students at this level.

If you conduct this exercise with the whole class, ask for several completions for each item. Students can call out their sentences. See the Introduction, p. xiii, for suggestions for handling open-completion exercises.

CHART 3-1: EXPRESSING FUTURE TIME: *BE GOING TO* AND *WILL*

• Both *be going to* and *will* are presented in this chart. They are often, but not always, interchangeable. Their differences in meaning are presented in Chart 3-5.

• The text emphasizes *be going to* first in the exercises and relates it to present and past verbs. Then the text deals with *will.*

• The use of *will* is sometimes called "the simple future tense," but, as noted above, *will* is actually only one of several modals and periphrastic modals used to express future time. What you could point out here is that *be going to* and *will* are used to express that an event is, in the speaker's mind, 100% certain to occur at a future time, as in examples (a) through (d). We can't, of course, always feel certain about future events, so other auxiliaries (see Chapter 5) are also frequently used for future time.

• Some conservative cultures resist the notion that any person can see into the future or dare to make predictions. Chart 3-4 presents *will probably, may,* and *maybe* as ways to communicate less certainty, which might satisfy some objections. As a side note on cultural attitudes toward predicting the future, three hundred years ago in Great Britain, predicting the weather was a crime punishable by death (burning at the stake as a witch).

• *Shall* is used with *I* and *we* in formal BrE, but in AmE and informal BrE, *will* is far more common. One use of *shall* is to show great determination, e.g., *We shall overcome* or *I shall return!* Otherwise, *will* is used with all subjects to express simple future time in AmE. Historically, there was no "rule" about *shall* being used with the first person and *will* with the second and third persons until the mid-seventeenth century. For centuries, no distinction existed in actual usage. The "rule" was originally formulated by prescriptive grammarians and passed on through generations of grammar textbooks.

CHART 3-2: FORMS WITH *BE GOING TO*

• *Going to* is sometimes pronounced /gɔnə/ or /gənə/, which—though not an accepted written form—may be represented in writing as *gonna.* Model *gonna* for your students so that they will be aware of it, but don't insist on its use by learners at this level. When learners force *gonna,* it may sound as though they are speaking careless, nonstandard English. The appropriate use of *gonna* will develop as the students gain experience with the language.

• One common error is the omission of *be:* INCORRECT: *I going to go to the market tomorrow.* (OR: *I going to the market tomorrow,* in which the present progressive is used to express future time. See Chart 3-7.)

☐ EXERCISE 2, p. 56. BE GOING TO. (Charts 3-1 and 3-2)

This exercise is a quick check on the written forms of *be going to:* statement, negative, question, and short answer.

ANSWERS: **2.** is Alex going to be . . . is going to be **3.** Are you going to finish . . . I'm going to finish **4.** are you going to call . . . am not going to call . . . am going to send **5.** is Dr. Price going to talk . . . is going to discuss [Try to avoid discussing the use of the present progressive to mean future time even though it is possible in this completion.]

☐ EXERCISE 3, p. 57. BE GOING TO. (Charts 3-1 and 3-2)

The purpose here is oral practice with typical conversational questions and answers about the future. Speaker B should be encouraged to answer truthfully, but some students enjoy using their imaginations and making up funny answers.

EXPECTED QUESTIONS: **1.** Where are you going to go after your last class today? **2.** Are you going to have pizza for dinner tonight? **3.** What are you going to do this evening? **4.** When are you going to visit my hometown? **5.** Are you going to visit (name of a place) sometime in the future? **6.** What are you going to do this coming Saturday? **7.** What time are you going to go to bed tonight? **8.** What are you going to wear tomorrow? **9.** Are you going to wear (your raincoat) tomorrow too? **10.** How long are you going to stay in this city? **11.** Are you going to take a trip sometime this year or next? **12.** Where are you going to go, and what are you going to do?

☐ EXERCISE 4, p. 58. Review of verb forms: past, present, and future. (Chapters 1 and 2; Charts 3-1 and 3-2)

This is a straightforward review of the forms of past, present, and future verbs: affirmative, negative, question, and short answer.

Students can work in pairs and then read their dialogues aloud. One pair can write their dialogue on the board for ease of discussion of the correct forms.

The sentences the students create can be silly and imaginative. This is an exercise on form; the emphasis is not on realistic dialogue, although the students are indeed practicing structures commonly used in typical everyday conversations. (It is helpful for students to concentrate principally on forms of structures at times; not every one of their utterances needs to be "real communication.")

Be sure to congratulate your students on their mastery of all the forms represented in this exercise!

SAMPLE COMPLETIONS: **1.** I fed birds in the park yesterday. **2.** . . . Do you feed birds in the park . . . ? **3.** Yes, I do. I feed . . . . **4.** Do you also feed goldfish in the park every day? **5.** No, I don't. I don't feed . . . . **6.** Did you feed goldfish . . . ? **7.** Yes, I did. I fed . . . . **8.** Did you also have a picnic in the park yesterday? **9.** No, I didn't. I didn't have a picnic . . . . **10.** Are you going to have a picnic in the park tomorrow? **11.** Yes, I am. I'm going to have a picnic . . . . **12.** Are you also going to feed the birds in the park tomorrow? **13.** No, I'm not. I'm not going to feed the birds in the park tomorrow.

☐ EXERCISE 5, p. 58. Present, past, and future. (Chapters 1 and 2; Charts 3-1 and 3-2)

This is a review of the simple present, present progressive, simple past, past progressive, and *be going to* (or *will* if a student wishes). Students may spontaneously use present tenses to express future time or use other verb forms, such as modal auxiliaries. That is fine.

Pair work gives maximum individual participation and practice, but after the students have practiced in pairs, you may wish to conduct an oral review with the whole class. Draw tense diagrams on the board to assist the review. Ask for more than one response to each item. Pursue interesting responses. To keep students alert and interested, occasionally ask one student what another student has said.

Other comments: In item 4, point out that *every day* (an adverbial expression) is spelled as two words. (It is spelled as one word when it is used as an adjective, e.g., *everyday activities.)* Items 6 and 8 *(the day before yesterday* and *the day after tomorrow)* may require a calendar written on the board to ensure clarity of understanding. Item 7 *(tonight)* can invite the use of present tenses if your class is taking place in the evening.

CHART 3-3: FORMS WITH *WILL*

• Model contractions with *will.* Include some examples of nouns and question words contracted with *will* in speech: *Tom'll be here soon. Where'll you be around eight tonight?* Mention that contractions are natural in conversations, both formal and informal. In fact, fluent speakers of English find it impossible not to use them; speech without contractions sounds stilted or bookish.

• After a consonant, the contraction "'ll" is pronounced as an additional syllable: /əl/. For example, *Bob'll* is pronounced like the word "bobble" or "bauble": /babəl/.

• The negative contraction *shan't (shall not)* occurs in BrE but rarely in AmE.

☐ EXERCISES 6 and 7, p. 59. Forms with WILL. (Chart 3-3)

The sentences in both exercises are intended as models for everyday spoken English. Ask the students to repeat after you. Point out to them that the "ll" is unemphasized, its sound low and fast; it's hard to discern unless one knows it's supposed to be there by being aware of the form, meaning, and use of *will.* One of the reasons learners study grammar is to enable them to understand normal contracted speech, e.g., understand that *dinner'll* is two words spoken as one, not a new vocabulary word, and expresses future time, as in *Dinner'll be ready soon.* You might point out that a common mistake in student production is a statement such as *Bye. I see you tomorrow.* Errors such as this arise because learners don't hear "ll," and they don't hear "ll" because they haven't learned to expect it.

EX. 6 ANSWERS:

2. We'll
3. You'll
4. She'll
5. He'll
6. It'll
7. They'll

EX. 7 ANSWERS:

2. Dinner'll
3. Mary'll
4. weather'll
5. party'll
6. Sam'll
7. friends'll
8. sun'll

CHART 3-4: SURENESS ABOUT THE FUTURE

• One uses *will* and *be going to* to express that one feels 100% sure about a future event, is confident that a certain thing will occur in the future. Even though one can never be sure about the future with absolutely certain knowledge, one can express one's confidence in future events by using *will* and *be going to.*

• One does not, however, always feel 100% confident about future activities and events. It is helpful for students to know how to qualify their statements about the future. Adding *probably* to *will* is one common way. Using *may* or *maybe* are other common ways. In Chapter 5, the students will learn other ways of qualifying their statements about the future by using other auxiliaries *(might, should, can,* etc.).

• The figures of 100%, 90%, and 50% to indicate degrees of certainty are approximate and figurative; they are not intended to be nor should be interpreted as statistically exact (as some students may want to do).

• As for placement of midsentence adverbs such as *probably,* if the question arises, tell the class that it is also sometimes possible to use *probably* in front of *will (Ann probably will go to the park tomorrow),* but tell them that the usual position is between the auxiliary and the main verb and suggest they use that placement in the exercise. At this level, the text asks students to gain mastery of usual, fundamental patterns of English. They can and will add variations as they gain experience and fluency.

☐ EXERCISE 8, p. 60. Sureness about the future. (Chart 3-4)

You might give the students these options to choose from in their responses: very or 100% sure, 90% sure, and 50% sure.

ANSWERS:

2. very sure
3. 90% sure
4. 50% sure
5. 90% sure
6. very sure
7. 50% sure
8. very sure
9. very sure (art museum)
50% sure (natural history museum)
10. 90% sure

☐ EXERCISE 9, p. 61. Sureness about the future: using PROBABLY. (Chart 3-4)

The items exemplify typical contexts in which people express less than 100% certainty about future events. Students don't need to prepare the answers prior to class discussion.

ANSWERS:

2. Rosa probably won't go / probably isn't going to go
She'll probably stay / is probably going to stay home and rest.
3. Sam will probably go / is probably going to go
He probably won't stay up / probably isn't going to stay up
4. Ms. Bok probably won't fly / probably isn't going to fly
She'll probably travel / is probably going to travel
5. Mr. Chu will probably call / is probably going to call . . . or e-mail
He probably won't wait / probably isn't going to wait
6. Gina probably won't run / probably isn't going to run
She'll probably skip / is probably going to skip

☐ EXERCISE 10, p. 61. Sureness about the future. (Chart 3-4)

This exercise seeks to prompt production of the target structures using real information that you elicit about the students' lives. Encourage the use of both *may/maybe* and *probably.* Discuss the distinction made in the directions about using *may/maybe* for guesses and *probably* if one is fairly sure.

Make up additional or alternative cues based on your students' situations and lives.

☐ EXERCISE 11, p. 62. Sureness about the future. (Chart 3-4)

Pair work allows for maximum student participation and practice. Teacher-led work allows for explication, modeling, correction, and interaction with a native (or near-native) speaker. Both are valuable approaches. Teacher-led oral exercises usually take less class time.

☐ EXERCISE 12, p. 62. Using WILL, BE GOING TO, and MAY. (Charts 3-1 → 3-4)

Divide the class into groups. Encourage the students to go beyond what is suggested in the items to discuss their ideas of what the future will be like. Perhaps each group could agree upon two or three original predictions (for one or more or all of the items) and report them to the rest of the class. The intention here is to start the students talking about the future; it is hoped that future verb forms will occur spontaneously and correctly.

CHART 3-5: *BE GOING TO* vs. *WILL*

• Ask the students about their future plans: "What do you plan to do tomorrow?" The question should generate examples of "prior plans" that require *be going to* rather than *will.*

• As a point of comparison, set up a situation that requires *will* rather than *be going to: I need some help. I need that piece of chalk. Who'll get it for me?* Have the students demonstrate volunteering by raising their hands and saying, "I'll get it for you."

• This chart's purpose is to point out specifically and as simply as possible when *be going to* and *will* have clearly recognizable differences in their use. Remind students that often there is no difference in meaning between *will* and *be going to.*

There are other differences between *will* and *be going to* and, in particular, other uses of *will* that the text does not address. As is true of most other modal auxiliaries, *will* is a complicated word with a variety of meanings and uses. The text does not view explanations of all the nuances in meaning and usage of *will* and *be going to* to be productive for ESL/EFL students, especially at this proficiency level. What the text intends is to engender a basic understanding and usage ability of the two, laying the groundwork for more sophisticated use of these structures as students gain experience with the language. (Teaching grammar at this level is largely a matter of laying the groundwork for growth in the students' linguistic skills.)

☐ EXERCISE 13, p. 63. BE GOING TO vs. WILL. (Charts 3-1 → 3-5)

This exercise has further examples of the grammar presented in Chart 3-5 and is intended for class discussion of the meanings of the two verb forms.

ANSWERS:

2. (1)
3. (2)
4. (1)
5. (1), (2)
6. (1)
7. (1), (2)
8. (1), (2), (2), (2)

☐ EXERCISE 14, p. 64. BE GOING TO vs. WILL. (Charts 3-1 → 3-5)

Many students would find it difficult to prepare this exercise before you have discussed Chart 3-5 and Exercise 13 in class. Students can prepare the exercise as seatwork, singly or in pairs, immediately after the discussion of Exercise 13.

ANSWERS:

3. will	**7.** will
4. am going to	**8.** will
5. will	**9.** am going to
6. are going to	**10.** will . . . will

CHART 3-6: EXPRESSING THE FUTURE IN TIME CLAUSES AND *IF*-CLAUSES

• Illustrate and identify a time clause. (See Chart 2-10, p. 48, of the *FEG 3e* student book.)

• Compare a main clause verb with a time clause verb that expresses future time. For example, both of the following express the same action (going to class tomorrow):

Main clause: *I am going to go to class tomorrow.*
Time clause: *Before I go to class tomorrow, . . .*

Write the main clause on the board. Then add *Before* at the beginning to change it to a time clause and demonstrate how the verb has to change.

To help students understand what a main clause is, demonstrate by pretending to come into the room and saying, "Before I go to class tomorrow, . . ." then stop as though you had finished your communication. They should feel that your statement is incomplete. Then say, "I am going to go to class tomorrow," and ask if they feel that that is a more complete statement. A main clause is a complete statement, but a time clause must be attached to a main clause.

Point out that the form of a verb in a time clause is simple present, but the meaning is future. Emphasize that *will* and *be going to* are not used in a time clause. Mistakes such as *before I will go to class tomorrow* and *after I'm going to eat dinner* are common. The learners may have logic on their side, but they must accept and learn traditional usages that have developed as English has evolved.

• There is a situation in which *will* is used in an *if*-clause. The text doesn't teach this use, but the question may arise. Sometimes when a person is making a deal or trying to reach an agreement about who will do what, *will* is used in the *if*-clause: *If you'll make the sandwiches, I'll pour the drinks.* *Will* in an *if*-clause is close to the meaning of a polite question with *will: Will you make the sandwiches? If you do, I will pour the drinks. Is that agreeable to you?*

☐ EXERCISE 15, p. 65. Future time clauses and IF-clauses. (Chart 3-6)

The focus is on verb forms in the subordinate clauses. Students need to identify the structure of the sentence in order to correct the verb form errors.

ANSWERS: **2.** . . . after she ~~will~~ **returns** from vacation next week. **3.** . . . as soon as my plane ~~will~~ **lands.** **4.** . . . until I ~~will~~ **find** something better. **5.** . . . as soon as you ~~will~~ **find** out anything about it. **6.** When you **are** in Australia next month, **7.** If it **isn't** cold tomorrow, . . . If it **is** cold tomorrow,

☐ EXERCISE 16, p. 66. Future time clauses and IF-clauses. (Chart 3-6)

ANSWERS: **2.** will call . . . returns **3.** won't be . . . come **4.** go . . . will prepare **5.** visits . . . will take **6.** will stay . . . calls **7.** doesn't come . . . will miss **8.** gets *(also possible:* is) . . . will eat . . . is . . . will be

☐ EXERCISE 17, p. 67. Future IF-clauses. (Chart 3-6)

Students might use something other than *will* or *be going to* in the main clause. Any verb expressing future time is fine: *can, should, might,* etc.

SUGGESTION: Before doing Exercise 17, you can invite the students to play "What if" with you. This is a kind of mental exercise. It is used by computer programmers, statisticians, financial planners, weather forecasters, and ordinary people every day. They try to imagine various results from certain conditions. (This can be done before Exercise 17 because it is not necessary for the students to change the verb form that you give them.) For example:

TEACHER: *What if I can't come to class tomorrow?*
SPEAKER A: *If you can't come, we won't have a lesson.*
SPEAKER B: *Or maybe we'll have another teacher.*
TEACHER (following B's idea): *What if you have another teacher tomorrow?*
SPEAKER C: *If we have another teacher, he or she probably won't give us homework.*
TEACHER (following C's idea): *What if you don't do any homework?*
Etc.

Change the topic after two or three students participate.

Point out that a "what if" question is a shortened form of "What will happen if . . . ?"

ANSWERS (verbs in if-*clauses only):*

1. If I have . . . .
2. If it rains . . . .
3. If it doesn't rain . . . .
4. If the teacher is . . . .
5. If I'm tired . . . .
6. If I'm not . . . .
7. If it is . . . .
8. If we don't have . . . .

☐ EXERCISE 18, p. 68. Future time clauses with BEFORE and AFTER. (Chart 3-6)

The students state intentions, perform actions, and describe these actions using adverb clauses of time.

☐ EXERCISE 19, p. 68. Future time clauses with UNTIL and AS SOON AS. (Chart 3-6)

This exercise connects real actions with the meanings of *until* and *as soon as* while providing an opportunity for listening and speaking practice. Listening carefully and being able to communicate heard information are important parts of this kind of exercise.

Only students whose English is of a high level compared to the rest of the class should be group leaders. Most classes would benefit from the teacher leading this exercise.

EXPECTED ANSWERS:

1. I'm going to sit at my desk until B knocks on the door. Then I'm going to get up and walk to the door. . . . A is going to sit at his/her desk until B knocks on the door. Then he/she's going to get up and walk to the door. . . . As soon as B knocks on the door, A is going to get up and walk to the door.
2. [Point out that *breath* is a noun and ends in voiceless *th; breathe* is a verb and ends in voiced *th.*] I'm going to hold my breath until B snaps his/her fingers. Then I'm going to breathe again. . . . A is going to hold his/her breath until B snaps his/her fingers. Then he/she is going to breathe again. . . . A is going to breathe again as soon as B snaps his/her fingers.
3. I'm going to clap my hands until B bows. Then I'm going to stop clapping . . . . A is going to clap his/her hands until B bows. Then he/she is going to stop clapping . . . . As soon as B bows, A is going to stop clapping his/her hands.

☐ EXERCISE 20, p. 69. Review of time clauses and IF-clauses. (Chapters 1 → 3)

ANSWERS:

1. a. goes . . . brushes
   b. goes . . . is going to e-mail / will e-mail
   c. went . . . took
   d. was taking . . . rang
   e. rang . . . jumped
   f. gets . . . is going to brush / will brush
   g. brushes . . . gets
2. a. get . . . drink
   b. get . . . am going to drink / will drink
   c. will not have . . . get
   d. got . . . drank
   e. was drinking . . . came . . . offered
   f. is probably going to drop / will probably drop . . . comes . . . am going to make / will make

☐ EXERCISE 21, p. 70. Writing about the past and the future. (Chapters 2 and 3)

You could use this for quick practice with time clauses and verb forms, having the students write short paragraphs of less than 100 words in class. You might concentrate on only these two areas when marking papers. It could also be used for homework, with each paragraph 200 to 250 words or more in length.

EXPANSION: You could also turn this exercise into a discussion of how to connect ideas with time words other than "time clause words" (i.e., subordinating conjunctions): *Before, after, when, while, until,* and *as soon as* introduce adverb clauses. *Next, then, later,* and *after that* do not introduce adverb clauses. They show the time relationships between two independent sentences: these words are sometimes followed by a comma.

To distinguish between *after* and *after that:*

Example: *I watched TV. After that, I went to bed.*

In the example, *that* is a pronoun that refers to the entire preceding sentence.

In this case, *after that* means "after I watched TV."

INCORRECT: *I watched TV. After I went to bed.*

REMINDER: In a paragraph-writing exercise, students will produce some sentences that can be used for teacher-made error-analysis exercises.

CHART 3-7: USING THE PRESENT PROGRESSIVE TO EXPRESS FUTURE TIME

• The use of the present progressive to express future time is common, especially with the verbs presented in the chart and other verbs that express planned activities. Some common ones are *bring, build, eat, call, finish, get, give, make, meet, move, send, start, visit.*

• The present progressive and *be going to* are used to talk about future events that the speaker has present knowledge of: *Do you have plans for this evening? Yes. I'm watching a baseball game on TV this evening.* (The speaker knows at the moment of speaking what his plans are for the future.) OR: *We're going to Thailand for our vacation.* (The speaker's vacation plans are a present reality.) OR: *Sara's having a baby in October.* (The speaker is expressing a future event based on present knowledge.)

When the present progressive is used to express future time, usually *be going to* is equally possible (but not vice versa: not all situations in which *be going to* is used can also be expressed by the present progressive). *I'm watching TV this evening* and *I'm going to watch TV this evening* have no difference in meaning.

☐ EXERCISE 22, p. 70. Using the present progressive to express future time. (Chart 3-7)

Point out the future time words or the context that gives a future meaning to the present progressive form.

ANSWERS:

1. A: are . . . doing *(future)*
   B: am going *(future)*
   B: am going . . . are . . . doing *(future)*
   A: am going . . . are going *(future)*
   B: am meeting *(future)*
2. A: are . . . taking *(present)*
   B: am taking *(present)*
   A: are . . . taking *(future)*
   B: am taking *(future)*
3. A: am going *(future)*
   B: are . . . going *(future)*
   B: Are . . . flying . . . taking/driving *(future)*
   A: am flying *(future)*
   A: am taking *(future)*
   B: am staying *(future)*
4. A: are . . . doing *(present)*
   B: am cutting *(present)*
5. A: am leaving *(future)*
   A: am spending *(future)* . . . is going *(present)* . . . am visiting *(future)*

☐ EXERCISE 23, p. 72. Using the present progressive to express future time. (Chart 3-7)

This exercise takes only a short time. Its intention is to have the students use the target structure in talking about their lives. After the pair work, you can ask students the questions at random so the class can get a sampling of their classmates' answers.

☐ EXERCISE 24, p. 72. Writing: using the present progressive to express future time. (Chart 3-7)

The purpose here is to practice expressing future time using a present verb form. Perhaps think of other situations besides travel plans in which native speakers would be likely to use the present progressive for future time and ask the students to write about those too: plans for this evening, plans for this weekend, plans for a coming student party, etc.

CHART 3-8: USING THE SIMPLE PRESENT TO EXPRESS FUTURE TIME

- The use of the simple present to express future time in an independent clause is limited to relatively few verbs, ones that deal with schedules and timetables.
- To help the students understand this special use of the simple present, tell them as a general rule it is used only when the activity is one that is typically written down, as on a schedule or timetable, and will occur at a definite time.

☐ EXERCISE 25, p. 73. Using present verb forms to express future time. (Charts 3-7 and 3-8)

Point out that the simple present can carry the same meaning as the present progressive or *be going to* in expressing future time, as in item 1. Also point out that its use in expressing future time is limited to special situations (outlined in Chart 3-8); it is not always interchangeable with the present progressive or *be going to* to express future time, as illustrated in item 2, where the situation does not deal with a schedule or timetable, but rather is simply a statement of intention about the future.

ANSWERS: **3.** b **4.** a, b **5.** b **6.** a, b **7.** a, b **8.** b

CHART 3-9: IMMEDIATE FUTURE: USING *BE ABOUT TO*

• The text treats *be about to* as an idiom; that is, its meaning is not predictable from the usual rules of grammar or usual meaning of the constituent vocabulary elements. In Chapter 13, the students are taught that gerunds, not infinitives, immediately follow prepositions. This is a special case (i.e., an "idiom"). In other words, *about* followed by an infinitive has a special meaning.

• *Be about to* is common in spoken English.

• To elicit examples from the class, start to perform some actions and ask the students what you are about to do: hold a piece of wadded up paper over a wastebasket; pick up an eraser and stand ready to erase the chalkboard; pull out a chair and make a movement toward sitting down, etc.

☐ EXERCISE 26, p. 74. Using BE ABOUT TO. (Chart 3-9)

ANSWERS: **1.** The chimpanzee is about to eat a banana. **2.** The man is about to leave/walk out the door. **3.** The airplane is about to land. **4.** The woman is about to answer the phone.

☐ EXERCISE 27, p. 74. Using BE ABOUT TO. (Chart 3-9)

POSSIBLE ANSWERS: **2.** She's about to open the door. **3.** He's about to finish the exam. **4.** She's about to wash her hands. **5.** He's about to leave/go outside. **6.** She's about to swat the fly. **7.** He's about to go to bed.

☐ EXERCISE 28, p. 75. Using BE ABOUT TO. (Chart 3-9)

This exercise provides spontaneous situational practice in which the students pretend to be about to do something (just as you did when you were presenting Chart 3-9). To facilitate practice, you might want to write cues on slips of paper and hand them out. Additional possibilities: pretend to be about to sneeze, turn off the ceiling light, put on a sweater/coat/etc.

☐ EXERCISE 29, p. 75. Preview: parallel verbs. (Chart 3-10)

This exercise can be used for seatwork and serves as an introduction to parallelism as presented in Chart 3-10.

ANSWERS: **2.** . . . and invited **3.** . . . and think **4.** . . . and studying **5.** . . . and turn

CHART 3-10: PARALLEL VERBS

• This unit introduces the concept of parallelism. Parallelism is revisited and expanded in Chapter 9 in units on connecting ideas with coordinating conjunctions.

• Errors in parallelism are common, with a second verb often found in the simple form or *-ing* form.

INCORRECT: *I opened the door and look around.*
INCORRECT: *A good teacher prepares interesting lessons and explaining everything clearly.*

☐ EXERCISE 30, p. 76. Parallel verbs. (Chart 3-10)

This exercise calls attention to parallel verbs for all the tenses presented to this point: simple present, present progressive, simple past, past progressive, simple future, and *be going to*.

In the answers given below, the auxiliary verbs in parentheses are typically omitted. You might want to point out what words have been omitted so that students can see the source of the correct verb forms (i.e., that *smoking* is correct in item 1 because it is part of the past progressive form).

ANSWERS: **1.** walked . . . was reading . . . (was) smoking **2.** is going to/will move . . . (is going to/will) look . . . graduates **3.** calls . . . complains **4.** is crying . . . (is) laughing **5.** get . . . am taking . . . (am) going [OR: am going to take . . . (am going to) go] **6.** dug . . . buried **7.** comes . . . am going to play . . . (am going to) jog [OR: am playing . . . (am) jogging] **8.** was carrying . . . (was) climbing . . . flew . . . sat . . . dropped . . . spilled [BrE: spilt] **9.** arrived . . . started . . . was watching . . . (was) feeling . . . knocked . . . asked . . . see . . . spend . . . are going to borrow . . . (are going to) go [OR: are borrowing . . . (are) going] . . . are taking . . . (are) going [OR: take . . . (are going to) go]

☐ EXERCISE 31, p. 77. Review: verb forms. (Chapters 1 → 3)

This exercise reviews present, past, and future verbs.

ANSWERS: **1.** ride . . . was raining . . . took . . . arrived . . . discovered **2.** opens . . . leave **3.** cut . . . is bleeding . . . will get **4.** am going / going to go . . . are going / going to go **5.** A: is ringing B: know A: Are you going to answer . . . Do you want . . . don't you want B: am expecting . . . don't want **6.** are you wearing / going to wear . . . am planning / plan . . . bought . . . is . . . will show . . . will get . . . bring **7.** A: is . . . are flashing B: know . . . know . . . see A: is going . . . Are you speeding B: am driving A: is passing **8.** A: Will the sun keep . . . will it eventually burn *(also possible:* be going to*)* B: will eventually burn . . . won't happen (*also possible:* be going to) **9.** will land / is going to land . . . think . . . will find / are going to find . . . don't expect / am not expecting . . . believe . . . will make / are going to make [*sentient* = able to experience feelings through the physical senses] [REMINDER: Ask students to describe what's happening in illustrations to encourage spontaneous language use.]

☐ EXERCISE 32, p. 79. Review: verb forms. (Chapters 1 → 3)

ANSWERS: **(1)** made . . . didn't have . . . weren't . . . wore **(2)** make . . . comes . . . buy **(3)** is . . . wear . . . wear **(4)** exist . . . wear . . . are **(5)** will probably be / are probably going to be . . . will wear / are going to wear . . . Will we all dress / Are we all going to dress . . . show . . . do you think

☐ EXERCISE 33, p. 80. Error analysis: summary review of present, past, and future time. (Chapters 1 → 3)

ANSWERS: **2.** . . . and I **passed** it. **3.** I **do** not like the food in the United **States**. **4.** I **used** to get up **5.** I study **hard** every day, but my **English** is not **improving**. **6.** Everyone **enjoys** **7.** . . . sang songs and **talked** to each other. **8.** I **studied** **English** in my school in **Hong** Kong before I **came** here. **9.** I like to travel. **I am going to** go to **10.** Now I **am studying** at this school and ~~I~~ living with my cousin. I ~~am~~ always meet my friends in the cafeteria, and we **talk** about our classes. **11.** When I wake up in the morning, I **turn** on the radio **before I** get up. **12.** I ~~am~~ live with . . . They **have** four **children**. **13.** . . . man **took** it . . . and **killed** it without mercy. **14.** . . . the weather **is** not ~~to be~~ cloudy, I **see/can see** a beautiful **15.** . . . children ~~they~~ are going to join me after I ~~will~~ finish

☐ EXERCISE 34, p. 81. Error analysis: summary review of present, past, and future time. (Chapters 1 → 3)

The rewritten paragraphs can be written on the board to facilitate discussion of the needed corrections. Another possibility is for you to hand out copies of the corrected passages so that students can correct their own or each other's rewritten paragraphs.

ANSWERS:

1. I want to tell you about Oscar. He **is** my cousin. He **came** here four years ago. Before he came here, he **studied** statistics in Chile. When he **left** Chile to come here, **he** came with four friends. They **studied** English in Ohio. Then he went to New **York and** stayed there for three years. He graduated from New York University. Now he **is studying** at this school. After he **finishes** his Master's degree, he **will** return to Chile.
2. Long ago in a faraway place, a lonely man **moved** into a new neighborhood. His first project **was** his new garden. He **began** to work on it right away. He **wanted** to make a perfect garden. One day some friendly neighbors and their children **visited** the man in his garden and **helped** him with the work. They **planted** flowers and **built** a small bridge across a little stream. All of them were very happy **while** they were building the bridge and **working** on the garden. The man was especially happy because he **was** no longer lonely. While the adults **were** working, some of their children **played/were playing** with a ball in the **garden. While** they were **playing**, one of them **stepped** on a flower. Suddenly the man **got** very angry and **told** everyone to leave. All the neighbors **left** and **went** back to their own homes. After that, the man **built** a wall around his garden and **locked** the gate. For the rest of his life, the man sat alone in his garden every evening and **cried**.

☐ EXERCISE 35, p. 81. Review: verb forms. (Chapters 1 → 3)

This exercise is meant to be a springboard for Exercise 36 by getting the students to think about fortune-telling.

ANSWERS:

1. does yours say
2. will be added
3. Are you planning
4. will prove
5. like
6. will overcome
7. don't understand
8. speak/are speaking
9. will just smile
10. will make
11. looks
12. will have

☐ EXERCISE 36, p. 82. Future time. (Chapter 3)

Following discussion of Exercise 35, have the students write fortunes (using *will*) that one might find in a fortune cookie. Place them in a container. Ask each student to draw out a fortune and read it aloud. Use this discussion of fortunes to lead into an explanation of the assignment for Exercise 36.

Ask your students if there are fortune-tellers in their cultures. Ask them if they believe there are people who can predict the future. Talk about fortune-tellers in your experience, perhaps discussing the North American stereotype of a middle-aged or older woman wearing scarves, brightly colored clothes, and a lot of gold jewelry who reads palms or tea leaves or gazes into a crystal ball.

The writing assignment suggests that the students write in second person, as though they were speaking to the person whose future they are predicting, but writing in third person would be fine too. Perhaps you can tell the students to write in the form of a letter to the person and to begin their writing by explaining (imaginatively) their powers for predicting the future.

This practice is intended to be written, but you could change it into an oral exercise done in small groups. One student at a time could be a fortune-teller and tell fortunes for others in the group.

Chapter 4: THE PRESENT PERFECT AND THE PAST PERFECT

ORDER OF CHAPTER	CHARTS	EXERCISES	WORKBOOK
Verb review and preview		Ex. 1	
Past participle	4-1	Ex. 2	
The present perfect	4-2 → 4-4	Ex. 3 → 9	Pr. 1 → 2, 4, 5, 7
Verb tense review		Ex. 10 → 17	Pr. 3, 6, 8
Using *since* and *for*	4-5	Ex. 18 → 22	Pr. 9 → 12
Present perfect progressive	4-6 → 4-7	Ex. 23 → 25	Pr. 13 → 14
Already, yet, still, anymore	4-8	Ex. 26 → 27	Pr. 15 → 16
Verb tense review		Ex. 28 → 34	Pr. 17
Past perfect	4-9	Ex. 35 → 38	Pr. 18 → 20
Cumulative review		Ex. 39 → 40	Pr. 21 → 22

General Notes on Chapter 4

• The perfective aspect of verb tenses is not unique to English, but it is not easy for learners to understand and control. It is a useful feature of the language because it gives us important information about the sequence of events, their completion or continuation, their duration, and their relationship to the present time or to another time in the past.

• The primary emphasis in the chapter is on the present perfect, which is a frequently used verb form and useful to students. The text actively encourages its use in the students' creative language production. The section on the past perfect, which is an infrequently used verb form, comes at the end of the chapter and is intended only as a minimal introduction.

• The grammar in this chapter on perfect verbs is difficult for many students at this proficiency level. You may choose to delay this chapter until later in the term. It is included here because many teachers prefer to present Chapters 1 through 4 as a single unit on verb tenses, but the chapters do not need to be taught in the order they are presented in the text. Less advanced classes might benefit from skipping to Chapters 5 and 6 at this point and then returning to Chapter 4 later. Chapter 5 (Asking Questions) does contain some exercise items with the present perfect and present perfect progressive; however, the fact that students have not studied these tenses prior to doing Chapter 5 does not present a pedagogical problem. It is beneficial for students to get exposure to structures prior to concentrated study of them.

• TERMINOLOGY: The terms "aspect" and "tense" are not used here, only "present perfect" and "past perfect."

☐ EXERCISE 1, p 83. Review and preview: present and past verbs. (Charts 3-1 → 3-6)

Compare the various tenses in the passage. Name the present perfect and past perfect when they occur in the blanks and explain that they are the focus of this chapter. Give an introductory overview of the two tenses. Some students may not be familiar with the use of *have* as an auxiliary verb. Most students at this level find these two verb tenses difficult to understand and use.

ANSWERS: **2.** am **3.** am studying **4.** have been **5.** arrived **6.** began **7.** came **8.** have done [If students ask about using the present perfect progressive here, tell them it is grammatically possible but not needed nor typical, and to wait until Chart 4-6 for a discussion of that verb form.] **9.** have met **10.** went **11.** met **12.** spoke **13.** didn't practice **14.** were **15.** came **16.** have met **17.** have met **18.** had never met (*also possible:* never met) **19.** know **20.** have become (or: are becoming)

CHART 4-1: PAST PARTICIPLE

• Chapter 4 is the first time in the text that the students are asked to use the past participle. The principal purpose of this chart is to define the term "past participle."

☐ EXERCISE 2, p. 84. Past participle. (Chart 4-1)

The verbs in this list are the ones used in the initial form-and-meaning exercises in this chapter. It is helpful for students to know these past participles while they are working on the form and meaning of the present perfect. Concentrated work on other irregular past participles begins in Exercise 10.

ANSWERS:

3. gone
4. had
5. met
6. called
7. fallen
8. done
9. known
10. flown
11. come
12. studied
13. stayed
14. begun
15. started
16. written
17. eaten
18. cut
19. read [pronounced "red"]
20. been

CHART 4-2: FORMS OF THE PRESENT PERFECT

• This is the first juncture in the text where the students are presented with *have* as an auxiliary in a verb tense. Point out that the past participle is the main verb.

• This chart keeps the focus on the forms of the present perfect, but it's helpful for you to explain the meanings of the examples, too, to prepare the students for the information in the following chart. Emphasize that the tense conveys the idea of "before now," i.e., "at an unspecified time in the past." The students don't need to wait until they read Chart 4-3 to be told that information. (A teacher can present a variety of interrelated information that a text needs to present step by step.)

• In (e), compare the two possible meanings of the contractions *she's* and *he's:*
COMPARE: *She'**s**/He'**s** (She **is**/He **is**) eating lunch.* vs. *She'**s**/He'**s** (She **has**/He **has**) eaten lunch.*
In (f), compare the two meanings of *it's:*
COMPARE: *It's (It **is**) cold today.* vs. *It's (It **has**) been cold for the last three days.*

☐ EXERCISE 3, p. 85. Forms of the present perfect. (Chart 4-2)

This is a straightforward exercise on form but also intended for teacher presentation of the meaning of the present perfect. Keep emphasizing that the tense conveys the idea of "before now," i.e., "at an unspecified time in the past." The items in this exercise all convey the idea "in one's entire lifetime up to now."

In item 1: *Have you ever eaten seaweed = In your entire lifetime, at any unspecified point, have you ever eaten seaweed?* The questioner is not interested in exactly when such a thing might have happened. The present perfect does not concern itself with exact points of time in the past; that's the job of the simple past.

ANSWERS: **2.** Have you ever stayed . . . have . . . have stayed **3.** Have you ever met . . . haven't . . . have never met **4.** Has Tom ever visited . . . has . . . has visited **5.** Has Ann ever been . . . hasn't . . . has never been . . . has not been

CHART 4-3: MEANINGS OF THE PRESENT PERFECT

- The present perfect relates past events to present time; it basically communicates the information that something occurred before the present time.
- Use the illustration of Jim and Ann to discuss the present perfect: question form, short answer, affirmative, negative. For example: *Has Jim (already) eaten lunch? Yes, he has. He's eaten lunch. Has Ann eaten lunch? No, she hasn't. She hasn't eaten lunch.* Continue to convey the meaning of "before now," i.e., "at an unspecified time in the past."
- The present perfect is a difficult tense for many students. The text moves slowly. Students need time to digest meanings and uses of the present perfect. They also need practice with the past participles of irregular verbs, which begins with Exercise 10.
- Note: Meaning #2 is the same meaning conveyed by the present perfect progressive: something began in the past and continues to the present. The difference is that the present perfect is used to express a situation (not an action) that began in the past and continues to the present when stative (non-action) verbs are used. *(I've known him for 20 years.)* The present perfect progressive is used to convey the same meaning for activities, but uses non-stative verbs. *(I've been waiting for Bob since 2 o'clock.)* Students don't need to be apprised of this at this point; they are given that information in a simplified form in Chart 4-6, p. 98, in the student book.

☐ EXERCISE 4, p. 87. Present perfect. (Chart 4-3)

The purpose of this exercise is to discuss the meaning of the sentences while acquainting the learners with the usual spoken contractions.

ANSWERS:

1. "Bob's been"
2. "Jane's been"
3. "The weather's been"
4. "My parents've been"
5. "Mike's already"
6. "My friends've moved"
7. "My roommate's traveled"
8. "My aunt and uncle've lived"

CHART 4-4: SIMPLE PAST vs. PRESENT PERFECT

- The problem for the teacher in presenting this chart is the fact that the simple past and present perfect are sometimes interchangeable in informal spoken English, especially in sentences containing *already,* as in example sentence (b). The use of the simple past in a sentence such as "I already finished my work" is common and acceptable, especially in American English. The text's intent is to draw clear distinctions between the two tenses for teaching purposes; students can blur and blend the two later as they gain experience with the language. Trying to explain to the students the ways in which the simple past and the present perfect can express the same meaning is more confusing than enlightening at this point, at least in the author's experience. Note that the simple past and present perfect are not interchangeable in examples (a), (c), and (d).

☐ EXERCISE 5, p. 87. Simple past vs. present perfect. (Chart 4-4)

So far you, the teacher, have been providing repeated explications of the meanings of the present perfect. Now the text assumes that the students have sufficient understandings of differences in meanings between the simple past and the present perfect that they can explain these themselves.

In discussion-of-meaning exercises, students find their own inventive ways of expressing meanings. Their explanations won't necessarily sound like yours or the text's, but once you discern the meaning, you can restate it slightly if necessary.

ANSWERS:

1. (a) uses the present perfect because no specific past time is mentioned. The others all mention specific times in the past, so the simple past is used.
2. (e) uses the simple past because there is a specific mention of time.
   (f) uses the present perfect because it conveys the idea "in my lifetime before now."
3. In (g), Ann no longer has her bike; the simple past conveys that something began and ended in the past. For example, Ann had a red bike from 1999 to 2001.
   In (h) Sue still has her bike; she acquired it two years ago from the present date.
4. Uncle Alex is dead. Grandpa is still alive.

☐ EXERCISE 6, p. 88. Simple past vs. present perfect. (Chart 4-4)

By this point, this exercise should be a piece of cake for the students, who should do the explaining during the discussion of this exercise. The text is trying to emphasize repeatedly that the present perfect and the simple past both express past occurrences, with the difference being unspecified vs. specified times.

ANSWERS:

SPECIFIED	UNSPECIFIED	
	☒	3. present perfect
☒		4. simple past
☒		5. simple past
	☒	6. present perfect
	☒	7. present perfect
☒		8. simple past
	☒	9. present perfect
☒		10. simple past

☐ **EXERCISE 7, p. 88. Simple past vs. present perfect. (Chart 4-4)**

Compare and discuss the two tenses in each item. (By now the students should be so familiar with the main points made in the chapter so far that they will be saying "ho-hum" when you talk about specified vs. unspecified times in the past.)

ANSWERS: **3.** have . . . have eaten . . . ate **4.** have already seen . . . saw **5.** have already written . . . wrote **6.** Has Antonio ever had . . . has . . . has had . . . had **7.** have already read . . . read **8.** have you visited . . . have visited . . . visited . . . was

☐ **EXERCISE 8, p. 89. Simple past vs. present perfect. (Chart 4-4)**

The purpose of this exercise is practice with the present perfect involving real information from the students' lives.

Ask a question that elicits the present perfect, then follow up with one that elicits the simple past as shown in the example. Pursue interesting responses; encourage spontaneous conversation.

Students' books should be closed. There is no need for them to read the questions. It's good for them to rely on their ears for understanding.

☐ **EXERCISE 9, p. 90. Present perfect. (Charts 4-2 → 4-4)**

Again this exercise provides practice with the present perfect involving real information from the students' lives. The grammar emphasis here is on adverbial expressions frequently used with the present perfect in both questions and statements. You might mention that *lots of times* is informal spoken language.

ANSWERS:

1.–3. have you ever been
5.–6. have you ever eaten
7.–9. have you ever ridden
10.–12. have you ever been in
13.–15. have you ever played
16. have you ever walked to
17. have you ever stayed up
18. have you ever bought

☐ **EXERCISE 10, p. 91. Irregular verbs. (Chart 2-5)**

Exercises 10 through 17 come in pairs. First the students produce—from memory, by guess, or by looking at Chart 2-7 (the reference list of irregular verbs)—the forms of the irregular verbs, and second they practice these verbs in questions and answers. These exercises can be done in pairs or groups. Not all of them need to be done on the same day; you might spread them over two to four days, conducting frequent oral reviews and quizzes as you go along. The text anticipates that the students will memorize the irregular verbs, which are more or less grouped according to similarity of form as a possible aid to memorization.

ANSWERS:

2. ate, eaten
3. gave, given
4. fell, fallen
5. took, taken
6. shook, shaken
7. drove, driven
8. rode, ridden
9. wrote, written
10. bit, bitten
11. hid, hidden

☐ **EXERCISE 11, p. 91. Practicing irregular verbs. (Charts 2-5 and 4-2 → 4-4)**

ANSWERS:

1. Have you ever taken
2. Have you ever ridden
3. Have you ever written
4. Have you ever given
5. Have you ever shaken
6. Have you ever bitten
7. Have you ever driven
8. Have you ever eaten
9. Have you ever hidden
10. Have you ever fallen
11. Have you ever seen

☐ EXERCISE 12, p. 92. Irregular verbs. (Chart 2-5)

ANSWERS:

1. broke, broken
2. spoke, spoken
3. stole, stolen
4. got, gotten (got)
5. wore, worn
6. drew, drawn
7. grew, grown
8. threw, thrown
9. blew, blown
10. flew, flown
11. drank, drunk
12. sang, sung
13. swam, swum
14. went, gone

☐ EXERCISE 13, p. 92. Practicing irregular verbs. (Charts 2-5 and 4-2 → 4-4)

ANSWERS:

1. flown
2. broken
3. drawn
4. swum
5. spoken
6. worn
7. gone
8. gotten (got)
9. stolen
10. grown
11. sung
12. drunk
13. thrown
14. blown

☐ EXERCISE 14, p. 92. Irregular verbs. (Chart 2-5)

ANSWERS:

1. had, had
2. made, made
3. built, built
4. lent, lent
5. sent, sent
6. spent, spent
7. left, left
8. lost, lost
9. slept, slept
10. felt, felt
11. met, met
12. sat, sat
13. won, won
14. hung, hung

☐ EXERCISE 15, p. 93. Practicing irregular verbs. (Charts 2-5 and 4-2 → 4-4)

ANSWERS:

1. lost
2. met
3. had
4. felt
5. sent
6. left
7. sat
8. spent
9. lent
10. slept
11. made
12. built
13. won
14. hung

☐ EXERCISE 16, p. 93. Irregular verbs. (Chart 2-5)

ANSWERS:

1. sold, sold
2. told, told
3. heard, heard
4. held, held
5. fed, fed
6. read, read
7. found, found
8. bought, bought
9. thought, thought
10. taught, taught
11. caught, caught
12. cut, cut
13. hit, hit
14. quit, quit
15. put, put

☐ EXERCISE 17, p. 94. Practicing irregular verbs. (Charts 2-5 and 4-2 → 4-4)

ANSWERS:

1. taught
2. held
3. found
4. cut
5. thought
6. heard
7. read
8. fed
9. told
10. quit [BrE: quitted]
11. bought
12. sold
13. hit
14. put
15. caught

☐ EXERCISE 18, p. 94. Preview: SINCE vs. FOR. (Chart 4-5)

Tell the students to cover Chart 4-5 with a sheet of paper and to do this exercise quickly as seatwork.

The purposes of a preview are (1) for students to arrive at their own conclusions about the forms and meanings of grammatical structures; (2) for students to become aware of what information they need to pay attention to in the following chart; and (3) for teachers to have a bevy of examples to use in introducing grammar points.

ANSWERS:

3. since
4. since
5. for
6. since
7. since
8. for
9. since
10. for
11. since
12. since
13. for
14. for
15. since
16. for

CHART 4-5: USING *SINCE* AND *FOR*

• Understanding the meaning and use of *since* helps students to understand the meaning and use of the present perfect.

• *Ever* is frequently used as an intensifier in front of *since*. The use of *ever* has little, if any, effect on the meaning of *since*. *I've lived here* ***ever since*** *May.*

• In example (a), *since* is used as a preposition, and in examples (f) and (g) as a subordinating conjunction. Subordinating conjunctions are generally called "time clause words" in this text or "words that introduce adverb clauses." *Since*-clauses can be related to the "time clauses" presented in Chart 2-10; a *since*-clause is an adverb clause of time.

• *Since* has another use not mentioned in this chart. It is also an adverb: *He got a job at the factory in 1975 and has worked there ever since.* The question may or may not arise.

• *Since* has another meaning: *because*. In this case, any tense can be used in the main clause. *Since* meaning *because* is presented not in this text but in *Understanding and Using English Grammar, Third Edition,* Chart 17-2. Example: *Bob's last name is Black.* ***Since*** *it's a common name, he never has to spell it for people. My last name is Bryzewski.* ***Since*** *it's an unusual name, I often have to spell it for people.*

• Try to keep the focus on the use of the present perfect with sentences containing *since*. It is true, however, that sometimes the simple present is used in the main clause rather than the present perfect. In this case, the simple present is usually used to express a general truth. For example, *Fewer people travel by train since the development of the automobile and airplane.* The text chooses not to teach this, as the instances in which the simple present is used are relatively infrequent. The past perfect can also be used in sentences with *since: I hadn't seen George since we were children.* It is possible that your more alert students may find and ask about such sentences. Explain, if necessary, that their grammar book is a guide to useful information about English for second language learners, not a compendium of all there is to know about English grammar. They truly don't want to know all there is to know about English grammar.

• In (h), it might help to explain that *for,* not *since,* is used with "countable periods of time" (e.g., *ten minutes, two hours,* etc.).

☐ EXERCISE 19, p. 95. SINCE vs. FOR. (Chart 4-5)

Students should complete the sentences with accurate information about themselves. Ask them to give accurate answers for item 1 also.

SAMPLE ANSWERS: **2.** since ten o'clock this morning . . . for an hour **3.** since August . . . for two months **4.** since I was eighteen years old . . . for three years **5.** since the beginning of this term . . . for four weeks.

☐ EXERCISE 20, p. 96. SINCE vs. FOR. (Chart 4-5)

Make it clear that Speaker A is to use *since* and that Speaker B is to use *for* to paraphrase Speaker A's response. If teacher-led, the exercise can go quickly. Group work would take longer, but of course involve more students in oral practice.

☐ EXERCISE 21, p. 96. Sentences with SINCE-clauses. (Chart 4-5)

ANSWERS: **2.** has changed . . . [since he **started** school] **3.** [Ever since I **was** a child], I have been afraid **4.** haven't slept . . . [since I **left** home three days ago] **5.** [Ever since Danny **met** Nicole], he hasn't been **6.** has had . . . [ever since he **bought** it] **7.** have you eaten [since you **got** up this morning] . . . have eaten **8.** had . . . was . . . [Ever since I **left** home at the age of fifteen], I have taken . . . have had . . . have learned

☐ EXERCISE 22, p. 97. SINCE vs. FOR. (Chart 4-5)

This can be a quick oral review or written homework.

Items 8 and 9 have stative passive verbs, so there are two past participles: *I have never* ***been married***. Some students may wonder about that. In the passive, the auxiliary *be* carries the tense form (e.g., *have been* for the present perfect) and is followed by a past participle (e.g., *married)*. You can refer students to Chart 10-7.

CHART 4-6: PRESENT PERFECT PROGRESSIVE

- As a way of introducing this chart, ask a student with a watch to time you when you begin to draw something on the board (something simple like a tree and flowers). As you are drawing, ask the students what you are doing (e.g., *You are drawing on the board)*. Continue drawing for 30 seconds or a minute and then, without stopping, ask the student with the watch how long you have been drawing. Point out that he/she can say "You are drawing on the board" but can't say "You are drawing on the board for 30 seconds." The tense has to shift to the present perfect progressive when duration is added to the description of the activity. Keep drawing and then ask, "Now how long have I been drawing?" and "What am I drawing now?" (as you switch from a tree to a bird perhaps) to continue to elicit the two tenses. If you prefer, ask a student to be the artist so that you can concentrate on leading the discussion.

- Try to avoid getting into differences between the present perfect and the present perfect progressive at this point, but remind students that some verbs (stative or non-action verbs) are not used in any progressive tenses, as is pointed out in examples (g) through (j).

☐ EXERCISE 23, p. 99. Present progressive vs. present perfect progressive. (Chart 4-6)

This exercise reinforces Chart 4-6 by emphasizing the relationship between the two tenses in order to demonstrate when and how the present perfect progressive is used.

ANSWERS: **2.** is waiting . . . has been waiting **3.** are talking . . . have been talking **4.** are doing . . . have been doing **5.** A: are you doing B: am working A: have you been working B: have been working

☐ EXERCISE 24, p. 99. Present perfect progressive. (Chart 4-6)

The questions are intended to spur the teacher's mind to come up with ways to elicit the present perfect progressive in teacher–student conversation. The questions do not need to be read verbatim. For example, in item 1, set up the situation verbally to lead up to the present perfect progressive questions: "What time is it now? What time did you get to class this morning? Does it seem like you've been here for a long time? How long *have you been sitting* here?"

CHART 4-7: PRESENT PERFECT PROGRESSIVE vs. PRESENT PERFECT

- The text seeks to make the distinction between these two tenses by comparing repeated action to duration.

- In examples (f) through (i), the text points out that in certain situations, there is little or no difference in meaning between the present perfect and the present perfect progressive. (It can be posited that the progressive emphasizes the continuous nature of the activity, while the present perfect is more concerned with a simple factual statement that something has existed for a certain length of time; however, the nuances of difference don't seem significant and are very difficult to pinpoint.)

- The fly in the ointment is often that the present perfect and the present perfect progressive have exactly the same meaning when they express the duration of an occurrence from the past to the present time, with the difference being that the present perfect progressive expresses the duration of "activities" and uses a fairly wide range of verbs, while the present perfect uses only stative verbs with *since* and *for* and expresses duration of "states" rather than "activities." This information can prove very confusing to many students. The chart presentation is fairly complicated for this proficiency level; it anticipates questions students might have, but the point doesn't need to be belabored.

- Not presented in this text is the information that the present perfect progressive can express an activity in progress recently, with no mention of duration. (E.g., *A: Hi, John. How's it going? B: Okay. I've* ***been studying*** *a lot, but finals are almost over.* See *Understanding and Using English Grammar, Third Edition,* Chart 3-2.)

☐ EXERCISE 25, p. 100. Present perfect vs. present perfect progressive. (Chart 4-7)

Notes on the example items follow. This information is intended as background in case students have questions. It seems more complicated in explication than is necessary and beneficial for students. (The teaching of grammar lays the foundation for growth as learners gain experience with the language. In the case of the grammar in question, an introduction to the form and meaning of the present perfect progressive encourages student awareness and usage, but no amount of explanation of grammar ensures mastery. That is not the intent of teaching grammar. It is important for both text and teacher to perceive the boundary between just enough information and too much information.)

Item 1: The present perfect is not possible. The sentence does not deal with the duration of an habitual activity (an activity that occurs every day or regularly), but rather with a present activity in progress. This item can be compared to an example of *walk* used to describe an habitual activity: *Mr. Lee has walked/has been walking his dog in the park every day since it was a puppy.*

Item 2: The present progressive is not possible because that tense (aspect) is not used to express repeated activities at unspecified times in the past. A "repeated activity" is not the same as an "habitual activity." A "repeated activity" occurs twice, several times, many times, but not on a regular or everyday basis.

Item 3: Usual or habitual activities can be expressed with either tense.

ANSWERS: **4.** have read **5.** have been reading **6.** have stayed **7.** has been crying **8.** has been teaching / has taught **9.** has been playing / has played . . . have been playing/have played **10.** has been working / has worked . . . has worked [This last blank is tricky for students; it uses the present perfect to describe completed actions at unspecified times in the past, so the present perfect progressive is not possible.]

CHART 4-8: USING *ALREADY, YET, STILL,* AND *ANYMORE*

- These words are hard to explain. In broad terms, *already* talks about events or situations that have occurred "before now" and may imply that they occurred sooner than expected. *Yet* also conveys the idea of "before now or up to now" and talks about events or situations that are expected to happen: *Jack hasn't come yet* indicates that the speaker expects Jack to come. *Still* indicates that an event or situation hasn't changed status; it continues to occur. *Anymore* indicates that an event or situation has changed status; it ceases to occur.
- The adverb *anymore* can also be spelled as two words: *any more.* For example, *He doesn't live there any more.* [NOTE: *Any more* is always spelled as two words when *any* is a pronoun or determiner. *Don't give me those books. I can't carry any more (books).*]

☐ EXERCISE 26, p. 102. ALREADY, YET, STILL, ANYMORE. (Chart 4-8)

Discuss the meanings of the sentences.

ANSWERS:

2. already
3. still
4. anymore
5. already
6. yet
7. still
8. yet
9. still
10. yet . . . still
11. already
12. still . . . anymore

☐ EXERCISE 27, p. 103. ALREADY, YET, STILL, ANYMORE. (Chart 4-8)

If you ask students to create sentences orally, ask for several completions for each. If you choose to have the students write, the assignment can be done relatively quickly in class, then sentences can be written on the board, read aloud, or handed in for correction.

SAMPLE RESPONSES: **1.** talk in my sleep . . . I don't **2.** take the test . . . studied **3.** you . . . living in town **4.** Don't water the flowers . . . watered them **5.** swim in the ocean . . . I . . . sunbathe on the beach

☐ EXERCISE 28, p. 103. Verb tense review. (Chapters 1, 2, and 4)

Encourage students to explain the meanings in their own words. See the *Introduction,* p. ix, for ways of handling discussion-of-meaning exercises.

SAMPLE ANSWERS: **1.** Rachel and Nadia are both taking English classes at present. We don't know how long Rachel has been taking the classes. Only the sentence about Nadia expresses duration (which is why the present perfect progressive is used). **2.** Ann is still in Jerusalem, but Sue is not. Sentence a. expresses duration, using a stative verb. Sentence b. discusses a situation that occurred at unspecified times in the past. **3.** Jack's visits occurred in the past. Matt is visiting his relatives at present. Sentence b. expresses duration. **4.** a. in progress right now b. habitually c. in progress from a time in the past to the present (duration) d. actions that occurred at unspecified times in the past **5.** habitually b. actions that occurred at unspecified times in the past c. actions that began and ended at a specific time in the past (last week) d. in progress right now e. in progress from a time in the past to the present (duration)

☐ EXERCISE 29, p. 104. Verb tenses. (Charts 4-2 → 4-8)

This exercise focuses on the relation between time expressions and verb tenses to reinforce the concept that verb tenses express time relationships.

Ask students to give real information about their actual lives. This exercise can be done orally or in writing.

☐ EXERCISE 30, p. 105. Review of verb tenses. (Chapters 1 → 4)

Students need time to work through this exercise. They could do it as seatwork in pairs prior to class discussion or simply as homework.

ANSWERS:

1. A: Do you have B: am planning A: Have you ever been B: was . . . lives / is living . . . go
2. B: is studying A: will she get / is she going to get / is she getting A: has she been studying A: Does she study
3. A: is talking B: is she talking A: have been talking
4. A: Do you know B: have . . . get . . . will call . . . (will) give B: will do
5. A: has been . . . . Has anyone seen B: saw . . . has been . . . will probably be / is probably going to be
6. A: have you worn / have you been wearing B: was A: Are you
7. A: Do you like B: have never eaten B: love A: is . . . have gone B: have never been . . . will be / is going to be . . . get
8. A: Do you smoke A: have you been smoking / have you smoked B: I have been smoking / have smoked . . . was . . . have been smoking / have smoked A: did you start B: was A: Do you want B: plan / am planning . . . have decided . . . intend / am intending A: will feel / are going to feel . . . stop / have stopped B: Have you ever smoked A: have never smoked . . . was . . . smoked . . . stole . . . went . . . got . . . have not had

☐ EXERCISE 31, p. 107. Error analysis. (Charts 4-1 → 4-8)

It is important for students to have adequate preparation time for error-analysis exercises (so that they have to scrutinize the sentences on their own, not just copy down what their classmates report).

ANSWERS:

2. I **have wanted** to learn English since I **was** a child.
3. Our class has **had** three tests since the **beginning** of the term.

4. I ~~have~~ started the English classes ~~since~~ three weeks ago, and I **have learned** some English since that time.
5. . . . , but I still **haven't found** a good way.
6. All of us **have learned** many **things** since we were children.
7. . . . Since then I **haven't talked** to her. (OR: **After that**, I didn't talk to her for three days.)
8. Since I was very young, I **have liked** animals.
9. I have been **studying English for** three and a half **months**.
10. I like **English very much**. **When** I was young, my father . . . but when I **moved** to another city, my father **didn't** find one for five years.
11. I almost **died** in an automobile accident five **years** ago. Since that day my life **has** changed completely.
12. In my country, women **have been** soldiers in the army since the 1970s.
13. I **met** Abdul in my first English class last June . . . We **have been** friends since that day.
14. . . . I **lived** (OR: **have lived**) there for twenty years.
15. My wife and I **were** in Italy two weeks ago.
16. . . . A lot ~~of~~ our friends **have visited** her since she **broke** her leg.
17. I **have been** busy every day since I arrived **in** this city.
18. I haven't to eaten any kind of **Chinese** food for a week.

☐ EXERCISE 32, p. 108. Verb tense review. (Chapters 1 → 4)

A long exercise such as this gives students the opportunity to experience how verb tenses are used in extended contexts, but it needs to be handled expeditiously in class. For you to write the answers on the board as the passage is being read aloud is helpful, for it allows students to check what they have heard when they are uncertain and allows you to comment during the reading of a paragraph when an incorrect completion is made by the reader and to answer any questions.

Another possibility is for you to photocopy the exercise with the answers written in and hand it out to the class. The most expeditious way is for the students to correct their own answers out of class and bring any questions to you the next day. A less expeditious way, but one that maximizes student speaking and listening practice, is to have the students work in small groups where only the leader has the photocopy with the correct answers and refers to it as the other members read the passage aloud.

NOTE: One of the purposes of the students' working with the long context in this exercise is to prepare them for their own creative writing assignment in the following exercise.

ANSWERS:

2. haven't been
3. haven't heard
4. have been
5. have been working
6. (have been) going
7. wrote
8. was going
9. (was) studying
10. have happened
11. were
12. lost
13. messed
14. got
15. showed
16. refused
17. felt
18. told
19. started
20. have been working / have worked
21. isn't/hasn't been
22. isn't/hasn't been
23. fetch [*fetch* = leave one place to get something in another place and bring it back]
24. have met
25. started
26. came
27. wanted
28. brought
29. put
30. was walking
31. pulled
32. started

33. looked
34. said
35. do you like
36. twitched [*twitch* = make quick little jerky movements, as a mouse's nose does when it is investigating something]
37. said
38. turned
39. said
40. are
41. know
42. enter
43. come
44. point
45. tell
46. try
47. buy
48. don't agonize
49. have learned
50. don't want
51. need
52. will prepare / is going to prepare
53. have decided
54. am working
55. (am) going
56. have always wanted
57. am
58. have
59. lost
60. made
61. have been
62. are
63. am really enjoying
64. will continue / am going to continue
65. will study / am going to study
66. will pursue / am going to pursue
67. have told
68. have grown
69. understand
70. made *(also possible:* has made)
71. believe
72. am finally taking OR have finally taken

☐ EXERCISE 33, p. 112. Writing: verb tense review. (Chapters 1 → 4)

This is an expansion activity: students can model their letters on the one in Exercise 32. This topic should encourage the use of a variety of verb tenses.

You probably won't want to assign both Exercise 33 and Exercise 34 (perhaps delay one or the other). Exercise 33 prompts informal writing; Exercise 34 prompts more formal writing.

☐ EXERCISE 34, p. 112. Writing: verb tenses. (Chapters 1 → 4)

These topics are intended to elicit a variety of verb tenses—including, it is hoped, correct and appropriate use of the present perfect.

Discuss paragraphing: form and purpose. A paragraph is indented from the left text margin. It contains one principal idea. When the writer moves on to a new idea, s/he begins a new paragraph. If your students are more advanced in their understanding of English rhetoric than these basics would assume, you could use these topics to assign a traditional five-part essay: introduction, three body paragraphs, conclusion.

CHART 4-9: PAST PERFECT

• Both the present perfect and the past perfect relate two points of time. The present perfect relates an event in the past to the present. The past perfect relates an event in the past to another event in the past that occurred at a different time.

• The past perfect is not an especially common and useful tense for language students at this level. The text's intention is a quick introduction to its form and meaning. A thorough understanding and usage mastery are neither sought nor expected. The students will come across the past perfect again in Chapter 14, where it is used in verb changes made from quoted to reported speech.

☐ EXERCISE 35, p. 114. Past perfect. (Chart 4-9)

This exercise can be prepared in pairs to encourage students to explain to each other the sequence of events in each item.

To help students visualize which event ended before the other one happened, refer frequently during class discussion to a diagram of the past perfect drawn on the board.

ANSWERS:

3. a. 1st
b. 2nd
4. a. 2nd
b. 1st
5. a. 1st
b. 2nd
6. a. 2nd
b. 1st
7. a. 1st
b. 2nd
8. a. 2nd
b. 1st

☐ EXERCISE 36, p. 115. Present perfect vs. past perfect. (Chart 4-9)

Use tense diagrams on the chalkboard to demonstrate the similar time relationships expressed by these two tenses: one communicates "before now," and the other communicates "before then."

ANSWERS:

3. have already slept
4. had already slept
5. have already met
6. had already met
7. have already seen
8. had already seen
9. have made
10. had made

☐ EXERCISE 37, p. 116. Past progressive vs. past perfect. (Chart 4-9)

ANSWERS:

2. A
3. A
4. B
5. B
6. A
7. B
8. B

☐ EXERCISE 38, p. 117. Present perfect, past progressive, and past perfect. (Chart 4-9)

ANSWERS:

2. have never been
3. had already heard
4. was still snowing
5. had passed
6. were making
7. Hasn't he come
8. had never been
9. was wearing . . . had never worn . . . hasn't worn

☐ **EXERCISE 39, p. 117. Verb tense review. (Chapters 1 → 4)**

On a multiple-choice test of this type, thirty seconds is usually allowed per item. If you do this exercise in class as seatwork, time the students, allowing five minutes, so that they can understand how quickly they need to work if taking a standardized test. If five minutes proves to be insufficient (and it probably will for students at this proficiency level), allow extra time so that students can benefit from working through the entire exercise. If your students are unlikely to ever take a multiple-choice test such as this, treat the tests as simply another exercise variety, having the students work in pairs or groups.

Exercises 39 and 40 cover the same content. They are divided into two exercises so that students can become aware of any problems they're still having with these tenses (in Exercise 39) and try again (in Exercise 40).

These are difficult multiple-choice tests. Be sure to congratulate your students on their expertise with English verb tenses! Even though they don't have mastery of the tenses yet, they have a very good base for linguistic growth.

ANSWERS:

1. C
2. B
3. D
4. A
5. C
6. C
7. A
8. D
9. B
10. B

☐ **EXERCISE 40, p. 118. Verb tense review. (Chapters 1 → 4)**

ANSWERS:

1. D
2. C
3. D
4. D
5. C
6. C
7. C
8. A
9. D
10. B

Chapter 5: ASKING QUESTIONS

ORDER OF CHAPTER	CHARTS	EXERCISES	WORKBOOK
Yes/no and information questions	5-1 → 5-2	Ex. 1 → 4	Pr. 1 → 6
Where, why, when, and *what time*	5-3	Ex. 5 → 7	Pr. 7 → 9
Who, who(m), and *what*	5-4	Ex. 8 → 10	Pr. 10 → 12
Contractions with question words	5-5	Ex. 11 → 13	
What + a form of *do*	5-6	Ex. 14 → 15	Pr. 13
What kind of	5-7	Ex. 16 → 17	Pr. 14
Which vs. *what*	5-8	Ex. 18 → 19	Pr. 15
Who vs. *whose*	5-9	Ex. 20 → 21	Pr. 16 → 17
Summary review		Ex. 22 → 23	
How	5-10 → 5-14	Ex. 24 → 36	Pr. 18 → 19
Summary review		Ex. 37 → 40	Pr. 20 → 21
How about and *what about*	5-15	Ex. 41 → 44	
Tag questions	5-16	Ex. 45 → 47	Pr. 22 → 23
Cumulative review		Ex. 48	Pr. 24 → 25

General Notes on Chapter 5

• Although questions were introduced in earlier chapters, this chapter summarizes those patterns, adds other types, and provides ample practice to help students gain control of and comfortable fluency with question words and forms. Questions occur principally in conversational English; exercises on form are followed by ones that encourage a lot of speaking practice.

• TERMINOLOGY: Information questions are also called WH-questions because they use the words *who, which, when, where,* and *how.* This chapter generally uses the term "helping verb" for an auxiliary, to distinguish it from the "main verb" in a sentence or clause.

☐ **EXERCISE 1, p. 120. Preview: asking questions. (Chapter 5)**

Ask students to create questions—any questions that will produce the given answers. Write the questions on the board (including any errors in form) and use them as the basis for introducing the principal grammar points in this chapter.

If you want to get an idea of your students' proficiency in the form and meaning of questions, ask them to write and hand in the questions (and the answers, too, to make it easier for you to correct). Copy questions with typical errors and create a photocopied worksheet for use in class the next day.

Students are expected to have some trouble with this exercise (incorrect word order, wrong question word, errors in verb forms, etc.). If they don't, this chapter can be covered very quickly!

The preview exercise in the *Workbook* may be a bit difficult for some students. You may wish to include a discussion of it in class at some point.

SAMPLE ANSWERS: **1.** Where did you go yesterday afternoon? **2.** Did you eat breakfast this morning? **3.** What time did you get up this morning? **4.** How long does it take to drive to (name of a place) from here? **5.** Why were you late for class? **6.** Which book is yours? **7.** Is Maria in class today? **8.** Whose book is this? **9.** Who(m) are you living with? **10.** How far is it from here to the post office? **11.** How often do you go to the fresh fruit market? **12.** What are you doing?

CHART 5-1: YES/NO QUESTIONS AND SHORT ANSWERS

• The students studied the forms of yes/no questions in conjunction with each verb tense presented in Chapters 1 through 4. See Chart 5-2 if students need a reminder of basic question word order: HELPING VERB + SUBJECT + MAIN VERB.

• Remind the students of the names of the tenses used in the examples and review how questions are formed: (a) simple present [discuss the use of *does* also], (b) simple past, (c) present perfect, (d) present progressive, and (e) the future with *will*.

• If you skipped Chapter 4 (Present Perfect and Past Perfect), you'll need to give a quick overview of the form of the present perfect at this juncture, explaining that *have* and *has* are used as auxiliary verbs. The present perfect occurs relatively infrequently in the exercise items in this chapter, so should not prove to be a problematic distraction. Use the examples and exercise items with the present perfect as a means of making a quick introduction to it, and tell your students they will concentrate on it more fully later in the term when you return to Chapter 4.

• Model the spoken form of the short answers. The emphasis is on the auxiliary verb *(Yes, I* ***do****. No,* ***I don't****.)*. Additional information not given in the chart: If a negative contraction is not used in a short answer, the emphasis is placed on *not* rather than on the verb *(No, I'm* ***not****. No, I do* ***not****.)*.

• The presentation pattern in this chart of *question + short answer + (long answer)* is used in the exercises on form in this chapter.

• Include an example with *can* in your discussion of this chart, relating it to *will* in question forms (both are modal auxiliaries). *Can* occurs in the exercises and in succeeding charts.

☐ **EXERCISE 2, p. 121. Short answers to yes/no questions. (Chart 5-1)**

This is an exercise on the form of yes/no questions and short answers. It can be done as seatwork or in pairs.

The directions tell students not to use a negative verb in the question. It is better that negative yes/no questions not be discussed with students at this level, as negative questions have complicated meanings and uses. (See *Understanding and Using English Grammar, Third Edition,* Chart B-4, p. A13.) The only negative questions practiced in this text are ones fronted by *why.*

"Uh huh" (item 6) is meant to represent the voiced but unspoken sound that signals *yes,* and "huh uh" (item 7) is meant to represent the sound of *no.*

ANSWERS: **2.** Does aspirin relieve pain? . . . it does. **3.** Do snakes have legs? . . . they don't. **4.** Can snakes move backward? . . . they can't. **5.** Is the United States in North America? . . . it is. **6.** Did you enjoy the movie? . . . I did. **7.** Will you be at home tonight? . . . I won't. **8.** Do you have a bicycle? . . . I do. **9.** Has Paul left? . . . he has. **10.** Did he leave with Kate? . . . he did.

☐ EXERCISE 3, p. 122. Short answers to yes/no questions. (Chart 5-1)

Having one student whisper to another is intended principally to add variation to student–student speaking/listening exercises. It is another way to encourage students to speak clearly and listen carefully—and have a little fun.

Give the students several more examples before dividing them into groups. Emphasize that the whisperer is whispering a true statement: in item 1, for example, the whisperer should use the name of someone who actually has curly hair.

Additional example to discuss with the class: *(. . .) doesn't have a pencil on his/her desk.* Point out that Speaker A (the whisperer) should be sure to choose the name of someone who does not have a pencil on his/her desk, and that Speaker B should not use a negative verb in the question.

SPEAKER A: *Josef doesn't have a pencil on his desk.* (whispered)
SPEAKER B: *Does Josef have a pencil on his desk?*
SPEAKER C: *No, he doesn't.*

Discuss additional examples as necessary to prepare the class for the group work.

EXPECTED QUESTIONS AND ANSWERS: **1.** Does (Maria) have curly hair? Yes, she does. **2.** Does (Omar) have a mustache? No, he doesn't. **3.** Is (Mr. Wong) sitting down? Yes, he is. **4.** Is the teacher talking to (Talal)? No, s/he isn't. **5.** Were (Olga) and (Pierre) in class yesterday? Yes, they were. **6.** Is this exercise easy? Yes, it is. *(also possible:* No, it isn't.) **7.** Does that book belong to (Stephan)? Yes, it does. **8.** Can an ostrich fly? No, it can't. **9.** Is (Graciela) wearing earrings? Yes, she is. **10.** Does this book have an index? Yes, it does. **11.** Is (Olga)'s grammar book open? No, it isn't. **12.** Do giraffes eat meat? No, they don't. [Speaker C may not know the correct answer. You might mention the use of *think so / not think so* to answer yes/no questions. See Chart 14-7.]

CHART 5-2: YES/NO QUESTIONS AND INFORMATION QUESTIONS

- One purpose of this chart is to relate the form of yes/no questions to the form of information questions so that the students can see the overall pattern in English. Make sure they understand that the inverted subject-verb form is the same in both kinds of questions—with the exception of examples (k) and (l), where the question word is the subject of the question.

- Write on the board the basic question pattern so students will have it as a reminder and reference throughout the discussion of this chapter:

(QUESTION WORD) + HELPING VERB + SUBJECT + MAIN VERB

- Model and discuss rising intonation at the end of a question.

☐ EXERCISE 4, p. 123. Yes/no and information questions. (Chart 5-2)

Draw a chart on the chalkboard with the question pattern headings:

(QUESTION WORD) + HELPING VERB + SUBJECT + MAIN VERB + (REST OF SENTENCE)
1. (a) (b)
2. (a) (b)
3. (a) (b)
Etc.

Ask the students to fill in the chart by writing on the board. Demonstrate how the pattern in questions is repeated again and again:

HELPING VERB + SUBJECT + MAIN VERB

Alternatively, draw a chart on paper, copy it, and pass it out; have the students fill it in as seatwork. No students should go any further in this chapter until they thoroughly grasp the basic question patterns in Chart 5-2 (with the possible exception of the pattern in examples (k) and (l)—which is dealt with in more depth in Chart 5-4).

ANSWERS: **1.** Does she live there? Where does she live? **2.** Do the students live there? Where do the students live? **3.** Did Bob live there? Where did Bob live? **4.** Is Mary living there? Where is Mary living? **5.** Were you living there? Where were you living? **6.** Are they going to live there? Where are they going to live? **7.** Will John live there? Where will John live? **8.** Can the students live there? Where can the students live? **9.** Has Jim lived there? Where has Jim lived? **10.** Has Tom been living there? Where has Tom been living?

CHART 5-3: *WHERE, WHY, WHEN,* AND *WHAT TIME*

- The text assumes that students are already thoroughly familiar with the meanings of the question words in this chart, but still need review and a lot of practice with the question patterns.
- Typical errors: *Where you went? Where did you went? Why you stayed home? Where your children do they go to school? Where go your children to school?*

☐ EXERCISE 5, p. 124. Information questions. (Charts 5-2 and 5-3)

ANSWERS: **2.** Where do your children go to school? **3.** What time/When does class begin? **4.** When [*but not* What time] did you meet the Smiths? **5.** Why is the cat staring at the hole in the wall?

☐ EXERCISE 6, p. 125. Yes/no and information questions. (Charts 5-2 and 5-3)

Pair work gives the students maximum opportunity for speaking practice. This exercise can also be written. Ask the students to write the entire dialogue, including the answer given in the text. Another possibility would be to have the students write the twelve questions in random order. Then these questions could be given to Speaker B, who would write in the appropriate responses from the text and the long answer. Speaker B could also be asked to correct Speaker A's question forms.

SAMPLE RESPONSES: **1.** A: When was your math final? B: The day before yesterday. My math final was the day before yesterday. **2.** A: Do you live in an apartment? B: Yes, I do. I live in an apartment. **3.** A: Why did you buy a new hat? B: Because I wanted to. I bought a new hat because I wanted to. **4.** A: What time do your classes begin each morning? B: At 8:30. My classes begin at 8:30 each morning. **5.** A: Is Jacob your brother? B: Yes, he is. Jacob is my brother. **6.** A: Where can I/you get fresh fruit? B: At a grocery store. You can get fresh fruit at a grocery store. **7.** A: When are you and Gisela going shopping at the new mall? [This sample uses the present progressive with a future meaning. Any verb with a future meaning is possible.] B: Tomorrow afternoon. Gisela and I are going shopping at the new mall tomorrow afternoon. **8.** A: Where is Mr. Nguyen from? B: Viet Nam. Mr. Nguyen is from Viet Nam. **9.** A: Can you play the piano? B: No, I can't. I can't play the piano. **10.** A: Why did you wear boots today? B: Because the weather is so cold today. I wore boots because the weather is so cold today. **11.** A: Do you want a cup of tea? B: Yeah, sure. Why not? Yeah, sure. I'll have a cup of tea. Why not? **12.** A: Do you think Ali would like to go to the concert with us? B: I don't know. Maybe. I don't know if Ali would like to go to the concert with us. Maybe. [This item requires a noun clause introduced by *if* in the long answer. Some students may have a question about this. Tell them they'll study it later and refer them to Chart 14-4.]

☐ EXERCISE 7, p. 125. Questions with WHY. (Chart 5-3)

Mention that in normal conversation a person would probably not ask the full *why*-question. The students understand that they are producing the full question in order to practice a grammar pattern here. Tell Speaker A to be alert to the proper form in Speaker B's *why*-question. The form of *why*-questions is troublesome for many students at this level.

Reinforce the idea that *Because I have to study for a test* is a short answer to a question, not a complete sentence that can stand by itself in written discourse.

SAMPLE RESPONSES: **1.** B: Why? Why did you eat two breakfasts this morning? A: Because I was very hungry. **2.** B: Why not? Why don't you like to ride on airplanes? A: Because I'm afraid they'll crash. **3.** B: Why? Why are you going to sell your guitar? A: Because I don't play it anymore and I need the money. **4.** B: Why? Why didn't you go to bed last night? A: Because I was studying for an exam. **5.** B: Why? Why are you happy today? A: Because I got a raise at work. **6.** B: Why? Why did you have to call the police last night? A: Because someone broke into my car. **7.** B: Why? Why can't you explain it to me? A: Because I don't have enough time. **8.** B: Why not? Why aren't you speaking to your cousin? A: Because she was rude to my wife. [*To be not speaking to someone* is an idiom meaning to be so angry at someone that you won't talk to her/him.]

CHART 5-4: QUESTIONS WITH *WHO, WHO(M)*, AND *WHAT*

- This grammar will be difficult unless students clearly understand subjects and objects. Refer to Chart 6-3 (Subjects, Verbs, and Objects) if necessary.
- *Whom* is rarely used in everyday discourse. Native speakers prefer *who: Who did you see at the party? Who did you talk to? Who does Bob remind you of?* Etc.

☐ EXERCISE 8, p. 126. Questions with WHO, WHO(M), and WHAT. (Chart 5-4)

The purpose of this practice is to help the students figure out if the word order is or is not inverted when the question word is *who* or *what.*

Help the students make the connection between subjects and objects in statements and in questions by showing that the answer *(someone/something)* parallels the grammatical function of the question word. The question word can be substituted for *someone/something.* If it is a subject, no change is made in word order. If it is an object, the word order is inverted.

ANSWERS:

3. Who knocked on the door? (s)
4. Who(m) did Sara meet? (o)
5. What did Mike learn? (o)
6. What changed Ann's mind? (s)
7. Who(m) is Ann talking about? (o) OR About whom is Ann talking? (o)

☐ EXERCISE 9, p. 126. Questions with WHO, WHO(M), and WHAT. (Chart 5-4)

Students should be asked to identify subjects and objects throughout. You might want to parse some of these items, pointing out the elements and patterns of the simple sentence in statements and questions.

ANSWERS: **2.** What did Mary see? **3.** Who saw an accident? **4.** Who(m) did Mary see? **5.** Who saw John? **6.** What happened? **7.** What did Alice buy? **8.** Who bought a new coat? **9.** What are you looking at? *(very formal:* At what are you looking?) **10.** Who(m) are you looking at? *(very formal:* At whom are you looking?) **11.** Who(m) did you talk to? *(very formal:* To whom did you talk?) **12.** What did Tom talk about? *(very formal:* About what did Tom talk?) **13.** What did the teacher look at? *(very formal:* At what did the teacher look?) **14.** Who looked at the board? **15.** Who(m) did the teacher look at? *(very formal:* At whom did the teacher look?) **16.** What is a frog? **17.** What is an amphibian? **18.** What do frogs eat?

☐ EXERCISE 10, p. 128. Questions with WHO, WHO(M), and WHAT. (Chart 5-4)

The purpose of this exercise is to encourage free response interaction between students. Encourage responses longer than one sentence. Encourage the questioner, Speaker A, to ask follow-up questions if s/he wishes.

ANSWERS: **1.** What [also possible but far less usual: *who,* meaning what author(s) do you like to read] **2.** Who(m) **3.** What **4.** Who(m) **5.** Who **6.** What **7.** What **8.** What **9.** Who(m) **10.** Who

CHART 5-5: SPOKEN AND WRITTEN CONTRACTIONS WITH QUESTION WORDS

• Emphasize that the contractions in examples (a) through (e) are **spoken** only, not written. Sometimes if students see a form written, as here, they assume it is a written form and don't pay attention to the information that these are representations of spoken English only.

☐ EXERCISE 11, p. 128. Spoken contractions with question words. (Chart 5-5)

The quotation marks below indicate that the contraction is usually spoken but rarely, if ever, written.

ANSWERS:

1. Where's
2. What's
3. "Why's"
4. Who's
5. "Who're"
6. "Where're"
7. "What're"
8. "Where'd"
9. "What'd"
10. "Why'd"
11. "Who'd"
12. "Where'll"
13. "When'll"
14. "Who'll"

☐ EXERCISE 12, p. 129. Information questions. (Charts 5-2 → 5-5)

Students should create written questions. Perhaps they can correct each other's questions prior to class discussion. Alternatively, they can hand the dialogues in if you ask them to use a separate sheet of paper and write both the question and the answer.

EXPANSION: Give the students this list of question words: *where, why, when, what time, who, what.* Tell them to make up an exercise for a classmate in which these words need to be used (and only these question words at this point). The format of the exercise they make up can be like Exercise 12 (or Exercise 9). Outline exactly what you have in mind when you make the assignment. Asking the students to make up exercises for their classmates is a good technique for many areas of grammar. It puts the student in the role of the teacher and enhances student learning.

SAMPLE ANSWERS: **1.** When did you see Omar? **2.** What did you buy when you went shopping? **3.** Who is your teacher? **4.** What time did you get up? **5.** Where did you go Saturday? **6.** Why did you stay home last night? **7.** What are you going to have for lunch? **8.** What is Roberto going to do after class today? **9.** When are you going to call your parents on the phone? **10.** Who do you enjoy spending time with during holidays?

☐ EXERCISE 13, p. 129. Asking for the meaning of a word. (Chart 5-4)

ANSWERS (definitions in parentheses):

1. What does *essential* mean? (extremely necessary)
2. What does *float* mean? (stay on the surface, not sink)
3. What does *mad* mean? (angry or insane)
4. What does *bury* mean? (put under the surface and cover up)
5. What does *beneath* mean? (under)
6. What does *grabbed* mean? (took quickly and firmly in one's hand)
7. What is an *orchard?* / What does *orchard* mean? (a field of fruit trees)
8. What is a *honeymoon?* / What does *honeymoon* mean? (a trip newlyweds take)
9. What is *small talk?* / What does *small talk* mean? (light, social conversation about unimportant things)
10. What are *hedges?* / What does *hedges* mean? (a row of trimmed bushes used as a boundary)

CHART 5-6: USING *WHAT* + A FORM OF *DO*

• Use your students' lives and activities to demonstrate *what* + *do* questions. For example, *What is Miguel doing? What was Yoko doing before she sat down? What did you do yesterday? What is Keh Kooi going to do after class today?* Show the relationship between the verb form in the answer and the form of *do* in the question.

☐ EXERCISE 14, p. 130. Using WHAT + a form of DO. (Chart 5-6)

This is an exercise on the form of the verbs in questions in which *what* + *do* is used to ask about activities.

ANSWERS: **2.** What did you do **3.** What are you going to do **4.** What do you want to do **5.** What would you like to do **6.** What are you planning to do **7.** What do you do **8.** What do you do **9.** What did the police officer do **10.** What does a bear do **11.** What should I do **12.** What does Mr. Rice do . . . What does Mrs. Rice do

☐ EXERCISE 15, p. 131. Using WHAT + a form of DO and verb tense review. (Chart 5-6)

Encourage conversational interaction.

CHART 5-7: USING *WHAT KIND OF*

• You might want to introduce the expression *what sort of* as well. It has the same meaning as *what kind of.*

• Use objects in the classroom to demonstrate what information can be elicited when *what kind of* is used. Ask students what kind of shoes they're wearing, what kind of watches they have, etc.

☐ EXERCISE 16, p. 132. Using WHAT KIND OF. (Chart 5-7)

This exercise is intended to give a basic survey of the information that can be elicited by asking *what kind of.* Emphasize the idea of specific kinds within a category. The question asks about a category. The answer supplies a specific kind.

ANSWERS: **3.** music . . . classical/jazz/etc. **4.** car . . . Ford, Toyota/etc. **5.** books . . . novels/nonfiction/etc. **6.–8.** *Free response.*

☐ EXERCISE 17, p. 133. Using WHAT KIND OF. (Chart 5-7)

Have the students walk around and interview each other, then write a report of the information they learned.

CHART 5-8: USING *WHICH*

• Demonstrate the difference between *which* and *what:* Put two books on a student's desk. Focus the attention of the class on the group of two books. Pick up one and ask, "Which one did I pick up, the grammar book or the dictionary?" For contrast, walk to another student's desk and pick up a pen or piece of paper, asking "What did I pick up?"

Explain that *which* is used when the speaker and listener(s) are thinking about the same known group (e.g., the books on Ahmad's desk), and that *what* is used when there is no known group. The answer to *what* can be anything that exists in the universe. The answer to *which* can only be something that is part of a limited and specific group.

• In the text, the examples and exercises deal only with *which* as an object of a verb or preposition, but *which* can also be used as the subject or part of the subject of a question.

Example: *Which book has the best information?* Perhaps pose to your students this philosophical question that is familiar to most English speakers: *Which came first, the chicken or the egg?*

• *Which* is also used in adjective clauses. *(The book, which no one liked, was required reading.)* See Chapter 12. You may or may not wish to mention this dual usage at this point.

☐ EXERCISE 18, p. 134. WHICH vs. WHAT. (Chart 5-8)

ANSWERS: **3.** Which **4.** What **5.** What **6.** which . . . which

☐ EXERCISE 19, p. 134. WHICH vs. WHAT. (Chart 5-8)

ANSWERS: **3.** Which pen / Which one / Which would you like? **4.** What did Chris borrow from you? **5.** What do you have in your hand? Which piece of candy / Which one / Which would you like? **6.** Which tie / Which one / Which are you going to buy? **7.** What did Tony get? **8.** What countries / Which countries did you visit? . . . Which country / Which one / Which did you enjoy visiting the most?

CHART 5-9: USING *WHOSE*

• The two principal ways of asking questions about possession are to use *whose* or *belong to:* *Whose (book) is this?* vs. *Who(m) does this (book) belong to?*

• *Whose* is also used in adjective clauses. (Example: *That's the man whose house burned down.*) See Chart 12-7 in the *FEG 3e* student book. The use of *whose* in questions is of much higher frequency than its use as a relative pronoun.

• In comparing the pronunciation of *whose* and *who's,* the text says that *who's* = *who is. Who's* can also be a contraction for *who has* when *has* is used as the auxiliary in the present perfect. (Example: *Who's been to Disneyland?)* You may or may not wish to mention this meaning of *who's.*

☐ EXERCISE 20, p. 136. Using WHOSE. (Chart 5-9)

One focus of this exercise is on distinguishing between *whose* and *who's*. Oral practice with *whose* alone follows in Exercise 21.

ANSWERS:

3. Whose notebook is
4. Whose tapes are
5. Who is
6. Whose clothes are
7. Whose coat is
8. Who is
9. Who is
10. Whose hair is

☐ EXERCISE 21, p. 137. Using WHOSE. (Chart 5-9)

This is an exercise on possessive nouns and pronouns (see Charts 6-11 and 6-12 in the *FEG 3e* student book) in addition to questions with *whose*.

Notice the two patterns for asking yes/no questions about possession using *be* and possessive nouns or pronouns. (Examples: *Are these Yoko's pens?* and *Are these pens Yoko's?)* Students can use whichever pattern they are comfortable with.

In discussing the examples in the text, point out that Speaker B's first response should be negative. In other words, Speaker A asks a question to which s/he knows that the answer is *no.*

☐ EXERCISE 22, p. 137. Review: information questions. (Charts 5-2 → 5-9)

This is a general review of question words and forms covered so far in this chapter. Encourage Speaker B to listen for any errors in Speaker A's grammar.

SAMPLE ANSWERS: **1.** Whose books are these? **2.** What are you going to do this evening? **3.** What kind of car do your parents drive? **4.** Who is the director of this English program? **5.** Whose dictionary is that? **6.** What does "little" mean? **7.** What kind of music is New Orleans famous for? **8.** Why didn't you come to class yesterday? **9.** Which pen do you want? **10.** Whose bookbag is that? **11.** When did you go downtown? **12.** What country was Gandhi from?

☐ EXERCISE 23, p. 138. Asking questions. (Charts 5-1 → 5-9)

You might have to clarify the directions because this is a one-of-a-kind exercise; the students aren't familiar with the format. Emphasize that Speaker A should choose an answer at random and then make up a question that will produce that answer.

CHART 5-10: USING *HOW*

- In general, *how* asks about manner, means, condition, degree, extent. It doesn't lend itself to a quick definition. Starting with this chart, the text introduces common uses of *how* in six separate charts so that students may slowly build their understanding of its meanings and uses.

☐ EXERCISE 24, p. 139. Using HOW. (Chart 5-10)

This exercise consists of further illustrations of the uses of *how* presented in Chart 5-10.

ANSWERS: **2.** How important is education? **3.** How do you get to school? **4.** How deep is the ocean? **5.** How are you going to get to Denver? **6.** How difficult was the test? **7.** How high is Mr. Everest? **8.** How did you get to school today?

CHART 5-11: USING *HOW OFTEN*

• COMPARE: *How often* is the common way to ask for general information about frequency, as in (a). The listener can respond in many different ways, as indicated by the sample answers in the chart. *How many times* is used to elicit more specific information about a given length of time and limits the way in which the listener can respond, as in (b).

☐ EXERCISE 25, p. 140. Using HOW OFTEN. (Chart 5-11)

This exercise focuses not only on questions with *how often* but, just as important, on common ways to answer such questions. Even though these frequency expressions are not presented in a separate chart, some of your teaching should focus on them.

CHART 5-12: USING *HOW FAR*

• This chart teaches expletive ***it*** for expressing distances as well as how to ask questions about distance. Elicit further examples of the grammar patterns in (b) by using local places your class is familiar with.

☐ EXERCISE 26, p. 141. Using HOW FAR. (Chart 5-12)

ANSWERS: **2.** How far is it from Montreal to Quebec? **3.** How far is it to the post office? **4.** How far did you get . . . ?

☐ EXERCISE 27, p. 141. Using HOW FAR. (Chart 5-12)

This exercise in intended for small group discussion of regional geography. The purposes are to familiarize the students with the geography of the surrounding area, make sure they know how to read a map in English and decipher a mileage chart, practice the target structures, and engage in directed conversation with their classmates.

Supply one road map to each small group. (Perhaps some of the students have road maps and can bring them to class. If not, it might require a small investment from a visual-aids budget.) Students can ask *how far* questions using place names on the map, make guesses about distance, and then figure out exact distances. Another possibility is for you to supply several pairs of place names (e.g., the names of this city and that city) and see which groups can figure out the correct distances from their maps. You could make it a game with prizes (such as chocolates or post cards).

CHART 5-13: LENGTH OF TIME: *IT* + *TAKE* AND *HOW LONG*

• In this section, the text is teaching expletive *it* + *take* for expressing length of time as well as teaching how to ask questions about length of time using *how long.*

• The text deals with infinitives following expletive *it* in Chapter 13.

☐ **EXERCISE 28, p. 142. Length of time. (Chart 5-13)**

This is a quick exercise on form: ***it*** + ***take*** + *infinitive.*

ANSWERS: **2.** It takes me twenty minutes to walk to class. **3.** It took Gino an hour and a half to finish the test. **4.** It will take us forty-five minutes to drive to the airport. **5.** It took Alan two weeks to hitchhike to Alaska. **6.** It takes me two hours to wash my clothes at the laundromat.

☐ **EXERCISE 29, p. 142. Length of time. (Chart 5-13)**

This is free-response reinforcement practice with ***it*** + ***take*** + *infinitive.* You can pose the questions, and several students can respond to each.

☐ **EXERCISE 30, p. 142. Length of time. (Chart 5-13)**

You may wish to model normal contracted speech, as represented below in the brackets for some of the items.

ANSWERS: **2.** How long will ["how long'll"] Mr. McNally be in the hospital? **3.** How long does it ["how long'uzit"] take to learn a second language? **4.** How long have ["how long've"] you been living here? **5.** How long did you live in Istanbul? **6.** How long have ["how long've"] you known Nho Pham? **7.** How long has ["how long's"] he been living in Canada? **8.** How long does a person have to do something consistently before it becomes a habit?

☐ **EXERCISE 31, p. 143. Length of time. (Chart 5-13)**

To clarify the instructions, write another example on the chalkboard and ask three students to model the form of the exercise for the rest of the class.

For optimal listening and speaking practice, only Speaker A's book should be open. The open book can be rotated as the students switch roles.

CHART 5-14: MORE QUESTIONS WITH *HOW*

- This chart consists of some miscellaneous common questions with *how.*
- In (d) through (f), the answer *so-so* means "not bad, but not good." It means things are okay, but one might wish they were better.
- In (f), *How's everything going?* is another way of asking *How's it going?*
- In the answers in (g), students might be interested in the derivation of *lousy.* It means "very bad," but the word itself comes from the noun *louse,* the plural of which is *lice.* Lice are international pests that infect humans. The literal meaning of *lousy* is "full of lice," but in everyday conversation, native speakers don't connect the word with the pest. They use it simply to mean *very bad* or *miserable.*
- Example (h) needs a little discussion and perhaps role-playing. Ask Speaker A to introduce B to C. Ask B and C to use *How do you do?* Have them shake hands at the same time. You might take a little time to talk about the forms of introductions in general, and compare the more formal *How do you do?* with the casual *Hi. Nice to meet you.*

☐ EXERCISE 32, p. 144. More questions with HOW. (Chart 5-14)

This exercise can be a spelling game in small groups. Many of the words on this list are frequently misspelled by second-language students—and native speakers as well.

Item 1: a mnemonic device of this oft-misspelled word is to remember it consists of three individual words: *to* + *get* + *her.*

Items 4, 5, 9, 13, and 15: Remind the class of the spelling rules they learned in Chart 2-5.

Item 6: The old spelling rule is: "i" before "e" except after "c" or when pronounced /ey/ as in *neighbor* and *weigh.* That rule accounts for the spelling of *receive* and *neighbor;* it does not, however, account for the spelling of *foreign* in item 8. Tell your students you sympathize with them in any difficulties they have spelling English words. Remind them they can always look words up in their dictionaries.

☐ EXERCISE 33, p. 144. More questions with HOW. (Chart 5-14)

Expand the exercise to include other words or phrases students may want to know in one another's languages.

In some languages there is no direct translation for *thank you.* Surveying the language groups in your class, discuss various ways of expressing thanks.

Some classes like to list all the ways to say "I love you" in as many languages as they can. Some students assiduously copy down each one.

☐ EXERCISE 34, p. 144. More questions with HOW. (Chart 5-14)

This is intended as a fun, change-of-pace exercise. Prepare the class for doing the exercise by pronouncing all the words in List A first. Have the students repeat them. Then pronounce one word and have the class tell you the number of the word you said. Open the discussion of the pronunciations. At least some students should spontaneously produce correct *how*-questions.

Following are the phonetic transcriptions for the exercise items:

LIST A:

(1) beat = /biyt/
(2) bit = /bɪt/
(3) bet = /bɛt/
(4) bite = /bayt/
(5) bait = /beyt/
(6) bat = /bæt/
(7) but = /bət/
(8) boot = /buwt/
(9) boat = /bowt/
(10) bought = /bɔt/

LIST B:

(1) zoos = /zuwz/
(2) Sue's = /suws/
(3) shoes = /šuwz/
(4) chews = /čuwz/
(5) choose = /čuwz/
(6) chose = /čowz/
(7) those = /ðowz/
(8) toes = /towz/
(9) doze = /dowz/
(10) dose = /dows/

NOTE: In List B, items (4) and (5) have the same pronunciation.

☐ EXERCISE 35, p. 144. Review of HOW. (Charts 5-10 → 5-14)

ANSWERS:

2. How long
3. How far
4. How many
5. How often
6. How far
7. How many
8. How fast
9. How many
10. How
11. How heavy
12. How . . . How

☐ EXERCISE 36, p. 146. Review of HOW. (Charts 5-10 → 5-14)

If you assign this as written homework, ask the students to write both the question and the answer to facilitate your task of reading their papers.

SAMPLE RESPONSES: **1.** How expensive is a ticket to a basketball game? **2.** How did you get to the airport? **3.** How long did the exam last? **4.** How old is your brother? **5.** When will class be over? **6.** How do you cut meat? **7.** How often do you eat lunch at the cafeteria? **8.** How far is the post office from here? **9.** How's everything going? **10.** How do you spell "written"? **11.** How cold does it get in Siberia? **12.** How is the food at Al's Restaurant?

☐ EXERCISE 37, p. 146. Review of questions. (Charts 5-1 → 5-14)

If there is any interest in baseball among your students, you might discuss a little baseball vocabulary as shown in the illustration: the outfield (left fielder, center fielder, right fielder), infield, first base, second base, two men on base. The net is protection for the spectators immediately behind home plate so they don't get hit by a foul ball.

EXPECTED COMPLETIONS: **2.** Which one are you going to **3.** Did you go to the game **4.** Did you go (to it) **5.** Did you go **6.** Who went **7.** Who(m) did you go **8.** Can you walk **9.** How far is it? **10.** How did you **11.** How long did (does) it take you to **12.** What time does the game **13.** How often do you go **14.** Why do you like to go **15.** What do you do

☐ EXERCISE 38, p. 148. Review of questions. (Charts 5-1 → 5-14)

This is a summary review exercise of Chapter 5. It can be used as a game, with teams getting points for well-crafted questions. Or it can be used as a written quiz (unannounced). Or it can be used as a quick oral review, with the class calling out possible questions. Or pairs can be assigned items to prepare to role-play for the class.

SAMPLE ANSWERS: **1.** What does "large" mean? **2.** When did you talk to Pedro? **3.** How often do you go to the market? **4.** How are you getting along? **5.** How do you get to school? **6.** Whose notebook is this? **7.** What kind of books do you like to read? **8.** How do you spell "beautiful"? **9.** Where do you like to go on the weekends? **10.** Why did you come to this school? **11.** How far is it to . . . ? **12.** What are you going to do after class today? **13.** How are you feeling? **14.** How do you do? **15.** How long does an average movie last? **16.** What time do you usually eat dinner? **17.** Who is your roommate? **18.** What is your favorite color? **19.** What's the weather like in Seattle in winter? **20.** Which book is yours? **21.** Whose book is that? **22.** How do you spell "occurred"? **23.** Who's coming with us tonight? **24.** How far is it to the nearest ATM machine? **25.** When was your son born? **26.** What is your sister's field of study? **27.** What are we doing? **28.** Where are you from? Where is it located? What is the principal product of Saudi Arabia? What is the capital of Saudi Arabia?

☐ EXERCISE 39, p. 148. Review of questions. (Charts 5-1 → 5-14)

Students will find this exercise easy and should be pleased with their own fluency.

SAMPLE ANSWERS: **1.** What kind of fruit do you like best? **2.** What country is south of the United States? **3.** How many times a week do you eat fish? **4.** What are you going to do tomorrow? **5.** How far is it from *(name of a place)* to *(name of a place)?* **6.** How long have you been living in this city? **7.** Who is sitting next to (Pedro)? **8.** What should I do this weekend? **9.** What do you do for a living? **10.** How do you spelled "happened"? **11.** How long does it take to go to your apartment from the airport? **12.** How are you getting along in your English classes?

☐ EXERCISE 40, p. 149. Review of questions. (Charts 5-1 → 5-14)

Tell the groups that they are "brainstorming" questions, i.e., saying whatever comes into their minds about the topic; groups brainstorm in order to come up with interesting and new ideas. *(Brainstorming* is AmE. In BrE, a *brainstorm* is something that occurs when you are unable to think clearly.)

Ask the groups to write down their most interesting questions to ask the rest of the class. Maybe you could give a prize for the best question or to the group with the best questions—explaining that you're looking for originality and insight and that your judgment is purely subjective.

The goal is creative, spontaneous use of the target structures in a fun and relaxed setting.

CHART 5-15: USING *HOW ABOUT* AND *WHAT ABOUT*

- *How about* and *what about* invite the listener to respond with how s/he feels about the idea the questioner suggests. The questioner is saying: "I think this is a possible idea for us/you to consider. What do you think?"
- The *-ing* form in examples (c) and (d) is a gerund. Gerunds are introduced in Chapter 13.
- In examples (e) and (f), *how about* and *what about* are "conversation continuers." They are used to promote the sharing of information in polite conversation. In some situations, if someone asks you if you are hungry, it is polite to ask if s/he is hungry, as in (f).

☐ EXERCISE 41, p. 149. HOW ABOUT and WHAT ABOUT. (Chart 5-15)

POSSIBLE COMPLETIONS: **2.** Let's get together Tuesday for lunch. . . . Wednesday? **3.** . . . Olga . . . the park . . . She . . . she has to work. . . . Fatima . . . . She might like to go with us. I'll ask her. **4.** . . . you . . . you . . . Yes, I think I'll have fish tonight, too.

☐ EXERCISE 42, p. 150. HOW ABOUT and WHAT ABOUT. (Chart 5-15)

This controlled-completion oral exercise allows students to experiment with *how/what about* in typical contexts and is intended to prepare them for pair work in the following two exercises.

☐ EXERCISE 43, p. 151. HOW ABOUT and WHAT ABOUT. (Chart 5-15)

Be sure to tell students how useful *how/what about* is in everyday informal conversations, such as they're practicing in this exercise.

☐ EXERCISE 44, p. 151. HOW ABOUT and WHAT ABOUT. (Chart 5-15)

The directions to Speaker A say to look "directly into the eyes of Speaker B." In some cultures, looking another person directly in the eye is not polite or has hierarchical implications. In much of the English-speaking world, people look each other straight in the eye. There is no need for international students of English to adopt English-speakers' cultural mannerisms, but it's good for them to be made aware of these mannerisms. And in the environment of the classroom, they may want to experiment with cultural mannerisms different from their own.

CHART 5-16: TAG QUESTIONS

• It's important for students to understand that a question with a tag indicates the speaker's belief about the validity of the idea being expressed. The speaker believes to be true what is expressed in the statement before the tag.

• Students are already familiar with the idea of a rising intonation at the end of a question. In the examples and exercises on tags, a rising intonation would be appropriate throughout.

The text keeps the focus on tag questions with rising intonations, but the footnote to the chart introduces tag questions with falling intonation, to be emphasized or not as you decide. In sum: If the speaker is truly seeking information, his/her voice rises: *This is your hat, isn't it?* If the speaker is expressing his/her opinion, the voice falls at the end: *This is a good class, isn't it.* (The period instead of a question mark here helps show a falling rather than rising intonation.) In this case, the speaker is simply making a comment and inviting conversation. S/he is not asking if this is a good class, whereas in the previous example the speaker is asking if the hat belongs to the listener.

• Other possible informal tags that turn statements into questions follow:

It's really cold today, ***eh****?*
This food is delicious, ***huh****?*
You borrowed my dictionary yesterday, ***no****?*

• Point out the "polarity" of tags, explaining what the plus and minus signs mean. (Plus is used for affirmative verbs, minus for negative verbs.)

☐ EXERCISE 45, p. 152. Tag questions. (Chart 5-16)

ANSWERS: **2.** didn't he . . . Yes, he did. **3.** wasn't he . . . Yes, he was. **4.** won't she . . . Yes, she will. **5.** can't you . . . Yes, I can. **6.** did he/she . . . No, he/she didn't. **7.** have you . . . No, I/we haven't. **8.** don't they . . . Yes, they do.

☐ EXERCISE 46, p. 153. Use of auxiliary verbs in tag questions. (Chart 5-16)

This is an exercise on both auxiliary verbs and pronouns.

ANSWERS:

2. can't they
3. doesn't he
4. is he
5. wouldn't you
6. doesn't she
7. hasn't she
8. doesn't she
9. shouldn't you
10. won't she
11. did you
12. isn't it
13. isn't it
14. aren't they
15. isn't it . . . can't they

☐ EXERCISE 47, p. 154. Tag questions. (Chart 5-16)

After you discuss the examples, tell the students to close their books. You give the cues.

ANSWERS:

1. wasn't s/he?
2. did s/he?
3. is s/he?
4. isn't s/he?
5. can s/he?
6. doesn't s/he?
7. won't s/he?
8. can't s/he?
9. doesn't s/he?
10. hasn't s/he?
11. didn't s/he?
12. doesn't s/he? [BrE: hasn't s/he?]

☐ EXERCISE 48, p. 155 Summary: creating and role-playing dialogues. (Chapter 5)

Assign one dialogue per pair. Have some or all of the pairs role-play their dialogues in front of the class or small groups. The given situations for the dialogues are intended to encourage students to ask questions of all types.

Chapter 6: NOUNS AND PRONOUNS

ORDER OF CHAPTER	CHARTS	EXERCISES	WORKBOOK
Preview		Ex. 1	Pr. 1
Pronunciation of final *-s/-es*	6-1	Ex. 2	Pr. 2 → 4
Plural forms of nouns	6-2	Ex. 3 → 4	Pr. 5 → 6
Subjects, verbs, and objects	6-3	Ex. 5 → 7	Pr. 7
Objects of prepositions	6-4	Ex. 8 → 9	Pr. 8 → 9
Prepositions of time	6-5	Ex. 10 → 11	Pr. 10
Word order: place and time	6-6	Ex. 12	Pr. 11
Subject–verb agreement	6-7	Ex. 13	Pr. 12 → 13
Using adjectives to describe nouns	6-8	Ex. 14 → 16	Pr. 14 → 15
Using nouns as adjectives	6-9	Ex. 17 → 18	Pr. 16
Summary review: nouns		Ex. 19 → 20	Pr. 17
Personal pronouns	6-10	Ex. 21 → 22	Pr. 18 → 20
Possessive nouns	6-11	Ex. 23 → 24	Pr. 21 → 22
Summary review: nouns + -s/-es		Ex. 25	
Possessive pronouns and adjectives	6-12	Ex. 26	Pr. 23 → 24
Reflexive pronouns	6-13	Ex. 27 → 30	Pr. 25 → 26
Summary review: pronouns			Pr. 27 → 28
Forms of *other*	6-14 → 6-16	Ex. 31 → 35	Pr. 29 → 32
Cumulative review		Ex. 36	Pr. 33 → 34

• Nouns are the basic tools for giving names to and talking about things and concepts. Learners need usage ability of not only nouns but associated words, such as pronouns, adjectives, and prepositions. The chapter seeks to provide an acquaintance with these basic structures and terms in English grammar and how they fit into the fundamental patterns of the simple sentence in English.

• TERMINOLOGY: Some books use the term "noun adjunct" for the word *vegetable* in the phrase *vegetable garden,* but this text simply calls it "a noun used as an adjective." A distinction is made between "possessive pronouns" (e.g., *my)* and "possessive adjectives" (e.g., *mine)*.

□ EXERCISE 1, p. 156. Preview: grammar terms. (Chapter 6)

This exercise depends upon the teacher to supply an introductory understanding of the concepts these grammar terms represent. Some students will be quite familiar with these terms, and some students will not be, in which case this exercise should catch their attention as to what they need to learn in this chapter.

When you discuss Exercise 1, you might use the following explanations.

In item 1: *shirt* is a thing. The traditional definition of a noun as a "person, place, or thing" can be useful to students. A noun can also be defined as a word that functions as a subject or object in a sentence. In this item, *shirt* is grammatically the object of the verb *wear* in the basic structure of a simple sentence: *subject* + *verb* + *object.* (See Charts 6-3 and 6-4 for explanations of subjects and objects.)

Item 2: *in* is a "little word" called a preposition. Prepositions are usually placed in front of nouns (or pronouns) and give information about place, time, and other relationships. Ask the students how many prepositions they can name (without looking at Chart 6-4).

Item 3: a pronoun refers to, and has the same meaning as, a noun. *He* and *Steve* are the same person in this item.

Item 4: an adjective describes (i.e., adds information about) a noun or pronoun; *thirsty* describes the subject *I.* If you say *Ali is thirsty,* then *thirsty* describes *Ali.* (Note: Some languages do not require a verb in this kind of statement, but English requires *be.)*

This preview contains basic simple sentences. If your students want to analyze them, they will find:

- All three patterns with main verb *be:*
  - ***be*** + *prepositional phrase of place* (items 2, 3, and 13)
  - ***be*** + *adjective* (item 4)
  - ***be*** + *noun phrase* (items 11 and 12)
- *Be* as auxiliary verb (item 3, second verb)
- Basic S + V + O in items 1, 5, 6, 9, 10, 14, 15
- Basic S + V (intransitive verb) in items 7 and 8

EXPANSION: Knowing some of the basic grammar terminology presented in this chapter will help students use dictionaries more effectively, where words are identified as nouns, pronouns, prepositions, adjectives, etc. Perhaps at the conclusion of this exercise, or at some later point in this unit, students could investigate in their own dictionaries where and how these grammar terms are used.

ANSWERS:

5. noun
6. noun
7. adjective
8. preposition
9. noun
10. adjective
11. noun
12. adjective
13. preposition
14. noun
15. pronoun

CHART 6-1: PRONUNCIATION OF FINAL *-S/-ES*

- Final *-s/-es* is troublesome for all ESL/EFL students. Paying special attention to its pronunciations can be helpful. In a way, students need to train themselves to be aware of hearing *-s/-es* as an aid to using it correctly in their own production, both spoken and written.
- Explain and model the pronunciation of the examples.
- To explain voiceless vs. voiced, tell the students to put their hand to their voice box to feel vibrations. A voiceless sound such as /t/ or /s/ comes from air being pushed through the tongue and teeth; a voiced sound such as /d/ or /z/ emanates from the voice box.
- Point out that in voiceless-voiced pairs such as /s/ and /z/, the tongue and teeth are in the same position. The only difference is the addition of the voice box to the /z/ sound.
- Some other voiceless vs. voiced pairs are /t/ and /d/, /p/ and /b/, /f/ and /v/.
- Define "buzz" (the sound a bee makes).
- The upside down "e" in the symbol /əz/ is called a "schwa."

□ EXERCISE 2, p. 157. Pronunciation of final -S/-ES. (Chart 6-1)

Clarify the information in Chart 6-1 by identifying voiced and voiceless sounds. For example, point out that final *-s* is pronounced /z/ in item 1 because /m/ is a voiced sound and pronounced /s/ in item 2 because /k/ is a voiceless sound.

ANSWERS:

3. /z/	**9.** /z/	**15.** /əz/
4. /z/	**10.** /z/	**16.** /əz/
5. /s/	**11.** /s/	**17.** /əz/
6. /z/	**12.** /əz/	**18.** /əz/
7. /s/	**13.** /əz/	**19.** /əz/
8. /z/	**14.** /əz/	

□ EXERCISE 3, p. 157. Preview: plural nouns. (Chart 6-2)

This preview exercise is intended to call students' attention to singular and plural nouns. Students using this text are already familiar with much of the grammar in this exercise, but some of the grammar is probably new to them (e.g., the use of the word *offspring)*.

EXPANSION: This practice can also be used in class discussion to identify the basic structures of the simple sentence.

S + V + O in items 1, 2, 3, 5, 7, 8, 9, 10
S + V + PrepPhr (of place) in item 4
S + *be* + Noun in items 6 and 10

ANSWERS: **2.** Boxes have six sides. **3.** Big cities have many problems. **4.** Bananas grow in hot, humid areas. **5.** Insects don't have noses. **6.** Lambs are the offspring of sheep. **7.** Libraries keep books on shelves. **8.** Parents support their child**ren**. **9.** Indonesia has several active volcano**es/s**. **10.** Baboons are big monkeys. They have large heads and sharp teeth. They eat leaves, roots, insects, and eggs.

CHART 6-2: PLURAL FORMS OF NOUNS

- You may wish to model the nouns in (a) to illustrate the three different pronunciations of final *-s/-es: birds* = *bird* + /z/; *streets* = *street* + /s/; and *roses* = *rose* + /əz/.

- In section (f), you may point out that *-s*, not *-es*, is added to nouns that end in *-o* when the noun is a shortened form (e.g., *auto* instead of *automobile*), when the noun is related to a musical term, and when the noun ends in two vowels. Or you can simply say that sometimes one adds *-s* and sometimes *-es;* when in doubt, look it up.

- Section (i) is included simply to inform the students that some oddities in the formation of plural nouns do exist. Words with foreign plurals are not emphasized in this text; they are dealt with more fully in *Understanding and Using English Grammar.* The four words in section (i) are difficult vocabulary for most students at this level. They will encounter the word *phenomena* again in Chapter 11 in the discussion of phenomena of nature that are used as noncount nouns. (You might want to note that these rather unusual nouns are in the process of being Anglicized; that is, they are often spoken with more regular forms: e.g., one bacteria, two cactuses, one phenomena. In formal writing, however, the forms in this chart are still preferred.)

☐ EXERCISE 4, p. 159. Plural nouns. (Chart 6-2)

ANSWERS:

2. libraries
3. children
4. leaves
5. wishes
6. fish
7. opinions
8. mice
9. sandwiches
10. men
11. women
12. flashes
13. tomatoes
14. teeth
15. halves
16. taxes
17. possibilities
18. thieves
19. heroes
20. geese
21. attorneys
22. butterflies
23. categories
24. mosquitoes/mosquitos
25. sheep
26. wolves
27. stitches
28. feet
29. pianos
30. beliefs

CHART 6-3: SUBJECTS, VERBS, AND OBJECTS

- This is, of course, a simplified explanation of the simple sentence, but the students need only a basic understanding of subjects, verbs, and objects.

- You may want to delay a discussion of intransitive vs. transitive verbs until Chapter 10, where the distinction is dealt with in connection with the passive form. If you decide to introduce the terminology here, you could point out that dictionaries might label intransitive verbs as **v.i.** or **V** or **I** and transitive verbs as **v.t.** or **V + O** or **T**.

☐ EXERCISE 5, p. 160. Subjects, verbs, and objects. (Chart 6-3)

This is a simple exercise, but the grammar it demonstrates is essential for students of this text to understand.

ANSWERS:

	S	V	O
3.	Cows	eat	grass.
4.	My dog	barked.	
5.	The dog	chased	the cat.
6.	Steam	rises.	
7.	Accidents	happen.	
8.	Most birds	build	nests.
9.	Our guests	arrived.	
10.	Teachers	assign	homework.
11.	My roommate	opened	the window.
12.	Jack	raised	his hand.
13.	Irene	is watching	her sister's children.

☐ EXERCISE 6, p. 160. Nouns and verbs. (Charts 6-2 and 6-3)

You might want to discuss the sentence structure of some of these items. Ask the students how they know the italicized word is a noun or a verb.

ANSWERS:

3.	n.	**7.**	n.	**11.**	n.
4.	v.	**8.**	v.	**12.**	v.
5.	v.	**9.**	v.	**13.**	v.
6.	n.	**10.**	n.	**14.**	n.

☐ EXERCISE 7, p. 161. Nouns and verbs. (Charts 6-2 and 6-3)

This practice requires a good understanding of the fundamental structure of the simple sentence and the grammatical functions of nouns and verbs. Students who are unable to complete it successfully may need extra help before they proceed in the chapter. Students who can't identify nouns and verbs will be at a great disadvantage throughout the rest of the text.

SAMPLE SENTENCES:

1. *Noun:* We walked home in the rain.
Verb: It rained yesterday.
2. *Noun:* Paint can be very expensive.
Verb: I will paint my bedroom this weekend.
3. *Noun:* I wore the tie you bought me.
Verb: I tied a string around the package.
4. *Noun:* The phone kept ringing last night, but I didn't get out of bed to answer it.
Verb: I'll phone you in the morning. *(an informal use)*
5. *Noun:* I bought my dress at a little shop in Los Angeles.
Verb: We shopped for furniture.
6. *Noun:* His face was familiar, but I couldn't remember his name.
Verb: I can't face my boss after the terrible mistake I made at work.
7. *Noun:* We couldn't drink the water because the stream was polluted.
Verb: I watered the vegetable garden this morning.
8. *Noun:* My sister drew a circle around the correct answer.
Verb: I will circle the correct answer to that question.
9. *Noun:* There's a fly on the ceiling.
Verb: I'm going to fly to Rome next week.

CHART 6-4: OBJECTS OF PREPOSITIONS

- What is a preposition? A simplified definition: A preposition is a word that occurs most often in front of nouns (or pronouns) to give information about place, time, and other relationships.
- Prepositions can also be humorously defined as "little words that cause second language learners a lot of trouble!"
- A definition may not be necessary or desirable. The text approaches recognition of prepositions (1) by supplying a list and simply telling the students that these words are prepositions, and (2) by demonstrating their grammatical structure and function in the examples and exercises.
- Appendix 2 contains preposition combinations with verbs and adjectives, with a reference list and exercises. The combinations are broken into small groups as an aid to learning. You may want to incorporate lessons from Appendix 2 into your class syllabus following the study of this unit. Students might use Appendix 2 to study one group of prepositions a week for the rest of the term.

□ EXERCISE 8, p. 162. Subjects, verbs, and objects. (Charts 6-3 and 6-4)

Ask the students to analyze (i.e., parse) the sentences prior to class discussion. They can work alone, in pairs, or in groups. It is important in using this textbook that learners be able to identify the basic elements of a simple sentence. (You might ask older or somewhat advanced students to think of how their own language connects the elements that are in these simple sentences. This might help them remember the differences in English.)

ANSWERS:

	S	V	PREP	O of PREP
2.	Sara	looked	at	the pictures.

	S	V	PREP	O of PREP	PREP	O of PREP
3.	Emily	waited	for	her friend	at	a restaurant.

	S	V	PREP	O of PREP
4.	The sun	rises	in	the east.

	S	V	O	PREP	O of PREP	PREP	O of PREP
5.	Sue	lost	her ring	in	the sand	at	the beach.

	S		V	PREP	O of PREP	PREP	O of PREP
6.	The moon	usually	disappears	from	view	during	the day.

	S	V	PREP	O of PREP	PREP	O of PREP	PREP	O of PREP
7.	Eric	talked	to	his friend	on	the phone	for	thirty minutes.

	S	PREP	O of PREP	V	PREP	O of PREP
8.	Children	throughout	the world	play	with	dolls.

	S	V	PREP	O of PREP	PREP	O of PREP
9.	Astronauts	walked	on	the moon	in	1969.

	S	PREP	O of PREP	V	PREP	O of PREP	PREP	O of PREP	PREP	O of PREP
10.	A woman	in	a blue suit	sat	beside	me	until	the end	of	the meeting.

☐ **EXERCISE 9, p. 162. Prepositions of place. (Chart 6-4)**

Have the students physically demonstrate the spatial relationships described by prepositions of place.

CHART 6-5: PREPOSITIONS OF TIME

- Your students might remember these prepositions with the help of a triangle written on the chalkboard or a large piece of heavy paper.

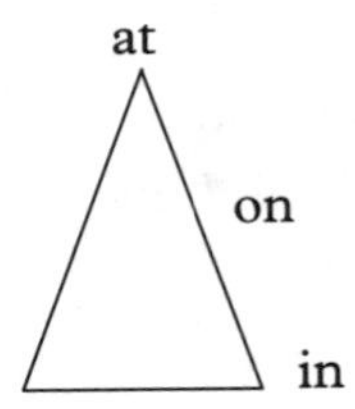

This triangle shows that *at* is related to the smallest, most specific point in time *(at 9:30, at noon,* etc.); *on* is related to a single day; and *in* is related to the longest, most general period of time *(in the evening, in 1997,* etc.). Some phrases, however, do not fit as well into this scheme (e.g., *at present, in the present, in a few minutes, in the afternoon* vs. *on Monday afternoon);* special attention should be paid to these.

☐ **EXERCISE 10, p. 163. Prepositions of time. (Chart 6-5)**

In items 3, 4, and 5, you may have to explain the difference between *in the present* (meaning *not in the past nor in the future), at present* (meaning *now, nowadays, for the time being),* and *at the present time* (meaning *for the time being, temporarily).* Using the triangle, show that *in* is more general than *at* in these phrases.

ANSWERS:

2. in
3. in
4. At
5. at
6. at
7. in
8. in
9. in
10. at
11. at
12. at
13. in
14. in
15. in
16. on
17. on
18. in
19. in . . . In
20. On . . . On
21. On
22. at

☐ **EXERCISE 11, p. 164. Prepositions of time. (Chart 6-5)**

ANSWERS:

1. in
2. at
3. in
4. in
5. on
6. in
7. on
8. in
9. in
10. at
11. on
12. at . . . in

CHART 6-6: WORD ORDER: PLACE AND TIME

• "Place before time" is a helpful phrase for students to know.

• For the most part, time expressions are placed at the beginning of a sentence if the writer wants to emphasize the time element, to vary his sentence structure for stylistic reasons, or to clarify a long and complicated sentence.

☐ EXERCISE 12, p. 164. Word order: place and time. (Chart 6-6)

ANSWERS: **1.** Alex works at his uncle's bakery on Saturday mornings. (OR: On Saturday mornings, Alex . . . .) **2.** I often take a walk in the park in the evening. (OR: In the evening, I . . . .) **3.** My plane arrived at the airport at six-thirty in the morning. (OR: At six-thirty in the morning, my plane . . . .)

CHART 6-7: SUBJECT–VERB AGREEMENT

• Singular–plural agreement is often a troublesome area for students. This chart presents only a few basics of subject–verb agreement.

• In (h): With *there* + *be,* nowadays a singular verb is common (informally) even when the subject is plural: *There's some books on the desk.* It certainly wouldn't hurt for the teacher to mention this peculiarity. This usage is dealt with in the more advanced text in this series, *Understanding and Using English Grammar, Third Edition,* Chart 6-4.

☐ EXERCISE 13, p. 165. Subject-verb agreement. (Chart 6-7)

The grammar dealt with in this exercise is troublesome for students and represents frequent sources of errors.

ANSWERS: **3.** My mother = S speaks = V **4.** My aunt and uncle = S speak = V *(no error)* **5.** Oscar = S speaks = V *(no error)* **6.** The students = S speak~~s~~ = V **7.** Every student~~s~~ = S speaks = V **8.** (There) are = V five students = S **9.** There's = V apartment = S *(no error)* **10.** Do~~es~~ = aux V people = S like = V **11.** The people = S speak~~s~~ = V **12.** (There) are = V kinds = S [As mentioned above, in informal spoken English one often hears *There is,* even among educated speakers: *There's many different kinds of fish* . . . . A singular verb here is not, however, generally considered correct grammar.] **13.** The neighbors = S ~~is~~ are = V **14.** (Every) student~~s~~ = S ~~have~~ has = V

CHART 6-8: USING ADJECTIVES TO DESCRIBE NOUNS

• The emphasis of this chart is on the terminology "adjective" and its function and form.

• Some languages inflect adjectives, i.e., change their form for number, gender, or some other category. Be sure to make clear that an adjective in English is neither singular nor plural and has no inflected endings.

☐ EXERCISE 14, p. 166. Adjectives. (Chart 6-8)

This exercise can be done quickly as a class or in groups. The goal is to make sure everyone in the class understands what an adjective is. The concept of adjectives will be revisited in the chapters on adjective clauses and comparisons.

Ask the students to identify the noun each adjective modifies.

ANSWERS:

2. dry
3. big
4. sharp
5. Dark . . . small
6. funny
7. Sensible . . . comfortable
8. soapy
9. local . . . stolen . . . illegal
10. primitive . . . wild

☐ EXERCISE 15, p. 167. Using adjectives with nouns. (Chart 6-8)

The emphasis here is on the placement and function of adjectives.

EXPECTED SENTENCES: **1.** Red roses are beautiful flowers. **2.** Cold rain fell from the dark clouds. **3.** The waiter poured hot coffee into my empty cup. **4.** The young girl in the blue dress was looking for a telephone. **5.** Annie sleeps on a soft bed in a quiet room. **6.** Mrs. Fox gave the hungry children some fresh fruit. **7.** After we finished our delicious dinner, Frank helped me with the dirty dishes. **8.** When Tom was getting a haircut, the inexperienced barber accidentally cut Tom's right ear with the scissors.

☐ EXERCISE 16, p. 167. Adjectives and nouns. (Chart 6-8)

With any luck, your students will create very funny passages to read aloud.

(The author remembers doing exercises like this years ago but doesn't remember the source of the idea. She would like to thank those who invented this format. It's a fun way to provide students with practice opportunities.)

CHART 6-9: USING NOUNS AS ADJECTIVES

- Nouns in this structure can be called "noun adjuncts" or simply referred to as "nouns that are used as adjectives."
- Common problems that arise with this structure are:
  (1) making the noun adjunct possessive: e.g., INCORRECT: *a flowers' garden;* and
  (2) making the noun adjunct plural: e.g., INCORRECT: *the shoes store.*
- Sometimes a noun describing another noun becomes a single compound noun: *firefighter, doorbell, earphone,* etc. Tell the students to use their dictionaries when in doubt about spelling a noun–noun combination as one word or two. (There is no hard-and-fast rule to predict the form.)

☐ EXERCISE 17, p. 168. Using nouns as adjectives. (Chart 6-9)

ANSWERS:

2. vegetable garden
3. television program
4. bean soup
5. vacation plans
6. newspaper articles
7. automobile factory
8. history lesson
9. mountain villages
10. flag poles

☐ EXERCISE 18, p. 169. Using nouns as adjectives. (Chart 6-9)

ANSWERS:

3. Airplanes
4. *(no change)*
5. *(no change)*
6. languages
7. Bicycles . . . Automobiles
8. *(no change)*

☐ EXERCISE 19, p. 169. Review: nouns. (Charts 6-1 → 6-9)

Students have to be alert to catch all the nouns that need to have a final *-s/-es* and to recognize those that do not because they are noun adjuncts. (Noun adjuncts are noted in brackets in the answers below.)

Students need time to prepare this exercise. They might enjoy putting their heads together and working in groups.

Note the pronunciation of final *-s/-es* during class discussion.

ANSWERS:

2. There are around 8,600 kind**s** of bird**s** in the world.
3. Bird**s** hatch from egg**s**. Baby [noun adjunct: birds that are babies are baby birds] bird**s** stay in their nest**s** for several week**s** or month**s**. Their parent**s** feed them until they can fly.
4. People eat chicken [noun adjunct] egg**s**. Some animal**s** eat bird [noun adjunct] egg**s**.
5. Fox**es** and snake**s** are natural enem**ies** of bird**s**. They eat bird**s** and their egg**s**.
6. Some bird**s** eat only seed**s** and plant**s**. Other bird**s** eat mainly insect**s** and earthworm**s**.
7. Weed**s** are unwanted plant**s**. They prevent farm [noun adjunct] crop**s** or garden [noun adjunct] flower**s** from growing properly. Bird**s** help farmer**s** by eating weed [noun adjunct] seed**s** and harmful insect**s**.
8. Rat**s**, rabbit**s**, and **mice** can cause huge loss**es** on farm**s** by eating stored crop**s**. Certain big bird**s** like hawk**s** help farmer**s** by hunting these animal**s**.
9. The feather**s** of certain kind**s** of bird**s** are used in pillow**s** and mattress**es**. The soft feather**s** from **geese** are often used for pillow**s** and quilt**s**. Goose [noun adjunct] feather**s** are also used in winter [noun adjunct] jacket**s**.
10. The wing [noun adjunct] feather**s** from **geese** were used as pen**s** from the sixth century to the nineteenth century, when steel [noun adjunct] pen**s** were invented.

☐ EXERCISE 20, p. 170. Review: nouns. (Charts 6-1 → 6-9)

Allow students time to do this as homework. (It might be best to have everyone write the whole exercise on paper.) Class discussion can be in groups as the students compare their analyses. Each student can read a sentence aloud and point out the changes, or write a corrected sentence on the chalkboard. Pay attention to pronunciation of final *-s/-es.*

ANSWERS: **(1)** Whale**s** . . . fish . . . fish . . . mammal**s** . . . **Mice** . . . tiger**s** **(2)** being**s** . . . example**s** . . . mammal**s** . . . Whale**s** . . . animal**s** **(3)** dog**s** . . . chimpanzee**s** . . . sea**s**, ocean**s** . . . river**s**, whale**s** **(4)** fish . . . Fish . . . egg**s** . . . offspring . . . Mammal**s** . . . birth **(5)** offspring **(6)** kind**s** . . . whale**s** . . . whale**s** . . . creature**s** **(7)** whale**s** . . . whale**s** . . . feet . . . meter**s** . . . length **(8)** ton**s** . . . kilogram**s** . . . whale**s** . . . elephant**s** **(9)** dinosaur**s** . . . heart . . . whale **(10)** size . . . car . . . vessel . . . aorta **(11)** person **(12)** being**s** . . . whale**s** . . . time**s** **(13)** people . . . whale**s** . . . enem**ies** . . . people **(14)** hunting . . . whale**s**

CHART 6-10: PERSONAL PRONOUNS: SUBJECTS AND OBJECTS

• This chart contains a lot of information, but it is assumed students are already familiar with personal pronouns (subject vs. object, singular vs. plural). You may wish to proceed directly to Exercise 21, using it as a preview to the chart.

• In examples (e) and (f), the use of *I* instead of *me* after *and* as an object pronoun seems to have taken the English-speaking world by storm. One can hear a lot of sentences like *Ann met Eric and I at the museum,* even from educated speakers. It's really quite an interesting linguistic phenomenon. You might mention to your students that they might hear native speakers misusing subject pronouns in this way as it is a common occurrence, but it is not yet accepted in formal writing. Perhaps someday it will be?

• Likewise, the use of *everyone . . . their* has become common in recent years. It now occurs in spoken language more often than *everyone . . . his/her.* This change may be an attempt to supplant the cumbersome *his/her* (which was adopted in the 1980s as more inclusive than the sexist *his)*.

☐ EXERCISE 21, p. 172. Personal pronouns: subjects and objects. (Chart 6-10)

ANSWERS:

2. me
3. I
4. I
5. it
6. them
7. me . . . us . . . We
8. them . . . They are
9. She . . . me
10. me . . . He . . . I

☐ EXERCISE 22, p. 172. Personal pronouns. (Chart 6-10)

This gives practice in identifying an antecedent and supplying the correct pronoun. To do so, the students must consider function, meaning, and form (subject vs. object, singular vs. plural, and gender).

During class discussion, ask students why they chose their answers.

ANSWERS:

3. They . . . her
4. it . . . it . . . him . . . he
5. it
6. they . . . them . . . they
7. them . . . they
8. it
9. it . . . It
10. them . . . They . . . They . . . them

CHART 6-11: POSSESSIVE NOUNS

- Proper placement of apostrophes in possessive nouns can be confusing, for native speakers as well as for second language learners. (Obviously, this is a problem only in the written language, not in speech.)
- Use ample examples to explain this chart, writing each on the chalkboard. For example, demonstrate *boys'* vs. *men's* and *girls'* vs. *women's.* Ask three male students to place their pens on one desk and three female students to place theirs on another. Then use the pens to demonstrate the meaning and placement of the apostrophe: *This is a man's pen. These are the men's pens. These are the boy's pens.* Etc.
- You may wish to point out that the apostrophe has more than one meaning and use. In this chart, it expresses possession (and its placement indicates number). In contractions, it indicates the omission of letters (e.g., *isn't* = *is not,* with the "o" omitted).
- In (h): *Tom's* can also be the contraction for *Tom has* in the present perfect form: ***Tom's** been here for two weeks.*

☐ EXERCISE 23, p. 174. Possessive nouns. (Chart 6-11)

This exercise and Practice 21 in the *Workbook* survey the basic uses of the apostrophe with the possessive forms of regular nouns, irregular nouns, and nouns that end in *-y/-ies.*

ANSWERS:

3. daughter**'s**
4. daughters**'**
5. man**'s**
6. woman**'s**
7. men**'s**
8. women**'s**
9. people**'s**
10. person**'s**
11. earth**'s**
12. elephant**'s**
13. teachers**'**
14. teacher**'s**
15. enemy**'s**
16. enemies**'**
17. Chris**'s** OR Chris**'**

☐ EXERCISE 24, p. 174. Possessive nouns. (Chart 6-11)

Point out that there is no difference in pronunciation between *king's* and *kings', babies'* and *baby's,* etc. They are different only in written form, not in spoken form.

ANSWERS:

3. Babies**'**
4. baby**'s**
5. caller**'s**
6. receptionist**'s** . . . callers**'**
7. yesterday**'s** . . . today**'s**
8. The pilots**'**
9. earth**'s**
10. Mosquitoes**'**
11. mosquito**'s**
12. animals**'**
13. animal**'s**

☐ EXERCISE 25, p. 175. Review of nouns + -S/-ES. (Charts 6-1 → 6-11)

This exercise reviews final *-s* vs. *-es,* irregular noun plurals, and possessive nouns.

ANSWERS: 3. lea**ves** 4. mother**'s** 5. Potat**oes** 6. birds . . . tee**th** 7. Tom**'s** 8. thie**ves** . . . Mr. Lee**'s** 9. Mountains . . . valleys 10. child**'s** 11. Children**'s** toys 12. actors**'** names 13. Teachers . . . people**'s** . . . ideas 14. monkeys . . . thumbs . . . hands . . . f**ee**t . . . thumbs . . . hands

CHART 6-12: POSSESSIVE PRONOUNS AND ADJECTIVES

- The term "possessive adjective" can be confusing. *My, your, our,* etc., are pronouns in that they are noun substitutes, but they function as adjectives, i.e., they modify nouns. In this way, they are different from *mine, yours, ours,* etc., which the text labels "possessive pronouns."
- The misuse of *it's* vs. *its* is common among native speakers as well as second language learners. If the author's own experience is representative, even educated native speakers often have to pause and figure out whether to use the apostrophe when they write *it* + *-s.* Students would welcome the information that even their teacher has to be careful when using *its* and *it's.*
- *It's* can also be a contraction for *it has* in the present perfect form: *It's been a long time since I last talked to him.*

☐ EXERCISE 26, p. 177. Possessive pronouns and adjectives. (Chart 6-12)

ANSWERS: **2.** his **3.** their **4.** my . . . yours . . . mine . . . Yours . . . your **5.** its . . . its **6.** It's **7.** Hers **8.** her **9.** your . . . It is . . . you **10.** a. They b. Their c. Our . . . theirs d. They're . . . there . . . they're . . . their **11.** mine **12.** yours

CHART 6-13: REFLEXIVE PRONOUNS

- Explain the form and meaning by using a mirror (a small pocket mirror will do). Incorporate Exercise 27 into the presentation of this chart. Perhaps mention that *reflexive* means "to bounce back or reflect," as light or images are reflected by a mirror.
- Briefly answer questions about the vocabulary listed at the bottom of the chart. Some notes:
  — *feel sorry for yourself* = engage in self-pity
  — *help yourself* = serve yourself (as in a cafeteria)
  — *pinch yourself* = (jokingly and figuratively) *I couldn't believe my good fortune. I had to pinch myself to make sure it was real.*
  — *work for yourself* = be self-employed
- Remind students that talking to themselves is a good way to practice English.

☐ EXERCISE 27, p. 178. Reflexive pronouns. (Chart 6-13)

Use the idea of this exercise while talking about Chart 6-13. Vary the leading questions you ask so that you cover all of the pronouns, singular and plural: *myself, ourselves,* etc.

☐ EXERCISE 28, p. 179. Reflexive pronouns. (Chart 6-13)

ANSWERS:
2. himself
3. yourself (*also possible:* yourselves) . . . themselves
4. ourselves
5. herself
6. himself
7. yourselves
8. yourself
9. myself
10. itself
11. themselves
12. myself

☐ EXERCISE 29, p. 179. Reflexive pronouns. (Chart 6-13)

This practice illustrates typical contexts of some of the common expressions listed in Chart 6-13. Vocabulary development is part of the intention of the exercise.

ANSWERS:

2. will cut yourself
3. introduced myself
4. was talking to himself
5. work for ourselves
6. taught themselves
7. killed himself
8. wished myself
9. is taking care of herself
10. believe in ourselves
11. felt sorry for myself
12. help themselves

☐ EXERCISE 30, p. 181. Reflexive pronouns. (Chart 6-13)

Orally, students can invent various sentences about themselves and their classmates. Encourage imaginative sentences. The exercise could also be written. The purpose is to further familiarize the students with common expressions in which reflexive pronouns are used.

CHART 6-14: SINGULAR FORMS OF *OTHER: ANOTHER* vs. *THE OTHER*

• The sole focus of this chart is to distinguish between *another* and *the other.* Additional forms of *other* are discussed in the next chart.

• Many learners erroneously put *the* in front of *another.* Point out that *another* is simply two words, *an* (meaning *one)* and *other,* written together. *An* is an article. *The* is an article. You use only one article in front of a noun, never two articles together. You can't say *This is the an apple.* Similarly, you can't put two articles together with *the* and ***an**other.*

☐ EXERCISE 31, p. 182. Singular forms of OTHER. (Chart 6-14)

ANSWERS: **2.** a. Another b. The other **3.** a. Another b. Another c. Another d. another **4.** The other **5.** Another . . . Another . . . Another . . . The other **6.** another **7.** the other **8.** the other [*Answer:* in the Pacific Ocean (Hawaii)] **9.** Another [*Others are* Switzerland, Germany, Luxembourg, and Belgium.]

CHART 6-15: PLURAL FORMS OF *OTHER: OTHER(S)* vs. *THE OTHER(S)*

• The key here is to distinguish between the use of *other(s)* as a pronoun and *other* as an adjective. Remind students that adjectives are not inflected: they have no added endings such as *-s*/*-es.*

☐ EXERCISE 32, p. 184. Forms of OTHER. (Charts 6-14 and 6-15)

This exercise suggests ways for you to use the classroom context to communicate the meaning and use of forms of *other,* both singular and plural.

EXPANSION: Another technique is to use Cuisinaire rods—sticks of wood or plastic of varied colors and lengths. Give each group of students some rods and have them describe the rods to each other using *others, another, the other,* and *the others.* A variation of this is to give identical sets of rods to two groups. One group builds something that the other group can't see. Then the builders must describe it accurately to the second group, who must try to copy the design with their rods. (This also provides practice in the use of prepositions of place.)

EXPECTED RESPONSES: **2.** This is one pen. This one is **another**. This one is **the other**. OR This is one pen. These are **the others**. **3.** This is one hand. This is **the other**. **4.** A hand has a total of five fingers. One is the thumb. **Another** is the index finger. **Another** is the middle finger. The ring finger is **another**. And **the other** finger, the last of the five, is the little finger. **5.** One of the names on the board is Anna. **The other** name is Roberto. **6.** One of the names on the board is Anna. **The others** are W, X, Y, and Z. OR **Others** are W and X. OR **Another** is W.

☐ EXERCISE 33, p. 184. Plural forms of OTHER. (Chart 6-15)

ANSWERS:

2. other
3. The others
4. The other
5. The other
6. The others
7. The others
8. The other
9. Other . . . others
10. The other
11. The others
12. a. Other
b. Others
c. Others
d. Other
13. The other . . . The others
14. Others
15. other . . . others . . . the other . . . other

CHART 6-16: SUMMARY OF FORMS OF *OTHER*

• The main point of this chart is to show when *other* has a final *-s* (i.e., only when it is a plural pronoun). A common problem is that learners add final *-s* to *other* when it is used as an adjective: e.g., INCORRECT: *I bought some others books.*

• This unit on *other* does not deal with all of its uses. See *Understanding and Using English Grammar, Third Edition,* Chart 8-6, for more information.

☐ EXERCISE 34, p. 186. Forms of OTHER. (Charts 6-12 → 6-16)

ANSWERS:

2. the other
3. Others
4. Other
5. Others . . . other . . . other
6. The other
7. another . . . others
8. another
9. The other
10. The others
11. Other

☐ EXERCISE 35, p. 187. Forms of OTHER. (Charts 6-12 → 6-16)

This exercise can be oral or written.

SAMPLE RESPONSES: **1.** blue . . . the other is red. **2.** Others ride the bus. **3.** one glass of water . . . he drank another one. **4.** several . . . Tagalog . . . the others are German and English. **5.** like to watch TV . . . others don't. **6.** two sisters . . . 30 . . . the other is 24. **7.** Ms. Gray. The other is Mr. Halprin. **8.** Juan and Pedro . . . Others are Maria and Luis. **9.** Some . . . Japan. Other . . . China, Indonesia, Turkey, and Colombia. **10.** soccer . . . Another . . . baseball. Others are tennis and golf.

☐ EXERCISE 36, p. 187. Error analysis: summary review of nouns and pronouns. (Chapter 6)

As in other error-analysis exercises in the text, the sentences in this exercise are adapted from actual student writing and represent common problems.

ANSWERS: **2.** I had some black **bean** soup for lunch. **It was** very good. **3.** The highways in my country are **excellent**. **4.** . . . **They're teachers**. **5.** Today many **women** are **miners**, **pilots**, and **doctors**. **6.** My wife likes all **kinds** of **flowers**. **7.** We often read **stories in** class and try to understand all the new **words**. I can't remember all of **them**. **8.** There are two **pools** at the park. One is for **children**. The **other** is for adults only. **9.** My brother has an **apple tree** orchard. **10.** The windows in our classroom **are** dirty. **11.** . . . I heard some **other important** news this morning. **12.** The population of my hometown in 1975 **was** about 50,000. Today **it is** more than 150,000. **13.** . . . **It's** in a bad neighborhood. **There is** trash on both **sides** of the street. I'm going to move to **another** neighborhood. **14. All** people **need** an education / Every **person needs** . . . . people can improve **their lives**. **15. When** Alice was a child, **she** lived in . . . Today **it** is a very big city with many **buildings** and **large** highways.

Chapter 7: MODAL AUXILIARIES

ORDER OF CHAPTER	CHARTS	EXERCISES	WORKBOOK
Preview		Ex. 1	Pr. 1
The form of modal auxiliaries	7-1	Ex. 2 → 3	Pr. 2
Can and *could*	7-2	Ex. 4 → 6	Pr. 3
May and *might; may* and *can*	7-3	Ex. 7 → 8	Pr. 4 → 6
Using *could* to express possibility	7-4	Ex. 9 → 12	Pr. 7
Polite questions	7-5 → 7-6	Ex. 13 → 16	Pr. 8 → 9
Should, ought to, had better	7-7 → 7-8	Ex. 17 → 23	Pr. 10 → 12
Have to, have got to, must	7-9 → 7-11	Ex. 24 → 30	Pr. 13 → 20
Imperative sentences	7-12	Ex. 31 → 34	Pr. 21 → 22
Let's and *why don't*	7-13	Ex. 35 → 39	Pr. 23
Prefer, like . . . better, would rather	7-14	Ex. 40 → 42	Pr. 24 → 25
Cumulative review		Ex. 43 → 44	Pr. 26 → 28

General Notes on Chapter 7

• Familiarity with the meanings of modal auxiliaries is important because these words communicate small but important differences in the user's attitude and feelings. Misuse of modal auxiliaries can result in confusion and even anger among people who are trying to communicate in either speech or writing. The chapter is organized on the basis of lexical meanings. Most exercises are interactive, emphasizing conversational forms.

• TERMINOLOGY: To keep terminology simplified for student purposes, the text uses the term "modal auxiliary" for both single-word (e.g., *must)* and periphrastic (e.g., *have to)* modals. The term "helping verb" is mentioned in the first chart as synonymous with "auxiliary."

☐ EXERCISE 1, p. 189. Preview: modal auxiliaries. (Chapter 7)

Paraphrase the sentences with modals to clarify their meaning. For example:

1. *Should I tell the boss about the accounting error?* = What do you think? Is it a good idea for me to tell the boss?
2. *You have to tell her.* = You have no choice. You must tell her. It is necessary for you to tell her.
3. *That error could get the company in big trouble.* = It's possible that the company could get in big trouble. Etc.

ANSWERS:

3. Ø **7.** Ø **10.** to
4. to **8.** Ø **11.** Ø
5. Ø **9.** Ø **12.** Ø
6. Ø

CHART 7-1: THE FORM OF MODAL AUXILIARIES

• This chart is simply an introduction to terminology and form. Subsequent charts in this chapter explain the expressions in detail.

• Discuss the meanings of the example sentences. Modals have a variety of meanings, as any glance at their definitions in a dictionary tells us. Mention that a modal can have different meanings. For example, in the sentence *I could meet you for coffee after class, could* means future possibility, whereas in example (b) in the chart, *could* expresses past ability. In example (c), *It may rain, may* expresses possibility, but in the sentence *You may pay by credit card but not by personal check, may* expresses permission.

• Point out for (j) and (k) that *study* is the main verb. The word *have* in *have to* and *have got to* is inflected for number and tense (***has*** *to*, ***had*** *to*, etc.). The main verb is never inflected after a modal. This is especially confusing for learners when the main verb is *have*. Examples: *He* ***ought to have*** *more patience. She* ***has to have*** *a new dress for graduation. Mr. Smith* ***had to have*** *his car repaired yesterday.*

☐ EXERCISE 2, p. 190. The form of modal auxiliaries. (Chart 7-1)

This is an exercise on form, but discuss meaning as you go along. Paraphrase the sentences for the students as a way of introducing them to the content of this chapter.

ANSWERS:

3. Ø **6.** to **9.** Ø
4. Ø **7.** Ø **10.** to
5. Ø **8.** to **11.** Ø

☐ EXERCISE 3, p. 191. Error analysis: the form of modal auxiliaries. (Chart 7-1)

ANSWERS: **2.** I must **study** for **3.** We couldn't **go** to **4.** I ~~am~~ have to improve **5.** You shouldn't ~~to~~ spend **6.** My mother can't **speak** . . . she can **speak** several other languages.

CHART 7-2: EXPRESSING ABILITY: *CAN* AND *COULD*

- *Can* is presented as expressing ability, but it is richer than that. Usually it expresses a subtle combination of ability and possibility. In this text, however, the term "possibility" is reserved for *may/might/could* (see Charts 7-3 and 7-4).
- It is not easy to define modals. The text seeks principally to give the students a general notion of their meaning and then provide, through the exercises, numerous situations in which they are used so that the students may become familiar with the range of meanings and nuances they can express.
- Mention that the "l" in *could, would,* and *should* is not pronounced.

☐ EXERCISE 4, p. 191. Expressing ability: CAN and CAN'T. (Chart 7-2)

Model the pronunciation of *can* and *can't*. *Can* is reduced to /kn/, spoken with a low tone and no stress. *Can't* is pronounced with a full vowel but not a strong final "t": /kæn/. However, in short answers they both receive full pronunciation and stress: *Yes, I can. No, I can't.*

Try to give the students a feel for the idea that *can* expresses a combination of ability and possibility.

ANSWERS:

2. can't . . . can
3. can . . . can't
4. can . . . can't
5. can . . . can't
6. can't . . . can

☐ EXERCISE 5, p. 192. Expressing ability: CAN and CAN'T. (Chart 7-2)

Pair up the students and let them talk to each other. One of the purposes of this practice is to provide relaxed time for directed conversation. The end result should be seven written sentences from each student containing the target structure. Of course, you don't need to follow the directions in the book. You can simply lead a general discussion with your class based on the given items.

NOTE *on item 6:* You might want to bring a deck of cards to class in case any of your students can perform card tricks. You might want to initiate a cross-cultural discussion of card-playing and see if there is any interest among your class.

NOTE *on item 8:* Students should take a piece of paper and fold it in half as many times as they can. In the author's experience, six is the maximum number with regular paper, while seven folds are possible with very thin tissue paper.

NOTE *on item 9:* As a follow-up activity, each student could try to draw a picture of another student, then the rest of the class could try to identify the subject of the portrait. Friendly conclusions may be drawn about who can and can't draw well.

☐ EXERCISE 6, p. 192. Expressing past ability: COULD and COULDN'T. (Chart 7-2)

SAMPLE RESPONSES: **1.** couldn't walk **2.** could play with my friends all day long in the summer **3.** could ride a bike **4.** could run a marathon **5.** In the past, I couldn't speak English very well

CHART 7-3: EXPRESSING POSSIBILITY: *MAY* AND *MIGHT* EXPRESSING PERMISSION: *MAY* AND *CAN*

• Review Chapter 3 by comparing *may/might* to *will: It will rain tomorrow* = the speaker is as close as possible to being 100% certain. *It may/might rain tomorrow* = the speaker gives it a 50% chance.

• The difference between the adverb *maybe* and the verb *may be* should be clarified for the class through several additional examples. Emphasize that the adverb *maybe* usually comes at the beginning of a sentence, while the verb *may be* comes in the main verb position following a subject.

• Make it clear that **two** meanings of *may* are being presented in this chart: possibility and permission. Listeners can ascertain the meaning from the speaking context.

• *Can* is regularly and correctly used to ask for and give permission, and it has been used that way for centuries. Using *may* for permission, however, communicates a certain tone of propriety and formality that may be absent from *can.*

• The negative contractions for *may* and *might* are *mayn't* and *mightn't.* They are rarely used.

☐ EXERCISE 7, p. 193. Expressing possibility: MAY, MIGHT, and MAYBE. (Chart 7-3)

Include *will* and *be going to* in the discussion to distinguish between degrees of certainty. For example, compare *I will/am going to go downtown* to *I may/might go downtown.*

You could ask students to close their books if you lead the discussion. Group work is also a possibility.

☐ EXERCISE 8, p. 194. Ability, possibility, and permission: CAN, MAY, and MIGHT. (Charts 7-2 and 7-3)

ANSWERS: **4.** may/might *(possibility)* **5.** can't *(ability)* **6.** may/can *(permission)* **7.** can't *(ability)* . . . Can *(ability)* . . . may/might *(possibility)* **8.** may not (cannot) *(permission)* . . . may (can) *(permission)* [In a formal situation such as this, native speakers would probably prefer *may* to *can.*] **9.** may/might *(possibility)*

CHART 7-4: USING *COULD* TO EXPRESS POSSIBILITY

• *Could* is a complex modal with several meanings and many nuances. Questions that students may ask about *could* are not as easy to answer as the charts may make it seem. Sometimes *could* is interchangeable with *may/might* for possibility, and sometimes it's not. The text seeks to minimize confusion by presenting *could* separately from *may/might.*

• When *could* is used in the negative to express possibility, it takes on the meaning of "99% impossible." For example: *That could be true.* = Maybe it is true and maybe it isn't. *That couldn't be true!* = I think it is impossible for that to be true. (COMPARE: The speaker would say *That isn't true* to express 100% certainty about impossibility.)

The use of *couldn't* to express impossibility is presented not in this text but in *Understanding and Using English Grammar, Third Edition,* Chart 10-2.

☐ EXERCISE 9, p. 195. Meanings of COULD. (Charts 7-2 and 7-4)

The purpose of this exercise is to distinguish between two meanings of *could* by relying on context. It should be noted that a context in which grammar is presented does not need to be long and involved. The dictum to teach "grammar in context" does not necessitate connected discourse in long paragraphs or dialogues. Indeed, clear but brief contexts often enhance students' ability to understand and learn aspects of English by allowing them to focus on particular forms and meanings without distraction. Concentrating on smaller contexts is an efficient language-learning device that leads to increased understanding and usage ability in larger contexts.

ANSWERS: **3.** could be = may/might be *(present time)* **4.** could swim = were able to swim *(past time)* **5.** could be = may/might be *(present time)* **6.** could arrive = may/might arrive *(future time)* **7.** could jump = was able to jump *(past time)*

☐ EXERCISE 10, p. 196. Expressing possibility: COULD, MAY, and MIGHT. (Charts 7-3 and 7-4)

Adapt the entries to your style of speaking and make a game out of this exercise. You could set this up as a team game with points for the greatest number of logical guesses and a bonus for the correct answer. Correct grammar should be required. Give extra clues as necessary so students can, without too much frustration, figure out what you're thinking about. The goal is for students to be able to use *could* frequently and naturally to express possibilities.

☐ EXERCISE 11, p. 196. Expressing possibility: COULD. (Chart 7-4)

Only the person giving the cues has an open book. Responders may need to think a bit to come up with viable possibilities for the given situations.

POSSIBLE RESPONSES:

1. She could put her grammar book over her head. She could put her sweater over her head. She could hold a newspaper above her head. She could ask to walk with someone who has an umbrella. She could wait until it stops raining.
2. They could cancel their tennis date. They could look for an indoor court. They could do something else together. They could shovel the snow off the court.
3. He could return to the shop where he bought it and ask for help. He could get on the Internet and look for directions in English. He could take a photography class. He could ask his Japanese friend to translate for him. He could figure out how it works by himself.
4. He could go to a hotel and explain his problem. He could beg for money. He could sleep in the train station and figure out what to do the next day. He could ask a policeman for help. He could try to earn some money. He could sell or pawn his wristwatch.

☐ EXERCISE 12, p. 197. COULD, MAY, MIGHT and WILL PROBABLY. (Charts 3-4 and 7-2 → 7-4)

This exercise can be written or oral.

SAMPLE RESPONSES:

1. Tonight I could go to the theater. Or I might go across town to visit my friends. Of course, I may go to a dance with my cousin. But I'll probably stay home and watch TV because I'm tired.
2. Next year, I might go home and get a job. But I could go to California and surf. I may go to Singapore and live with my cousin. But I'll probably stay here and finish my studies.

3. My friend Talal may visit me this weekend, but I'm not sure. He might visit his brother. He could also simply decide to stay home. But he'll probably come to visit me.
4. One hundred years from now, people may have mini-helicopters instead of cars. They may fly instead of drive to work. Cars could be obsolete in a hundred years. But cars will probably still be more common than personal helicopters.

CHART 7-5: POLITE QUESTIONS: *MAY I, COULD I, CAN I*

• Modal auxiliaries allow the speaker to show politeness. Discuss the difference between *Give me your pen* vs. *May I please borrow your pen? Give me your pen* may sound aggressive and could imply that the speaker feels s/he is superior to or has authority over the listener. The use of modals allows the speaker to show respect for the listener.

• Compare the meanings of *could* that the text presents.

*I **could** run fast when I was younger.* = past ability. (Chart 7-2)
***Could** I help you?* = polite question. (Charts 7-5 and 7-6)
*It **could** start raining any minute.* = possibility. (Chart 7-4)

• Contrary to what some of us were taught as children, the use of *can* to request permission is common and acceptable—as any dictionary reveals. The use of *can* instead of *may* does, however, signal a subtle difference in the relationship between the speaker and the listener: *can* may signal familiarity and equality; *may* keeps a polite distance. *Can* is less formal than *may.*

☐ EXERCISE 13, p. 197. Polite questions: MAY I, COULD I, and CAN I. (Chart 7-5)

You might want to take the role of Speaker A, the person who answers the phone. Then, after discussing the exercise in class, set up additional telephone role-plays. For example: Assign Speaker A to place a call to Speaker B but talk to Speaker C (Speaker B's roommate). Tell Speaker A to call a school office for certain information and have Speaker B play the role of the school's secretary, who must look up the information and call back later. Etc.

ANSWERS:

1. May/Could I speak *(possibly too informal:* Can I talk)
2. May/Could I speak *(too informal:* Can I talk)
3. Can I talk *(also possible:* May/Could I talk/speak)
4. May/Could/Can I help
5. May/Could/Can I speak . . . May/Could I take
6. May/Could/Can I speak . . . May/Could I leave
7. May/Could/Can I speak

☐ EXERCISE 14, p. 199. Polite questions: MAY I, COULD I, and CAN I. (Chart 7-5)

This exercise can be done fairly quickly with the teacher giving the cues.

CHART 7-6: POLITE QUESTIONS: *WOULD YOU, COULD YOU, WILL YOU, CAN YOU*

- The use of *may* is an occasional problem with this pattern, as noted in the chart.
- If you want to assign "degrees of politeness," *would* and *could* could be called the politest. *Will* is possibly a little less polite; *would* is softer. *Can* loses a slight degree of politeness by signaling familiarity rather than respectful distance. For the students' purposes, however, any of these modals will allow them to show appropriate politeness when making a request as compared to an imperative such as *Open the door.*
- Even polite modals can be made threatening or angry by the speaker's tone of voice.

☐ EXERCISE 15, p. 200. Polite questions: WOULD/COULD/WILL/CAN YOU. (Chart 7-6)

POSSIBLE POLITE QUESTIONS: **2.** Would/Could/Will/Can you answer the phone for me? **3.** Would/Could/Will/Can you turn it down? **4.** Would/Could/Will/Can you please turn the volume up? **5.** Would/Could/Will/Can you please pick some up? **6.** Would/Could/Will/Can you please say that again [*Walabaaxitinpundoozit* is meant to represent an uncomprehended utterance.] **7.** Would/Could/Will/Can you please tell me where the nearest post office is?

☐ EXERCISE 16, p. 201. Summary: polite questions. (Charts 7-5 and 7-6)

Pairs can create short dialogues for each of the items. These can be very short role-plays. If time permits, students can use the situations and characters to create "dramas." Students can write a script if they wish.

If students don't come up with creative ideas on their own, expand the situations by giving fuller directions. For example, in item one tell Speaker A that s/he is an impatient clerk and Speaker B that s/he is a customer who can't make up his/her mind about what she wants. In item 2, tell "Mr. Jenkins" that he is an unreasonable and unsympathetic boss talking to a persistent and ill employee.

CHART 7-7: EXPRESSING ADVICE: *SHOULD* AND *OUGHT TO*

- When advice is given with these modal expressions, they indicate that results usually implied rather than stated will occur if a certain course of action is taken. These results may be good or bad.
- *Ought to* is often pronounced /ədə/ or /atə/.
- *Should* can also be used to express expectations. (For example: *Mary left at ten. She should arrive by ten-thirty.)* This usage is not introduced in this text. See *Understanding and Using English Grammar, Third Edition,* Chart 10-10.

☐ EXERCISE 17, p. 202. Expressing advice: SHOULD and OUGHT TO. (Chart 7-7)

POSSIBLE RESPONSES: **1.** Maybe you should / ought to eat a sandwich. **2.** You should / ought to put your coat on. **3.** You should / ought to / had better see a dentist. **4.** You should / ought to drink a glass of water. / You should / ought to hold your breath. **5.** You should / ought to go back to the restaurant and ask about them. **6.** Maybe you should / ought to open the windows. **7.** You should / ought to take an aspirin. **8.** You should / ought to call the police. **9.** You should / ought to take them back to the store. **10.** You should / ought to use a dictionary when you write.

CHART 7-8: EXPRESSING ADVICE: *HAD BETTER*

• *Had better* is a little stronger than *should* and *ought to.* In the negative, *had better not* usually communicates a threat of bad results, and the affirmative *had better* may also imply a warning that is not conveyed by *should* and *ought to.*

Had better is also commonly used simply to give friendly advice among peers. *Had better* is not used to give advice to a superior, but *should* and *ought to* can maintain a polite enough distance to allow for such. For example, one might say to one's boss, "I think you should consider Mr. Loo for that project." One would not say to one's boss, "I think you'd better consider Mr. Loo for that project."

☐ EXERCISE 18, p. 203. Expressing advice: HAD BETTER. (Chart 7-8)

POSSIBLE BAD CONSEQUENCES: **2.** If you don't change clothes, you'll make a bad impression. **3.** If I don't call the credit card company, I'll be held responsible for charges someone else makes on my card. **4.** If you don't put ice on it, it will swell. **5.** Someone might steal it if you don't lock it.

☐ EXERCISE 19, p. 203. Expressing advice: HAD BETTER. (Chart 7-8)

This exercise can be teacher-led or assigned as pair work.

POSSIBLE RESPONSES: **1.** You'd better pay it. If you don't, the electric company will shut off your electricity. **2.** You'd better leave here by seven. If you don't, you won't get to the airport in time. **3.** You'd better make reservations. If you don't, you might not be able to get a table. **4.** S/He'd better not go to a movie. If s/he does, s/he may not be ready for his/her test. **5.** You'd better go home and go to bed. If you don't, you'll get worse. **6.** S/He'd better be on time in the future. If s/he isn't, s/he will lose her/his job.

☐ EXERCISE 20, p. 204. Expressing advice: SHOULD, OUGHT TO, and HAD BETTER. (Charts 7-7 and 7-8)

ANSWERS: **2.** Anna shouldn't **wear** shorts **3.** I should ~~to~~ go to the post office today. **4.** I ought **to pay** my bills today. **5.** You'd ~~had~~ better ~~to~~ call **6.** You ~~don't~~ should**n't** stay up **7.** You'd ~~to~~ better not **leave** your key **8.** . . . He ought **to find** a new apartment.

☐ EXERCISES 21 and 22, pp. 204–205. Giving advice. (Charts 7-7 and 7-8)

In these two exercises, the students do all the talking, and the teacher is silent (unless giving directions or answering a question).

☐ EXERCISE 23, p. 206. Giving advice. (Charts 7-7 and 7-8)

It is hoped that in this unstructured group work, the students will engage in meaningful conversations and share actual problems they are having. But, if not, they will still get some good conversation practice.

CHART 7-9: EXPRESSING NECESSITY: *HAVE TO, HAVE GOT TO, MUST*

- *Must* generally carries a forceful meaning, often too forceful to use in everyday conversation about everyday affairs, in which case *have to* and *have got to* are usually used to convey the notion of necessity. The text emphasizes the use of *have to* and *have got to* to express necessity.
- Model the usual pronunciation of *have to* and *have got to* and let the students experiment producing it, but don't insist that they use the contracted forms. Contracted speech develops as the students become aware of it and gain experience with English.

☐ EXERCISE 24, p. 206. HAVE TO, HAVE GOT TO, MUST, and SHOULD. (Charts 7-7 → 7-9)

This exercise is meant to be a teaching springboard for questions, practice, and discussion. Elicit several responses for each item. Expand the items with leading questions of your own. Model spoken forms. Distinguish between *should* (advisability) and *must / have to / have got to* (necessity).

☐ EXERCISE 25, p. 207. Summary: expressing advice and necessity. (Charts 7-7 → 7-9)

This exercise is intended for group discussion but works equally well as a writing assignment. If done as group work, the group could prepare written advice together. You might want to ask them to underline the modals they use.

You might want to discuss how impolite it is to call someone stupid.

CHART 7-10: EXPRESSING LACK OF NECESSITY: *DO NOT HAVE TO* EXPRESSING PROHIBITION: *MUST NOT*

- Use gestures and tone of voice to reinforce the distinction between these two forms. For *do not have to,* shrug your shoulders and look nonchalant. For *must not,* use facial expressions and gestures that show sternness. For example, English speakers often shake their head from side to side or shake their index finger up and down (mostly to small children) to gesture *must not.*

☐ EXERCISE 26, p. 208. Lack of necessity (DO NOT HAVE TO) and prohibition (MUST NOT). (Chart 7-10)

ANSWERS:

3. doesn't have to	**8.** don't have to
4. must not	**9.** don't have to
5. doesn't have to	**10.** must not
6. must not	**11.** don't have to
7. must not	**12.** must not . . . don't have to . . . must not

☐ EXERCISE 27, p. 209. Summary: expressing advice, possibility, and necessity. (Charts 7-4 and 7-7 → 7-10)

SAMPLE RESPONSES:

1. Steve had better decide what his priorities are. He could take an art history course now, but he has got to take the required chemistry course sometime. He ought to see if he can find a better chemistry teacher. He should consider changing his major. He might prefer a liberal arts major.

2. Matt and Amy should wait until they're older to get married. They should get to know each other better. Matt ought to have a job before they marry. They could be making a big mistake getting married now. They had better get an education so that they can find good jobs. They might be happy now, but it won't last if they have a lot of money problems.

3. Georgia shouldn't keep the money. She'd better go back into the store and return the money. She ought to return the money so she can teach her son about honesty. As a parent, she's got to be a good role model. She must not be an honest person/must be in a bad financial situation.

4. Parents should/shouldn't let their children choose their own friends. Frog and Rabbit should continue to be friends/should respect their parents' wishes and end their friendship. Frog and Rabbit should try to talk with their parents about their friendship. They could suggest that the two families meet to get to know one another. Parents shouldn't teach their children to be prejudiced. People shouldn't judge other people by their appearance.

CHART 7-11: MAKING LOGICAL CONCLUSIONS: *MUST*

- Compare: *She must be sleepy* = the speaker is 95%–99% sure.
  She is sleepy = the speaker is 100% sure.
- Point out that this chart has three different meanings of *must:* logical conclusion, necessity, and prohibition.

☐ EXERCISE 28, p. 211. Making logical conclusions: MUST and MUST NOT. (Chart 7-11)

POSSIBLE CONCLUSIONS: **1.** She must be happy. **2.** She must have a cold. **3.** He must be married. **4.** He must be cold. **5.** He must have mice in his apartment. **6.** He must be hot. **7.** She must like to watch movies. **8.** She must be smart. / She must study a lot. **9.** He must be strong.

☐ EXERCISE 29, p. 211. Making logical conclusions: MUST and MUST NOT. (Chart 7-11)

All the completions include *must.* The students need to decide whether the completions should be negative or affirmative.

ANSWERS: **3.** must **4.** must not **5.** must **6.** must not **7.** must **8.** must not **9.** must [You might want to point out the progressive modal *(must be doing)* and note that, like the present progressive, it expresses the idea of an activity in progress.]

☐ EXERCISE 30, p. 212. Making logical conclusions: MUST and MUST NOT. (Chart 7-11)

EXPECTED ANSWERS: **2.** She must love books. She must like books better than people. She must not like to talk to people. **3.** She must be busy all the time. She must not have a lot of spare time. **4.** He must be a computer addict. He must not have a happy home life. **5.** She must not want to go to a movie. She must be tired. **6.** She must be upset. She must not want to talk to her parents right now. She must want to be alone.

CHART 7-12: GIVING INSTRUCTIONS: IMPERATIVE SENTENCES

- Discuss the form of imperative sentences. Explain the concept of the "understood *you*" as the subject of an imperative verb, with *you* being the listener(s). For example, in (a): *Open the door!* = *You* (i.e., the soldier the speaker is addressing), *open the door!*
- The addition of *please* and a pleasant tone of voice can make an imperative sentence quite polite, as in *Please open the door.* When making a polite request, however, the students can be assured they are using a high level of politeness if they use *would* or *could* (e.g., *Could you please open the door?*). *Please open the door* in the wrong tone of voice can seem unfriendly or haughty.
- Demonstrate varying tones of voice that can be used with imperative sentences, from barking out an order to requesting politely.

☐ EXERCISE 31, p. 213. Imperative sentences. (Chart 7-12)

It is assumed that students are familiar with imperative sentences. This exercise allows them to explore what one person might say to another using an imperative sentence and how the second person might respond.

During class discussion, you might elicit several possible completions for each item.

POSSIBLE COMPLETIONS: **2.** Take this medicine for a week and call me if you don't get better. **3.** Don't forget to write a thank-you note to your aunt. [*Don't worry* = an imperative] **4.** Please pick up your toys and put them away on the shelf. **5.** Button your shirt. **6.** Help your mother with the dishes. **7.** Don't ask Tom to come with us. **8.** Hand me that plate. [*would you?* = a polite tag] **9.** Don't use the car today. **10.** Take this report to the accounting office. **11.** Don't wear your boots in the house.

☐ EXERCISE 32, p. 214. Imperative sentences. (Chart 7-12)

This number puzzle is intended principally for fun and variety.

☐ **EXERCISE 33, p. 214. Writing activity. (Chart 7-12)**

The focus is on imperative sentences in written advice. Using item 1, you might write a practice list of advice on the board, copying down what the students tell you to write.

This exercise could be used for class discussion with no writing. Item 7 is not appropriate for some cultural groups, but young people from other cultures have fun with the topic. A brief cross-cultural discussion of dating and courtship might develop, depending upon the cultural groups in your class.

☐ **EXERCISE 34, p. 215. Writing activity. (Charts 7-1 → 7-12)**

This topic encourages informal, everyday use of modals and imperatives.

CHART 7-13: MAKING SUGGESTIONS: *LET'S* AND *WHY DON'T*
• Relate *let's* and *why don't* to *should.* In (a) and (b), the speaker is saying "We should go to the beach. Going to the beach is a good idea."   • The speaker isn't using *why* to ask for a reason. The listener would not respond to these questions by giving a reason. *Why don't* is an idiomatic use of *why.*   • Model intonation with *Why don't* sentences: the intonation usually falls instead of rises as is normal with questions. *Why don't* sentences are suggestions, not really questions.

☐ **EXERCISE 35, p. 215. Making suggestions with LET'S and WHY DON'T WE. (Chart 7-13)**

The first item is intended to illustrate in "real life" how *let's* and *why don't* are used to make suggestions, prompting the responses *Let's do it as a class* and *Why don't we do it in pairs?* Ask several individual students their opinions and go with the majority.

☐ **EXERCISE 36, p. 215. Making suggestions with WHY DON'T YOU. (Chart 7-13)**

POSSIBLE SUGGESTIONS: **1.** Why don't you have a glass of water? **2.** Why don't you take a nap? **3.** Why don't you see a dentist? **4.** Why don't you open a window? **5.** Why don't you take geology? **6.** Why don't you give her a book?

☐ **EXERCISE 37, p. 216. Making suggestions with LET'S and WHY DON'T. (Chart 7-13)**

This exercise is intended to increase students' awareness of the common ways of making suggestions and give them some directed listening practice. And too, this is a change-of-pace exercise to add variety to classroom activities.

ANSWERS: **1.** B: Why don't you have a strong cup of tea? **2.** A: Let's rent a video. **3.** B: Why don't you put on a sweater? **4.** B: Why don't we go to *(name of a local place)?* A: Let's go to *(name of a local place)* instead. **5.** B: Why don't you take some aspirin? B: Then why don't you lie down and rest? **6.** A: Why don't we go dancing tonight? A: Then why don't we go to a movie? A: Well then, let's go to a restaurant for dinner.

☐ EXERCISE 38, p. 217. Making suggestions with LET'S and WHY DON'T WE. (Chart 7-13)

SUGGESTION: Have students work in pairs prior to class discussion. Then for each item, ask several pairs to say their dialogues without looking at their texts.

SAMPLE COMPLETIONS: **2.** Why don't we go to the swimming pool? **3.** Let's get a sandwich. **4.** Let's do something fun, like go to Las Vegas. **5.** Why don't we go together Tuesday morning? . . . Let's go Tuesday afternoon. **6.** Let's go hiking. **7.** Why don't we leave here around four o'clock? **8.** Why don't we go to a movie? **9.** Let's eat out tonight. . . . Let's make something special at home instead.

☐ EXERCISE 39, p. 218. Making suggestions with WHY DON'T YOU. (Chart 7-13)

SAMPLE RESPONSES: **1.** Why don't you go out to dinner at a fancy restaurant? Why don't you go to the new jazz club? Why don't you get tickets for a play or a concert? **2.** Why don't you join a fitness club? Why don't you take a long walk every day? Why don't you ride your bike more often? **3.** Why don't you ask Professor Black if you can turn it in tomorrow? Why don't you cut class? **4.** Why don't you call the apartment manager and ask him/her to let you in? Why don't you go to dinner and a movie until your roommate gets home? Why don't you spend the evening with a friend? **5.** Why don't you call your friend and discuss the problem? Why don't you write your friend a letter to explain how you feel? **6.** Why don't you join an amateur sports team? Why don't you take a short vacation? Why don't you join a hiking club? **7.** Why don't you speak only English all day long? Why don't you listen to the TV news every day? Why don't you read a novel written in English?

CHART 7-14: STATING PREFERENCES: *PREFER, LIKE . . . BETTER, WOULD RATHER*

- The forms of these patterns need special attention when the chart is presented in class to make sure the students understand them clearly. Elicit additional examples from the class and write them on the chalkboard, pointing out the characteristics of each pattern.

- *Would rather* may be new to some students. Perhaps do a chain exercise to introduce the pattern orally:

TEACHER:	*What would you rather do than study?*
SPEAKER A:	*I'd rather watch TV than study.*
TEACHER:	*What would you rather do than watch TV?*
SPEAKER B:	*I'd rather read a book than watch TV.*
TEACHER:	*What would you rather do than read a book?*
SPEAKER C:	*Etc.*

- The "*-ing* verb" referred to in the explanation in this chart is a gerund. It is also possible to use an infinitive after *like;* the text chose to present only the gerund pattern here. Using an infinitive with *like . . . better than* can lead to awkward sentences that a native speaker would be likely to avoid.

☐ **EXERCISE 40, p. 219. Expressing preferences. (Chart 7-14)**

ANSWERS:

4. to	**7.** to	**10.** than
5. than	**8.** than	**11.** to
6. than	**9.** than	**12.** than

☐ **EXERCISE 41, p. 219. Expressing preferences: WOULD RATHER. (Chart 7-14)**

In this exercise, students use the target structures while speaking about their personal preferences.

☐ **EXERCISE 42, p. 220. Expressing preferences: WOULD RATHER. (Chart 7-14)**

Make up silly questions that your class would relate to and enjoy. "Would you rather be a dumb blonde or a nerd?" "Would you rather be Frankenstein or Dracula?" Etc.

☐ **EXERCISE 43, p. 220. Cumulative review. (Chapter 7)**

A multiple-choice test is simply another kind of exercise. If you want to give students practice in taking multiple-choice tests, allow 30 seconds per item.

ANSWERS:

1. C	**8.** B	**15.** B
2. A	**9.** C	**16.** B
3. A	**10.** B	**17.** A
4. B	**11.** B	**18.** C
5. C	**12.** A	**19.** A
6. B	**13.** C	**20.** C
7. C	**14.** A	**21.** A

☐ **EXERCISE 44, p. 223. Review: auxiliary verbs. (Chapters 1 → 7)**

This practice covers the auxiliary verbs presented from the beginning of the text through this chapter, with an emphasis on modals.

POSSIBLE COMPLETIONS: **3.** Would **4.** must not **5.** Did **6.** May (Could/Can) . . . Could (Would/Can) **7.** Could/Would . . . is **8.** should / ought to / had better **9.** are . . . am **10.** has to / must / has got to **11.** Don't **12.** are . . . Do . . . Could/Would **13.** May/Could . . . must **14.** Is **15.** must/should . . . cannot/will not

Chapter 8: CONNECTING IDEAS

ORDER OF CHAPTER	CHARTS	EXERCISES	WORKBOOK
Preview		Ex. 1	
And, but, or, so	8-1 → 8-3	Ex. 2 → 9	Pr. 1 → 10
And, but + auxiliary verbs	8-4	Ex. 10 → 12	Pr. 11 → 12
And + *too, so, either, neither*	8-5	Ex. 13 → 18	Pr. 13
Because	8-6	Ex. 19 → 22	Pr. 14 → 18, 20
Even though/although	8-7	Ex. 23 → 26	Pr. 19, 21
Summary review		Ex. 27 → 28	Pr. 22

General Notes on Chapter 8

• Because most students need to write English for academic or business purposes, this chapter focuses on basic conventions of standard written English. These include parallelism, punctuation, coordination, and subordination. Students who are not interested in improving their skills in written English can use this chapter selectively.

• TERMINOLOGY: An **independent clause** is also called a **main clause**. A **dependent clause** may also be called a **subordinate clause**. An **adverb clause** may also be called a **subordinating adverbial clause**.

This chapter presents **compound sentences** in which *and, but, or,* and *so* are **coordinating conjunctions**, and **complex sentences** in which *because, even though,* and *although* are **subordinating conjunctions**. None of this terminology is used in the text except for **conjunction**, which is applied only to *and, but, or,* and *so.*

The punctuation mark at the end of a statement is called a **period** in American English, but a **full stop** in British English.

☐ EXERCISE 1, p. 225. Preview. (Chapter 8)

This exercise previews the two principal grammar points presented in this chapter: the use of coordinating conjunctions *(and, but, or,* and *so)* and subordinating conjunctions *(because* and *even though/although)*. Integral to this grammar is an understanding of the structure of a simple sentence and independent vs. dependent clauses.

It is essential for learners using this text to be able to identify subjects and verbs. However, complementary structures (e.g., direct objects, indirect objects, predicate nominatives, objective complements) are neither named nor discussed in the text. You may wish to refer students to Charts 6-2, 6-3, and 6-8, which present the fundamentals of a simple sentence:

S + V
S + V + O
S + ***be*** + *noun phrase, adjective,* or *prepositional phrase*

In this exercise, the only grammatical analysis the students are being asked to make is to find subjects and verbs as aids in identifying a sentence. Many native speakers can pick out subjects and verbs but don't know the terminology for the various complementary structures in English; these native speakers can, nonetheless, recognize the beginning and end of a sentence. The goal is the same for ESL/EFL students.

Coordinating conjunctions connect grammatical elements of equal status. This exercise previews the two uses of coordinating conjunctions: (1) in compound phrases and (2) as connectors for two independent clauses. Students have to identify compound subjects and compound verbs as well as compound sentences. The term "compound" is not used in the text; students only need to identify the coordinated words. (For example, in item 2, they need to recognize that the subject consists of *ants* and *butterflies* connected by *and.)* If you feel, however, that additional terminology such as "compound" or "coordinating" would help you and your students, you certainly should introduce it.

EXPECTED CORRECTIONS:

1. Butterflies are insects**.** **A**ll insects have six legs.
2. *(no change)*
3. Ants**,** butterflies**,** cockroaches**,** bees**,** and flies are insects.
4. Butterflies and bees are insects**.** **S**piders are different from insects.
5. Spiders have eight legs**,** so they are not called insects.
6. Most insects have wings**,** but spiders do not.
7. Bees are valuable to us**.** **T**hey pollinate crops and provide us with honey.
8. *(no change)*
9. Insects can cause us trouble**.** **T**hey bite us**,** carry diseases**,** and eat our food.
10. Insects are essential to life on earth**.** **T**he plants and animals on earth could not live without them**.** **I**nsects may bother us**,** but we have to share this planet with them.
11. *(no change)*
12. Because insects are necessary to life on earth**,** it is important to know about them.

CHART 8-1: CONNECTING IDEAS WITH *AND*

• *And* is a coordinating conjunction. It connects parallel elements, i.e., elements having the same structure. These elements may be compound subjects, verbs, or objects or may be two independent clauses. (It is also possible to use *and* to connect three independent clauses: *I walked, he ran, and Mary drove.* That use is not taught in the text, which keeps the focus on avoiding comma splices between two independent clauses: *I walked, he ran.* = a comma splice. Example (h) in this chart is also a comma splice, which is a type of run-on sentence.)

• Chart 3-10 in Chapter 3 presents the concept of parallel verbs. Chart 8-1 extends parallelism to nouns and adjectives. You may wish to use the term "parallel" and explain its meaning by drawing two parallel lines, then three, then four—showing that the form of each element is identical to the others. Then draw two parallel lines and another line that is not parallel (/ / \ ) to make an analogy to grammar. For example, if the first two elements are adjectives (represented by the first two lines), the third in a series (represented by the non-parallel line) should not be a noun. All the elements connected by *and* must be the same.

INCORRECT: *She is kind, affectionate, and a grandmother.*
CORRECT: *She is a kind, affectionate grandmother.* OR
She is kind, affectionate, and wise.

• The use of a comma before *and* in a series, as in example (b), is a matter of style. Some style manuals say to omit it as unnecessary punctuation. Others say to include it for clarity. This text takes the latter view, but either is correct. In the *ANSWERS* to the exercises and practices in this unit, the comma is shown before *and* in a series.

• For students unfamiliar with the punctuation of English, Chart 8-1 can be confusing. Write examples on the board and identify the parallel elements connected by *and.* Go over the structure elements and punctuation as many times as necessary. Once students truly understand this chart, the use of the comma and the period will seem much less mysterious; run-on sentences should start disappearing from their writing. You might mention to your class that many native-speaking students in high school and college make punctuation errors in their writing and have to study this same grammar in their own English classes.

• In normal speech, *and* is unstressed and is often reduced to /ən/. Model normal contracted speech for your students.

☐ EXERCISE 2, p. 226. Connecting ideas with AND. (Chart 8-1)

This exercise deals only with parallel elements within a sentence, i.e., within one independent clause. It does not deal with connecting independent clauses.

ANSWERS: **3.** wide and deep = *adj + adj (no commas)* **4.** wide, deep, and dangerous = *adj + adj + adj* **5.** Goats and horses = *noun + noun (no commas)* **6.** Giraffes, anteaters, tigers, and kangaroos = *noun + noun + noun + noun* **7.** played games, sang songs, and ate birthday cake = *verb + verb + verb* **8.** played games and sang songs = *verb + verb (no commas)* **9.** mother, father, and grandfather = *noun + noun + noun* . . . brother and sister = *noun + noun (no commas)* **10.** moos like a cow, roars like a lion, and barks like a dog = *verb + verb + verb*

☐ EXERCISE 3, p. 227. Connecting ideas with AND. (Chart 8-1)

This is a simple exercise on punctuation. Students could correct each other's papers.

SAMPLE ANSWERS: **1.** My favorite sports are football, baseball, and basketball. **2.** My father is honest, generous, and compassionate. **3.** I would like to visit Paris, Beijing, Cairo, and Bogota. **4.** This city is large and noisy. **5.** I got up at 6:30, took a walk, and ate breakfast. **6.** The most important people in my life are my mother, father, sister, grandfather, and aunt. **7.** Good food and good friends make me happy. **8.** The people in my country are friendly, hardworking, and generous.

☐ EXERCISE 4, p. 227. Punctuating with commas and periods. (Chart 8-1)

This exercise focuses on punctuation of independent clauses but also deals with parallel elements within a sentence. If your students will ever need to write English in school or in their jobs, they will need to be able to discern the structure of sentences like these and punctuate them correctly. Proper punctuation is a value in English rhetoric. Not all cultures deem punctuation to be of equal importance in proper language use by educated writers. (In fact, British usage of commas is somewhat less rigid than American.)

Punctuation marks are signals to the reader. In most cases, they mark boundaries of segments that in speech are marked by pauses or intonation changes. For example, a comma often signals a pause in speech. A period usually signals an even longer pause as well as dropping of the voice.

While most rules of punctuation are straightforward, some conventions are, as in the spoken language, flexible within limits. Learners should control the basic rules of use presented here before they experiment with any options.

Students may ask if they can begin a sentence with *and.* The answer is yes, although not in very formal writing (e.g., certain academic writing). In other registers, from personal letters to magazine articles, beginning a sentence with a coordinating conjunction is common. In item 4, it is possible to write *I talked to Ryan about his school grades. And he listened to me carefully.*

ANSWERS: **3.** I talked**. H**e listened. **4.** I talked to Ryan about his school grades**,** and he listened to me carefully. **5.** The man asked a question**. T**he woman answered it. **6.** The man asked a question**,** and the woman answered it. **7.** *(no change)* **8.** Rome is an Italian city**. I**t has a mild climate and many interesting attractions. **9.** You should visit Rome**. I**ts climate is mild**,** and there are many interesting attractions. **10.** The United States is bounded by two oceans and two countries**. T**he oceans are the Pacific to the west and the Atlantic to the east**,** and the countries are Canada to the north and Mexico to the south. **11.** The twenty-five most common words in English are: *the***,** *and***,** *a***,** *to***,** *of***,** *I***,** *in***,** *was***,** *that***,** *it***,** *he***,** *you***,** *for***,** *had***,** *is***,** *with***,** *she***,** *has***,** *on***,** *at***,** *have***,** *but***,** *me***,** *my***,** and *not.*

CHART 8-2: CONNECTING IDEAS WITH *BUT* AND *OR*

- If the students understood Chart 8-1, they should have no problems with this chart. It expands what they learned about using *and* to two other coordinating conjunctions, *but* and *or.*
- In normal speech, *or* is unstressed: /ər/.

☐ EXERCISE 5, p. 228. Connecting ideas with AND, BUT, and OR. (Charts 8-1 and 8-2)

The focus of this exercise is on both meaning and structure. To select the correct conjunction, students need to decide on the relationship between the given ideas. Using punctuation appropriately depends on understanding the underlying structure.

ANSWERS: **4. ,** but **5.** but **6. ,** and **7.** and **8. ,** but **9.** or **10. ,** or

☐ EXERCISE 6, p. 229. Punctuating with commas and periods. (Charts 8-1 and 8-2)

ANSWERS: **2.** Cats are mammals, but turtles are reptiles. **3.** Cows and horses are farm animals, but zebras and giraffes are wild animals. **4.** Cows and horses are farm animals. Zebras, giraffes, and lions are wild animals. **5.** Cars use roads. Trains run on tracks. **6.** Cars, buses, and trucks use roads, but trains run on tracks. **7.** Most vegetables grow above the ground, but some are roots and grow under the ground. Corn, beans, and cabbage grow above the ground, but carrots and onions grow under the ground. **8.** *(no change)* **9.** Nothing in nature stays the same forever. Today's land, sea, climate, plants, and animals are all part of a relentless process of change continuing through millions of years. **10.** Mozart was a great composer, but he had a short and difficult life. At the end of his life, he was penniless, sick, and unable to find work, but he wrote music of lasting beauty and joy.

CHART 8-3: CONNECTING IDEAS WITH *SO*

- Like other coordinating conjunctions, *so* connects two independent clauses. Unlike *and, but,* and *or,* the word *so* is not used to connect parallel elements within a clause.
- In addition to *and, but, or,* and *so,* there are other coordinating conjunctions: *for, nor,* and *yet.* They are not introduced in this text. See *Understanding and Using English Grammar, Third Edition,* Chart 16-3.

☐ EXERCISE 7, p. 230. SO vs. BUT. (Charts 8-2 and 8-3)

This exercise contrasts cause-and-effect and opposition. The students will encounter this contrast again in the unit on *because* vs. *even though.*

ANSWERS:

3. so	**6.** but	**9.** but
4. but	**7.** so	**10.** so
5. so	**8.** but	

☐ EXERCISE 8, p. 231. Punctuating with commas and periods. (Charts 8-1 → 8-3)

Identify parallel structures that do not require commas (those with two elements) as well as the ones that do.

In this challenging exercise, students have to recognize structure even though they may not be familiar with all the vocabulary. You might point out that being able to recognize the structure in which a word is used can be helpful when one is guessing at its meaning.

Congratulate your students on their ability to recognize basic sentence structures in English, as demonstrated by their ability to punctuate them correctly. You might mention that there are some native speakers at the university level who cannot punctuate this exercise correctly and need remedial study.

You might also point out how much easier it is to read this passage when it is properly punctuated. Punctuation has very practical purposes.

ANSWERS: **2.** Asiatic elephants are native to the jungles and forests in India, Indonesia, Malaysia, Thailand, China, and other countries in southeastern and southern Asia. **3.** Elephants spend a lot of time in water and are good swimmers. They take baths in rivers and lakes. They like to give themselves a shower by shooting water from their trunks. **4.** After a bath, they often cover themselves with dirt. The dirt protects their skin from the sun and insects. **5.** A female elephant is pregnant for approximately twenty months and almost always has only one baby. **A** young elephant stays close to its mother for the first ten years of its life. **6.** Elephants live peacefully together in herds**,** but some elephants (called *rogues)* leave the herd and become mean**. T**hese elephants usually are in pain from decayed teeth**,** a disease**,** or a wound.

☐ EXERCISE 9, p. 232. Punctuating with commas and periods. (Charts 8-1 → 8-3)

This unpunctuated passage is difficult to read; the reader has to slow down and decipher the sentence structures. Again stress how important proper punctuation and capitalization are in making written English easier to read.

ANSWERS:

(1) **A** few days . . . to Chicago.
(2) **W**e didn't . . . first hour**,** but near
(3) . . . highway construction**. T**he traffic . . . at all**. M**y friend
(4) . . . and waited**. W**e talked . . . jobs**,** our families**,** and . . . traffic**. S**lowly
(5) traffic started to move.
(6) **W**e . . . of the road**. T**he right blinker was blinking.
(7) **T**he driver . . . the line of traffic**. C**ar after car
(8) . . . get in line**. I** decided to do a good deed**,** so I
(9) motioned . . . ahead of me**. T**he driver
(10) . . . thanks to me**,** and I waved back at him.
(11) **A**ll cars . . . down the road**. I** held out
(12) . . . to pay my toll**,** but the tolltaker . . . me on**. S**he told me
(13) . . . paid my toll**. W**asn't
(14) *(no change)*

CHART 8-4: USING AUXILIARY VERBS AFTER *BUT* AND *AND*

• The focus in this chart is on which auxiliary to use to echo the main verb. In (f) through (j), point out that *either* is used with a negative auxiliary verb and *too* is used with an affirmative auxiliary. The information in this chart is preparatory to the presentation of the patterns with *and + too, so, either, neither* in the next chart, where the emphasis is on word order.

• Some strict traditionalists insist that a comma must precede *too.* Today one increasingly sees *too* used without the comma in both popular and academic publications. It's curious that traditional usage does not mandate a comma before *either,* which has exactly the same adverbial function as *too.* A comma is possible in the sentence "Jack came to the meeting, too" but not in the sentence "Mary didn't come to the meeting either."

☐ EXERCISES 10 and 11, pp. 233–234. Using auxiliary verbs after BUT. (Chart 8-4)

For the first few items, ask the students to tell you the full meaning of the auxiliaries they supply. For example, in item 1, *don't = don't read a lot of books.*

EX. 10 ANSWERS:	*EX. 11 ANSWERS:*
3. won't	**3.** is
4. don't	**4.** isn't
5. does	**5.** can't
6. are	**6.** does
7. can't	**7.** did
8. hasn't	**8.** won't
9. is	**9.** doesn't
10. doesn't	**10.** hasn't

☐ EXERCISE 12, p. 234. Using auxiliary verbs after AND or BUT. (Chart 8-4)

Some students may not yet understand when and how to use *too* and *either*. Their use was barely touched upon in Chart 8-4. More information is presented in the chart that follows this exercise, making it a preview.

ANSWERS:

4. are too
5. aren't either
6. aren't
7. didn't either
8. does too
9. isn't
10. won't either
11. wasn't
12. is too
13. can

CHART 8-5: USING *AND* + *TOO, SO, EITHER, NEITHER*

- The patterns in this chart are used principally in conversation. They are ways of sharing experiences and opinions. First, the patterns are presented and practiced in connected clauses with *and;* then they are practiced in the more typical dialogue form shown in examples (e) through (h).
- To some arbiters of correct English usage, the responses in (i) and (j) are substandard and grammatically unacceptable. However, native speakers, including educated speakers, often use these expressions in normal conversation.

☐ EXERCISES 13 → 15, pp. 235–236. AND + TOO, SO, EITHER, NEITHER. (Chart 8-5)

EX. 13 ANSWERS:

1. a. James does too
   b. so does James
2. a. Ivan doesn't either
   b. neither does Ivan
3. a. Omar is too
   b. so is Omar
4. a. James isn't either
   b. neither is James

EX. 14 ANSWERS:

2. so does X OR X does too
3. neither can X OR X can't either
4. neither was X OR X wasn't either
5. so did X OR X did too
6. neither does X OR X doesn't either
7. so will X OR X will too
8. neither is X OR X isn't either
9. so does X OR X does too
10. so has X OR X has too

EX. 15 ANSWERS:

2. salt isn't either / neither is salt
3. cats do too / so do cats
4. gorillas don't either / neither do gorillas
5. the teacher did too / so did the teacher
6. the teacher was too / so was the teacher
7. I haven't either / neither have I
8. penguins can't either / neither can penguins

☐ EXERCISE 16, p. 237. AND + TOO, SO, EITHER, NEITHER. (Chart 8-5)

Because this exercise is designed to prepare the students for the pair work in the following exercise, the directions ask for the use of only *so* or *neither* in an effort to simplify the students' task. If you wish, discuss the use of *too* and *either* also, as well as the informal rejoinders *me too* and *me neither.*

ANSWERS:

3. So do I.
4. Neither do I.
5. Neither did I.
6. Neither have I.
7. So did I.
8. So should I.
9. Neither can I.
10. So can I.

☐ EXERCISE 17, p. 237. SO and NEITHER. (Chart 8-5)

The directions ask only for *so* and *neither,* but the patterns with *too* and *either* could also be used if the students wish, as well as the informal rejoinders *me too* and *me neither.*

Speaker A should judge the appropriateness of Speaker B's response.

Mention to the students that this dialogue format is the usual way these patterns are used: one person makes a statement, and the other person uses these expressions to show interest in what the first speaker has said and to share information. Other ways of showing interest and continuing the conversation (but without sharing information) would be to respond by saying *Oh?* or *Really?* See the footnote on this page (p. 237).

☐ EXERCISE 18, p. 238. TOO, SO, EITHER, NEITHER. (Chart 8-5)

You might want to delay this exercise, using it for review the next day or the following week. After the pair work, students could role-play some of the items.

CHART 8-6: CONNECTING IDEAS WITH *BECAUSE*

• The students were introduced to adverb clauses of time in Chapter 2. This is the first chart, however, in which the term "adverb clause" is used. One of the purposes of this chart is to define an adverb clause. You might want to connect the term with the time clauses the students studied in Chapter 2 so that they get an overview of this important English structure.

• The first part of this chapter dealt with compound sentences. Now the text turns to complex sentences. Both kinds of sentences allow the speaker/writer to connect and show relationships between ideas.

• *Because of* is not presented in this text. See *Understanding and Using English Grammar, Third Edition,* Chart 19-1. In brief, *because* introduces an adverb clause. *Because of* is a two-word preposition followed by a (pro)noun object. A common error is the use of *because of* instead of *because.*

INCORRECT: *He drank some water because of he was thirsty.*

☐ EXERCISE 19, p. 239. Adverb clauses with BECAUSE. (Chart 8-6)

The items in this exercise are essentially additional examples to help explain the grammar presented in Chart 8-6. Ask the students to identify the main clause and the adverb clause. The adverb clauses are underlined below.

ANSWERS:

2. The children were hungry <u>because there was no food in the house</u>.
   <u>Because there was no food in the house</u>, the children were hungry.
3. <u>Because the bridge is closed</u>, we can't drive to the other side of the river.
   We can't drive to the other side of the river <u>because the bridge is closed.</u>
4. My car didn't start <u>because the battery was dead</u>.
   <u>Because the battery was dead</u>, my car didn't start.
5. Larry and Patti laughed hard <u>because the joke was very funny</u>.
   <u>Because the joke was very funny</u>, Larry and Patti laughed hard. [In English, the sounds of laughter are often represented by "ha ha" and "hee hee." Ask your students how the sounds of laughter are represented in their languages.]

☐ EXERCISE 20, p. 240. Adverb clauses with BECAUSE. (Chart 8-6)

Again point out how practical punctuation is: it clarifies the meaning by marking structures for the reader, in the same way a speaker would mark structures by using pauses and intonations. Note for the students that in item 1, a speaker would drop the intonation after "young" and pause.

ANSWERS:
2. Mr. El-Sayed had a bad cold. **B**ecause he was not feeling well, he stayed . . . .
3. Judy went to bed early because she was tired. **S**he likes to get . . . .
4. Frank put his head in his hands. **H**e was angry and upset . . . .

☐ EXERCISE 21, p. 240. BECAUSE and SO. (Charts 8-3 and 8-6)

ANSWERS:
2. The room was hot**,** so I opened the window.
3. It was raining**,** so I stayed indoors.
4. Because Jason was hungry**,** he ate.
   OR Jason ate because he was hungry.
5. Because the water in the river is polluted**,** we can't go swimming.
   OR We can't go swimming because the water in the river is polluted.
6. Because my watch is broken**,** I was late for my job interview.
   OR I was late for my job interview because my watch is broken.

☐ EXERCISE 22, p. 240. Review: conjunctions and adverb clauses. (Charts 8-1 → 8-6)

The students must understand compound and complex structures to complete this exercise. Punctuation is being used mainly as a tool for teaching the students to look at underlying sentence structures.

In items 11 and 12 especially, point out how correct punctuation makes comprehension easier. Sentences that are run together without correct punctuation are confusing. It's the writer's job to clarify the meaning by marking the structures appropriately with commas and periods.

ANSWERS: **2.** Jim was hot and tired**,** so he sat in the shade. **3.** Jim was hot**,** tired**,** [optional comma] and thirsty. **4.** Because he was hot**,** Jim sat in the shade. **5.** Because they were hot and thirsty**,** Jim and Susan sat in the shade and drank tea. **6.** *(no change)* **7.** Jim sat in the shade**,** drank tea**,** [optional comma] and fanned himself because he was hot**,** tired**,** [optional comma] and thirsty. **8.** Because Jim was hot**,** he stayed under the shade of the tree**,** but Susan went back to work. **9.** Mules are domestic animals**. T**hey are the offspring of a horse and a donkey**. M**ules are called "beasts of burden" because they can work hard and carry heavy loads. **10.** Because mules are strong**,** they can work under harsh conditions**,** but they need proper care. **11.** Ann had been looking for an apartment for two weeks**. Y**esterday she went to look at an apartment on Fifth Avenue**. S**he rented it because it was in good condition and had a nice view of the city**. S**he was glad to find a new apartment. **12.** The word "matter" is a chemical term**. M**atter is anything that has weight**. T**his book**,** your finger**,** water**,** a rock**,** air**,** [optional comma] and the moon are all examples of matter**. R**adio waves and heat are not matter because they do not have weight**. H**appiness**,** daydreams**,** [optional comma] and fear have no weight and are not matter.

CHART 8-7: CONNECTING IDEAS WITH *EVEN THOUGH / ALTHOUGH*

• What the students learned about adverb clauses with *because* in Chart 8-6 is extended here to the use of *even though* and *although.*

• Understanding the relationship expressed by *even though/although* is difficult for some students.

• A common mistake among learners is to use both *although* and *but* in the same sentence. This sends confusing signals to the reader because *although* indicates subordination and *but* indicates coordination. INCORRECT: *Although I was hungry, but I did not eat.*

• *Though* is not presented here in order to keep the focus on adverb clauses. *Though* has various adverbial uses:

(1) It can be used in the same ways as *even though* and *although: Though I was hungry, I did not eat.*
(2) *I was hungry. I didn't eat, though.* (principally spoken English)
(3) *I didn't eat anything, though my wife did.* (a use similar in form and meaning to *but)*
(4) *Jack looked as though he were ill.*

The text seeks to simplify the students' (and teachers') task by focusing only on *even though* and *although.* Some students, depending on their familiarity with English, may spontaneously use *though* instead of *although* or *even though,* which is fine.

☐ EXERCISE 23, p. 242. EVEN THOUGH vs. BECAUSE. (Chart 8-7)

The emphasis here is on meaning. Rephrase the sentences to make sure the students understand the relationship expressed by *even though* compared to *because.*

ANSWERS:

3. Even though
4. Because
5. Even though
6. Because
7. because
8. even though
9. Even though . . . because

☐ EXERCISE 24, p. 242. EVEN THOUGH / ALTHOUGH and BECAUSE. (Charts 8-6 and 8-7)

To check on their understanding, ask the students to explain some of the items in their own words. It's a good way to discuss the meaning of these structures.

ANSWERS:

2. A
3. C
4. B
5. A
6. C
7. C
8. C
9. B
10. C

☐ EXERCISE 25, p. 243. EVEN THOUGH vs. BECAUSE. (Charts 8-6 and 8-7)

This is not an easy exercise. Some students may be more comfortable with their books open. You might want to explore both yes and no answers for each item.

ANSWERS:

1. Yes, I stayed up late even though I was tired. No, I didn't stay up late because I was tired.
2. Yes, I'd like a glass of water because I'm thirsty. No, I don't want a glass of water even though I'm thirsty.
3. Yes, I want a candy bar because I'm hungry. No, I don't want a candy bar even though I'm hungry.

4. Yes, I eat a lot of vegetables because they're good for you. No, I don't eat a lot of vegetables even though they're good for you. [*You* means "any person," no one in particular.]
5. Yes, I would like to be an astronaut because space exploration is exciting. No, I wouldn't like to be an astronaut even though space exploration is exciting.
6. Yes, I want to own a gun even though they're dangerous. No, I don't want to own a gun because they're dangerous.
7. Yes, I eat at *(name a local restaurant)* because it is inexpensive (OR: even though it is expensive). No, I don't eat at *(name of a local restaurant)* even though it is inexpensive (OR: because it is expensive).
8. Yes, I buy *(name of a local delicacy)* even though it is / they are expensive. No, I don't buy *(name of a local delicacy)* because it is / they are expensive.
9. Yes, I want to swim in *(name of a local river)* because it isn't polluted / even though it is polluted. No, I don't want to swim in *(name of a local river)* because it is polluted / even though it isn't polluted.
10. Yes, I want to go to *(the beach / the swimming pool)* with *(. . .)* and you this afternoon even though I can't swim. No, I don't want to go to *(the beach / the swimming pool)* with *(. . .)* and you this afternoon because I can't swim.
11. Yes, I want to go to *(the beach / the swimming pool)* with *(. . .)* and you because I love to go swimming. No, I don't want to go to *(the beach / the swimming pool)* with *(. . .)* and you this afternoon even though I love to go swimming.
12. Yes, I like living here in winter because the winters are warm. (OR: Yes, I like living here in winter even though the winters are cold.) No, I don't like living here in winter because the winters are cold. (OR: No, I don't like living here in winter even though the winters are warm.)
13. Yes, I want to see *(name of a recent movie)* because it had good reviews. No, I don't want to see *(name of a recent movie)* even though it had good reviews.
14. Yes, I want to draw a picture of you on the board because I'm a good artist. (OR: Yes, I want to draw a picture of you on the board even though I'm not a good artist.) No, I don't want to draw a picture of you on the board because I'm not a good artist. (OR: No, I don't want to draw a picture of you on the board even though I'm a good artist.)
15. Yes, I'm going to see my family over *(name of the next holiday)* because they live nearby. [OR: Yes, I'm going to see my family over *(name of the next holiday)* even though they don't live nearby.] No, I'm not going to see my family over *(name of the next holiday)* because they live far away. [OR: Yes, I'm going to see my family over *(name of the next holiday)* even though they live far away.]

☐ EXERCISE 26, p. 244. EVEN THOUGH and BECAUSE. (Chart 8-7)

As with other open completion exercises, a good technique is to assign this exercise as homework. Then in class, discuss each item by having several students read their sentences aloud or write them on the board. The rest of the class should correct their own sentences using what they learn from the discussion of others' completions. You can collect the papers or not. See the *Introduction,* p. xiii, for suggestions for handling this kind of exercise.

SAMPLE ANSWERS: **1.** I like our classroom even though it doesn't have any windows. **2.** I like my home because it has lots of windows. **3.** I agreed to go to the movies with Pedro even though I don't like movies. **4.** I didn't accept Pedro's invitation to go to a movie because I don't like movies. **5.** Because we have a test tomorrow, we should study tonight. **6.** Even though it's raining, we should go to the zoo. **7.** Even though I was tired, I didn't go to bed because I had to study **8.** Because it was raining, we canceled the picnic at the park, but the children wanted to go to the park anyway because they wanted to feed the ducks. [This item is likely to produce an overly long and awkward sentence, but it presents a fun and challenging structure for students to figure out.]

☐ EXERCISE 27, p. 244. Error analysis. (Charts 8-1 → 8-7)

ANSWERS: **2.** Gold**,** silver**,** and copper ~~they~~ are metals. **3.** The students crowded around the bulletin **board because** their grades were posted there. **4.** I had a cup of coffee, and so **did** my friend. **5.** My roommate didn't go. Neither **did** I. (OR: I **didn't either**.) **6.** Even **though** I **was** very exhausted, I didn't stop working until after midnight last night. **7.** The teacher went **to** the meeting, and **two** of the students did **too**. **8.** ~~Although~~ I like chocolate, but I can't eat it because I'm allergic to it. (OR: Although I like chocolate, ~~but~~ I can't eat it because I'm allergic to it.) **9.** Many tourists visit my country **because it has warm** weather all **year and many** interesting landmarks. **10.** Because the weather . . . all year**,** ~~so~~ many tourists (OR: **T**he weather . . . all year**,** so many tourists) **11.** . . . breakfast**,** and everybody else in my family **does** too. **12.** A hardware store sells tools**,** nails**,** plumbing supplies**,** paint**,** ~~and~~ etc. **13.** . . . in late September**,** we had to cancel . . . had our passports**,** visas**,** airplane tickets**,** and hotel reservations. **14.** . . . stress on our jobs**. M**y job is stressful . . . comfortable**. I**t is noisy**,** hot**,** and dirty**. E**ven though I try to do my best**,** my boss . . . bad performance reports**.** I need to find another job. **15.** I like animals**.** I have a little dog at home**. H**er name is Linda**. S**he is brown and white.

☐ EXERCISE 28, p. 245. Punctuating with commas and periods. (Chapter 8)

This is a cumulative review exercise of the compound and complex structures covered in this chapter.

ANSWERS:

(1) What is the most common substance on earth? **I**t isn't wood**,** iron**,** or sand**. T**he most common substance on earth is water**. I**t occupies more than seventy percent of the earth's surface**. I**t is in lakes**,** rivers**,** and oceans**. I**t is in the ground and in the air**. I**t is practically everywhere.

(2) Water is vital because life on earth could not exist without it**. P**eople**,** animals**,** and plants all need water in order to exist**. E**very living thing is mostly water**. A** person's body is about sixty-seven percent water**. A** bird is about seventy-five percent water**. M**ost fruit is about ninety percent water.

(3) Most of the water in the world is saltwater**. N**inety-seven percent of the water on earth is in the oceans**. B**ecause seawater is salty**,** people cannot drink it or use it to grow plants for food**. O**nly three percent of the earth's water is fresh**. O**nly one percent of the water in the world is easily available for human use.

(4) Even though water is essential to life**,** human beings often poison it with chemicals from industry and agriculture**. W**hen people foul water with pollution**,** the quality of all life—plant life, animal life, and human life—diminishes**. L**ife cannot exist without fresh water**,** so it is essential for people to take care of this important natural resource.

Chapter 9: COMPARISONS

ORDER OF CHAPTER	CHARTS	EXERCISES	WORKBOOK
Preview		Ex. 1	
Comparisons with *as . . . as*	9-1	Ex. 2 → 6	Pr. 1 → 5
Comparative and superlative	9-2 → 9-3	Ex. 7 → 13	Pr. 6 → 11
Comparatives	9-4 → 9-6	Ex. 14 → 19	Pr. 12 → 15
Unclear comparisons	9-7	Ex. 20	Pr. 16
Using *more* with nouns	9-8	Ex. 21	Pr. 17
Repeating a comparative	9-9	Ex. 22	Pr. 18
Double comparatives	9-10	Ex. 23	Pr. 19 → 20
Superlatives	9-11	Ex. 24 → 28	Pr. 21 → 22 Pr. 24 → 25
Summary review		Ex. 29 → 31	Pr. 23, 26 → 27
The same, similar, different, like, alike	9-12	Ex. 32 → 35	Pr. 28 → 31
Cumulative review		Ex. 36 → 37	Pr. 32

General Notes on Chapter 9

• Students will learn a variety of structures to express comparison, contrast, and related ideas.

• The assumption is that students have already been introduced to simple phrases of comparison. This chapter both reviews and expands on those forms, emphasizing idiomatic usage.

• TERMINOLOGY: The terms "comparative" and "superlative" are used traditionally here and associated with *-er/more* and *-est/most,* respectively.

☐ EXERCISE 1, p. 247. Preview of comparisons. (Chapter 9)

This exercise can be used as an oral introduction to the functions of comparisons, especially those using *as . . . as*, comparatives, and superlatives. Elicit sentences from the class. Preview the grammar in this chapter. Note problems your students are having. Following are some typical errors in the use of comparison structures:

INCORRECT: *Line B is the* ***longer*** *of all.*
INCORRECT: *Line B is the longest* ***from*** *all.*
INCORRECT: *Line C is* ***shortest*** *than line B.*
INCORRECT: *Line C is shorter* ***that*** *line B.*
INCORRECT: *Line C is* ***more short*** *than line B.*
INCORRECT: *Line C is* ***more shorter*** *than line B.*
INCORRECT: *Line C is shorter* ***as*** *line B.*
INCORRECT: *Line D is as short* ***than*** *line E.*
INCORRECT: *Line D is short as line E.* (omission of first *as)*
INCORRECT: *Line E is* ***very*** *shorter than line B.*

SAMPLE RESPONSES:

2. Rick looks as happy as Jim.
Rick and Jim look happier than Mike and David.
David looks sadder than the others.
David looks the saddest of all.
Mike is happier than David but not as happy as Rick or Jim.
Jim is the happiest of the four boys.
OR Rick looks just about as happy as Jim.
Etc.

3. Canada is the largest of the four countries.
Brazil is almost as large as Canada.
Brazil is larger than Egypt and Spain put together.
Spain is the smallest of the four countries.
Spain is much smaller than Brazil or Canada.
Etc.

4. The second question is the hardest of all.
The first and fourth questions are the easiest.
The fourth question is just as easy as the first question.
The third question is harder than the first or fourth but easier than the second.
Etc.

5. C is the best handwriting.
A is the worst handwriting.
C is better than either A or B.
A is worse than B. B is worse than C.
A isn't nearly as good as C.
Etc.

9-1: MAKING COMPARISONS WITH *AS . . . AS*

• Discuss the examples. Then for reinforcement, ask the students to cover the chart and tell you about the four people in the pictures. Or use the ages of three students in your class and a child (possibly yours or a student's) to elicit the same structures as in the examples.

• The use of the modifiers *quite, nearly, almost,* and *just* may be difficult for some learners and require special teaching attention. Return to Exercise 1 and elicit comparisons that use these modifiers, or make up additional situations for oral work by using objects/people in the classroom or pictures drawn on the board. A topic that easily lends itself to comparison is people's heights (e.g., *Ali isn't quite as tall as Roberto,* etc.). If you use this situation, make sure you know your students well enough to be assured that the shortest person in the group to be compared is not sensitive about being short. Other things that could be compared are hair length, book size, or size of circles drawn on the board, to name a few. Practices in the *Workbook* also emphasize use of modifiers with *as . . . as.*

• In the negative, *so* can be used instead of the first *as* with no change in meaning: *not so . . . as* has the same meaning and use as *not as . . . as.* For example, *Line A is not so long as line B = Line A is not as long as line B.* The use of *so* in negative comparisons is no longer as common in everyday English as it once was. Many people use *not as . . . as.*

☐ EXERCISE 2, p. 249. Comparisons with AS . . . AS. (Chart 9-1)

ANSWERS:

2. not nearly as
3. just as
4. almost as / not quite as
5. not nearly as
6. just as
7. almost as / not quite as

☐ EXERCISE 3, p. 249. Comparisons with AS . . . AS. (Chart 9-1)

EXPECTED COMPLETIONS: **3.** A lake isn't (nearly) as . . . an ocean **4.** Honey is just as . . . sugar **5.** Money isn't (nearly) as . . . good health **6.** Children usually aren't as . . . adults **7.** A solar system isn't (nearly) as . . . a galaxy **8.** People aren't (nearly) as . . . monkeys **9.** reading a novel is just as / isn't nearly as . . . listening to music

☐ EXERCISE 4, p. 250. Comparisons with AS . . . AS. (Chart 9-1)

This exercise includes clause completions for *as . . . as* comparisons. The use of subjects and verbs in comparison clauses is not discussed in Chart 9-1, but will be addressed in Chart 9-4 in relation to comparatives. Some items in this exercise ask students to come up with expressions with *as . . . as* that they might have encountered before. For example, *as fast as I can* is a common expression that the students may already be familiar with.

POSSIBLE COMPLETIONS: **3.** as fast as I can **4.** as sour as a lemon **5.** as wide as a river **6.** as difficult as I (had) expected **7.** as often/much as you can **8.** as (young) as you feel **9.** as easy as you might think / as easy as it looks **10.** as long to drive to the airport as it takes to fly to Chicago

☐ EXERCISE 5, p. 251. Comparisons with AS . . . AS. (Chart 9-1)

These comparisons are included mostly for fun and vocabulary development. The native speaker may find these expressions trite, but second language learners often find them entertaining. If the students learn a few of these phrases, it does not mean their writing will become trite and hackneyed. These phrases are so common that almost any native speaker can supply the traditional completion to the comparison. The ones in this exercise are only a few out of many such phrases. Some others: *proud as a peacock, easy as pie, quiet as a mouse, happy as a clam, dead as a doornail, good as gold, sly as a fox, wise as an owl, busy as a bee.*

In these traditional phrases, the first *as* is sometimes dropped: *He's strong as a bull.*

ANSWERS:

2. a bull/an ox
3. a bird
4. a mule
5. a rock
6. the hills
7. a cat
8. a feather
9. a kite
10. a wet hen

☐ EXERCISE 6, p. 252. Comparisons with AS . . . AS. (Chart 9-1)

This exercise can be oral or written. Many sentences involve ideas that are a matter of the speaker's opinion.

SAMPLE SENTENCES: **1.** Clean air is . . . clean water. **2.** The desks in this classroom are . . . seats in a movie theatre. **3.** Accounting is . . . marine biology. **4.** Apple pie is . . . blueberry pie. **5.** Algebra is . . . calculus. **6.** Children are . . . adults. **7.** Frozen broccoli is . . . fresh broccoli. **8.** People in cities are . . . people in small towns. **9.** Wood is . . . stone. **10.** An apple is . . . a pear. **11.** I exercise . . . **12.** I don't exercise . . . **13.** I need to go to the bank . . . **14.** Cooking is . . . **15.** I speak English . . .

9-2: COMPARATIVE AND SUPERLATIVE

- This chart introduces the concepts and terminology of comparisons with *more/-er* and *most/-est.* A presentation of forms follows in Chart 9-3.
- Be sure that the students note that the article *the* must be part of a superlative.

☐ EXERCISE 7, p. 252. Error analysis: comparative and superlative. (Chart 9-2)

This exercise contains some typical errors in the form of comparatives and superlatives. It serves as a preview to Chart 9-3. Discuss the meanings.

ANSWERS: **2.** Alaska is **the** largest **3.** Texas is ~~the~~ larger **than** France. **4.** . . . comfortable **than** new shoes. **5.** I like Chinese food ~~more~~ better than French food. **6.** A pillow is **softer than** a rock. **7.** I am **younger** than my brother. My sister is **the youngest** person

☐ EXERCISE 8, p. 253. Comparative and superlative. (Chart 9-2)

This exercise should open up conversation that is not limited to the specific target structures it seeks to elicit. This kind of exercise is a time for students to talk freely. The talk should center around the task at hand. The exercise anticipates that the students will have to ask each other questions (e.g., *Whose ring is that? Could you please hand me the book and the notebook so I can see which is heavier?* Etc.).

After you demonstrate how this exercise should proceed, you can form the students into groups to maximize each student's speaking opportunities. The leader of each group should make sure that both the comparative and the superlative are practiced.

9-3: COMPARATIVE AND SUPERLATIVE FORMS OF ADJECTIVES AND ADVERBS

• Discuss the chart to help the students understand how comparative and superlative forms relate to the number of syllables in the adjective or adverb.

• The text concentrates almost solely on adjectives in comparisons. You might want to give a quick overview of the basic uses of adjectives (to modify nouns) and adverbs (to modify verbs). Examples:

Adjective: *Mrs. Bender is a* ***wise*** *woman.*
Adverb: *Mrs. Bender acts and speaks* ***wisely****.*

• Students might note that the comparative and superlative forms for *good* (adjective) and *well* (adverb) are the same: *better* and *the best.* For example: In the sentence "Anna speaks good English," *good* is an adjective modifying the noun "English." In the sentence "Anna speaks English well," *well* is an adverb modifying the verb "speaks." The comparative form of the two is the same:

Adjective: *Anna speaks better English than I do.*
Adverb: *Anna speaks English better than I do.*

The basic distinction between *good* and *well* is that *good* is an adjective and *well* is an adverb. However, confusion sometimes occurs because *well* can also be an adjective meaning "healthy, not sick." In the sentence "Anna is well," *well* is an adjective describing the noun "Anna." It means that Anna is not sick; she is a well person.

As a further side note on a question that often arises, the expressions "feel well" and "feel good" are both correct, for *feel* is a linking verb and thus can be followed by an adjective; either adjective, *well* or *good,* is correct. In the sentence "I don't feel well," *well* limits the meaning to physical health, whereas the statement "I don't feel good" could refer to one's emotional state and/or to one's physical health.

☐ EXERCISE 9, p. 254. Comparative and superlative forms. (Charts 9-2 and 9-3)

Ask students to construct sentences for some of these items. Point out the spelling of words that require a doubled consonant or a change from *y* to *i* before *-er/-est.*

ANSWERS: **2.** better, the best **3.** lazier, the laziest **4.** hotter, the hottest **5.** neater, the neatest **6.** later, the latest **7.** happier, the happiest **8.** more dangerous, the most dangerous **9.** more slowly, the most slowly **10.** more common, the most common OR commoner, the commonest **11.** more friendly, the most friendly OR friendlier, the friendliest **12.** more careful, the most careful **13.** worse, the worst **14.** farther/further, the farthest/furthest

☐ EXERCISE 10, p. 254. Comparatives. (Charts 9-2 and 9-3)

ANSWERS:

2. funnier
3. more dangerous
4. more confusing
5. cleaner
6. darker
7. prettier
8. wetter

EXPANSION ACTIVITY: Divide the class into two teams. Each team will try to score points.

SCORING: (1) One point for the correct *meaning* of the given adjective.
(2) One point for the correct *comparative form* of that adjective.
(3) One point for a clear *sentence* with the comparative form.

Example: dependable

TEACHER: What does *dependable* mean?

TEAM: *Dependable* means "responsible, reliable, trustworthy." For example, it describes people who do their jobs well every day.

TEACHER: Yes. That's one point. Now, comparative form?

TEAM: *more dependable than*

TEACHER: Correct. That's one point. And a sentence with one of those forms?

TEAM: Vegetables are more dependable than fruit.

TEACHER: What? That doesn't make any sense. No point.

TEAM: Adults are more dependable than children.

TEACHER: Good. One point. Your total points as a team: Three.

The teams should prepare for the contest by discussing the words in the list, looking them up in the dictionary if necessary, and making up possible sentences.

List of adjectives to choose from:

absent-minded	*confusing*	*fresh*	*pleasant*
active	*cute*	*friendly*	*polite*
attractive	*dangerous*	*heavy*	*soft*
bright	*delightful*	*hectic*	*sour*
calm	*dim*	*high*	*straight*
clever	*easy*	*humid*	*wild*
common	*flexible*	*intelligent*	*wonderful*

☐ EXERCISE 11, p. 255. FARTHER and FURTHER. (Chart 9-3)

Point out that *further* can mean "additional" (as in item 2), but *farther* does not.

ANSWERS: **3.** farther/further **4.** further **5.** farther/further **6.** further

☐ EXERCISE 12, p. 256. Comparatives. (Charts 9-2 and 9-3)

This practice could be assigned for written homework. Some of the comparisons may not be immediately obvious and may require time for the student to think through. This practice could also be used in small groups.

EXPECTED RESPONSES: **2.** A pool is shallower than a lake. **3.** An elephant's neck is thicker than a giraffe's neck. **4.** Sunlight is brighter than moonlight. **5.** Iron is heavier than wood. **6.** Walking is easier / more relaxing / more enjoyable than running. **7.** A river is wider and deeper than a stream. **8.** Rubber is more flexible than wood. **9.** Nothing is more enjoyable than sitting in a garden on a quiet summer's day. **10.** A butterfly's wing is thinner than a blade of grass.

☐ EXERCISE 13, p. 256. Comparatives. (Charts 9-2 and 9-3)

NOTE: A speaker who uses *but at least* is usually looking for positive or optimistic comparisons.

SAMPLE RESPONSES: **1.** . . . it's bigger than a cockroach. **2.** . . . it's larger than a closet. **3.** . . . it's more comfortable than sitting on a rock. **4.** . . . it's more intelligent than a fish. **5.** . . . it was easier than this one. **6.** . . . it's cleaner than a dirt floor. **7.** . . . it's more expensive than a pencil. **8.** . . . it's heavier than this dictionary. **9.** . . . it's brighter than gray. **10.** . . . it's closer to X than Y (is).

9-4: COMPLETING A COMPARATIVE

• The use of object pronouns (e.g., *me* and *him)* after *than* is common and today generally acceptable. In the sentence "Tom is older than me," some grammatical analyses consider *than* a preposition that is correctly followed by the objective case. Some older prescriptive grammars didactically state that *than* is a conjunction that must be followed by the subjective case even when the verb is not expressed: *Tom is older than I (am)*. The text skirts the issue by calling the use of object pronouns after *than* "informal." Guide your students according to their best interests. (There are still some traditionalists, especially in academic settings, who consider the use of object pronouns after *than* substandard and proof of a lack in one's education.)

• If native speakers use a subject pronoun after *than,* they often also include the auxiliary verb. In other words, it's typical for many native speakers to say "I'm older than he is" rather than "I'm older than he." The text does not state this observation, but through example encourages the use of auxiliary verbs with subject pronouns following *than.* You might want to make special mention of this pattern to your students.

☐ EXERCISE 14, p. 257. Completing a comparative. (Chart 9-4)

Encourage the inclusion of an auxiliary verb if a subject pronoun follows *than.*

ANSWERS:

2. she is/her
3. they are/them
4. he can/him
5. he did/him
6. he can/him
7. mine . . . hers
8. theirs . . . ours

☐ EXERCISE 15, p. 258. Comparative and superlative forms. (Charts 9-3 and 9-4)

The game format is intended, in general, to add an element of fun as a motivator in reviewing forms and creating contexts for the target structures. If time is limited, you can of course dispense with the game aspect. If you do divide the class into teams, it is probably best that you be the moderator and assign the points. The "rules" of the game are just complicated enough that small groups with a leader might spend unnecessary time trying to figure out the format and worrying about how to assign points.

Students have their own inventive ways of defining words; dictionary definitions are not required.

SAMPLE DEFINITIONS:

1. *absent-minded* = forgetful
2. *active* = busy, moving, not quiet
3. *attractive* = good-looking
4. *bright* = shining, not dark

5. *calm* = quiet, not nervous
6. *clever* = smart, intelligent
7. *common* = usual, typical
8. *confusing* = difficult to understand
9. *cute* = pretty [principally AmE]
10. *dangerous* = possibly harmful, risky
12. *dim* = not bright
13. *easy* = not hard
14. *flexible* = bends easily
15. *fresh* = new, not salty
16. *friendly* = kind, helpful
17. *heavy* = of great weight
18. *hectic* = very busy, full of hurrying and activity [Students are unlikely to be familiar with this word. Choose it only if you're looking to challenge your more advanced students.]
19. *high* = tall [*High* and *tall* are not exact synonyms. *High* is generally not used for living beings, whereas *tall* is. *High* conveys that the speaker is thinking of the distance (often a large distance) something reaches above ground: *a high mountain, a high ceiling, a nest high in a tree. Tall* often conveys the idea of length from top to bottom: *a tall tree, a tall person, a tall ladder.* Opposites: *high ≠ low; tall ≠ short.*]
20. *humid* = slightly moist
21. *intelligent* = smart, having a good mind
22. *pleasant* = nice
23. *polite* = having good manners, courteous
24. *soft* = not hard
25. *sour* = an acid taste
26. *straight* = without a bend, angle, wave, or curve
27. *wild* = not tame(d)
28. *wonderful* = unusually good, terrific

9-5: MODIFYING COMPARATIVES

- A fairly common error is the use of *very* with a comparative:

  INCORRECT: *My brother Raul is very older than me.*

- The use of *far* as an intensifier with comparatives may seem odd to some learners. Emphasize that in this usage, *far, much,* and *a lot* (not *a lot of*) have the same meaning and function.

☐ EXERCISE 16, p. 259. Modifying comparatives. (Chart 9-5)

ANSWERS:

3. very
4. much / a lot / far
5. very
6. much / a lot / far
7. much / a lot / far
8. very

9-6: COMPARISONS WITH *LESS . . . THAN* AND *NOT AS . . . AS*

• In the use of *less,* the text fails to state one exception. The explanation should state that *less* (not *as . . . as)* is used with adjectives and adverbs of more than one syllable except for two-syllable adjectives that end in *-y,* such as *easy, happy, hungry.*

INCORRECT: *less easy than, less happy than, less hungry than*
CORRECT: *not as easy as, not as happy as, not as hungry as*

Exceptions to this exception are *friendly* and *angry,* which can be used with either *less* or *not as . . . as.*

INCORRECT: *less easy than, less happy than, less hungry than*
CORRECT: *less friendly than, less angry than*

Sometimes the text may err on the side of simplification in an attempt to present basic patterns without too many exceptions.

☐ EXERCISE 17, p. 259. LESS . . . THAN and NOT AS . . . AS. (Chart 9-6)

ANSWERS: **3.** B **4.** A, B **5.** B **6.** A, B

☐ EXERCISE 18, p. 260. MORE/-ER, LESS, and NOT AS . . . AS. (Charts 9-1 → 9-6)

EXPECTED RESPONSES: **4.** A sidewalk isn't as wide as **5.** Arithmetic isn't as difficult as / is less difficult than **6.** A hill isn't as high as **7.** Bottled water is clearer and cleaner than **8.** . . . weather isn't as pleasant as / is less pleasant than **9.** . . . chair is more comfortable than **10.** . . . path isn't as dangerous as / is less dangerous than **11.** Toes aren't as long as fingers. **12.** Toes aren't as useful as / are less useful than **13.** Toes aren't as long or useful as **14.** Fingers are longer and more useful than

☐ EXERCISE 19, p. 260. MORE/-ER, LESS, and NOT AS . . . AS. (Charts 9-1 → 9-6)

Tell students this is a free association exercise: they should mention anything that comes to mind as points of comparison. Students may spontaneously produce sentences in which *more* is used with nouns to make comparisons: e.g., *The sun produces more energy than the moon does.*

SAMPLE RESPONSES: **1.** hotter / not as hot as, larger/not as big as, more important to plants, brighter, farther away from earth, etc. **2.** younger, smaller, more playful, less responsible, more independent, noisier, less knowledgeable, etc. **3.** more expensive / less expensive, food is better, easier to get a reservation at, service is faster, ambience is better, etc. **4.** (Comparisons depend on the two people chosen.)

9-7: UNCLEAR COMPARISONS

• Sometimes a verb is required after *than* in order to make a comparison clear. The intention of the text is to make students aware that sometimes confusions can occur if comparisons are not properly completed.

☐ EXERCISE 20, p. 261. Unclear comparisons. (Chart 9-7)

ANSWERS: **2.** . . . better than he likes his wife. OR . . . better than his wife does. [The latter is assumed to be what the writer meant to say. The first completion shows humorously what can happen if a comparison is not properly completed.] **3.** . . . more than he helps Debra. OR . . . more than Debra does. **4.** . . . more than I pay my dentist. OR . . . more than my dentist does.

9-8: USING *MORE* WITH NOUNS

• *More* is frequently used with nouns, functioning as the comparative form of the adjectives *many* and *much.* Sometimes, as in (d), it functions as a noun substitute.

• *More* is used with plural (not singular) count nouns and with noncount nouns.

• In comparatives with nouns, the opposite of *more* is either *less* or *fewer.* In formal or, one might say, educated English of the past, *fewer* is said to be used with count nouns and *less* with noncount nouns.
Examples:

There are ***fewer students*** (count noun) *in this class than in that class.*
Mr. Black assigns ***less homework*** (noncount noun) *than Mr. Green.*

In actual usage, *less* seems to be used with nearly every noun. In common usage, many native speakers would say *There are less students in this class than that class.* The use of *fewer* is becoming rarer in everyday language, but there are those, including the authors of this *Teacher's Guide,* to whom the use of *less* with count nouns does not "sound right." You may or may not choose to discuss the use of *less* vs. *fewer* with nouns; it depends upon the level and interests of your students.

☐ EXERCISE 21, p. 261. Comparatives with nouns, adjectives, and adverbs. (Charts 9-2, 9-3, and 9-8)

Ask the students to identify nouns, adjectives, and adverbs in the list.

ANSWERS:
4. more information
5. happier
6. more happily
7. more happiness
8. more mistakes
9. more responsibly
10. more responsibilities
11. more responsible
12. quicker
13. more salt
14. more doctors

9-9: REPEATING A COMPARATIVE

• You might mention that repeating the comparative once is generally sufficient, but in oral story-telling traditions, a speaker might repeat a comparative several times for effect. For example: *The wolf stopped abruptly when she saw the rabbit. Had the rabbit seen her? No, she decided. Slowly the wolf crept toward the rabbit. She crept* ***closer and closer and closer and closer****. Alas, the rabbit sensed the wolf's presence too late. The wolf pounced, and that was the end of the rabbit.*

☐ EXERCISE 22, p. 262. Repeating a comparative. (Chart 9-9)

ANSWERS: **2.** bigger and bigger **3.** better and better **4.** louder and louder **5.** angrier and angrier / more and more angry **6.** longer and longer **7.** more and more discouraged **8.** colder and colder / warmer and warmer **9.** harder and harder . . . wetter and wetter **10.** weaker and weaker

9-10: USING DOUBLE COMPARATIVES

• It is important to discuss the meaning of this structure. It expresses a cause-and-effect relationship.

• The idiom in (e) is for fun. The vocabulary *merry–merrier* will probably need to be explained. The one in (f) is very common and should be useful in the students' creative production.

• This is an infrequent pattern. It is included more in the interest of assisting reading comprehension than in expectation that the students will adopt the pattern in their own production.

☐ EXERCISE 23, p. 264. Double comparatives. (Chart 9-10)

ANSWERS: **2.** The closer . . . the warmer **3.** The sharper . . . the easier **4.** The noisier *(also possible:* the more noisy) . . . the angrier *(also possible:* more angry) **5.** more shrimp . . . the pinker **6.** . . . faster she drove, the more nervous I became. **7.** . . . more he thought about his family, the more homesick he became. **8.** . . . the darker the sky grew, the faster we ran to reach the house.

9-11: USING SUPERLATIVES

• A useful way to explain the superlative is to say that it compares one part of a group to all other things or people in that group.* In (a), a city, Tokyo, is being compared to all other large cities in the world. In (b), David is being compared to all other people the speaker knows and has ever known. In (c), the group consists of three books, with one book being compared to the other two.

• The emphasis in the text is on how superlatives are completed.

☐ EXERCISE 24, p. 265. Superlatives. (Chart 9-11)

ANSWERS: **3.** the most beautiful . . . in **4.** the worst . . . in **5.** the farthest/furthest . . . in **6.** the best . . . of **7.** the biggest . . . in **8.** the oldest . . . in **9.** the most comfortable . . . in **10.** the most exhausted of

---

*The group can consist of only two things or people (especially in informal English), but usually consists of three or more. The superlative is often distinguished from the comparative by saying that the comparative compares two things or people, whereas the superlative compares three or more things or people. That explanation has a certain simplistic usefulness, but in actual (usually informal) usage, the superlative is often used when only two units are being compared: *I think both these books are good, but the red one is the best.* OR *We have two daughters. Our oldest daughter lives and works in Toronto. The youngest is still in high school.*

☐ EXERCISE 25, p. 266. Superlatives. (Chart 9-11)

ANSWERS: **2.** the cleanest air **3.** The highest mountains on earth **4.** the biggest bird **5.** The two greatest natural dangers **6.** the most popular forms of entertainment **7.** The three most common street names **8.** The longest river in South America

☐ EXERCISE 26, p. 266. Completing superlatives with adjective clauses. (Chart 9-11)

ANSWERS: **2.** the nicest times she's ever had **3.** the most difficult courses I've ever taken **4.** the worst mistakes I've ever made **5.** the most beautiful buildings we've ever seen **6.** the easiest tests I've ever taken

☐ EXERCISE 27, p. 267. Using ONE OF with superlatives. (Chart 9-11)

Patterns with ***one of*** + *superlative* are common and useful but can also be a source of grammatical errors. Typical mistakes:

INCORRECT: *One of the most beautiful* ***country*** *in the world is Switzerland.*
INCORRECT: *One of the most beautiful countries* ***are*** *Switzerland.*

SAMPLE RESPONSES:

1. One of the most beautiful countries in the world is Switzerland. Switzerland is one of the most beautiful countries in the world.
2. One of the most famous people in the world is the president of the United States. The president of the United States is one of the most famous people in the world.
3. One of the best movies I've seen recently is an old favorite, *Casablanca. Casablanca* is one of the best movies I've seen recently. One of the worst movies I've ever seen is *Creatures from the Deep. Creatures from the Deep* is one of the worst movies I've ever seen.
4. One of the most exciting things I've ever done is fly a glider. Flying a glider is one of the most exciting things I've ever done.
5. One of the most wonderful people I've ever known is my friend Jane. My friend Jane is one of the most wonderful people I've ever known.
6. One of the happiest days in my life was my wedding day. My wedding day was one of the happiest days in my life.
7. One of the most interesting animals in the world is the koala bear. The koala bear is one of the most interesting animals in the world.
8. One of the most important people in the history of my country is Abraham Lincoln. Abraham Lincoln is one of the most important people in the history of my country.
9. One of the best experiences I've ever had was parasailing. Parasailing is one of the best experiences I've ever had.
10. One of the most important people in my life is my mother. My mother is one of the most important people in my life.

☐ EXERCISE 28, p. 267. Superlatives. (Chart 9-11)

Students can write their answers as seatwork, then compare them in small groups and write the best ones on the chalkboard for discussion by the class.

SAMPLE ANSWERS: **2.** The most popular sport in my country is soccer. **3.** The largest city in France is Paris. **4.** The Mikado Garden is the best restaurant in this city. **5.** Mr. Green is one of the most interesting people I've ever met. **6.** The most valuable thing I have is my great-grandmother's wedding ring. **7.** The three most important things in life are good health, family, and peace. **8.** The most serious problems in the world today are war and poverty.

☐ EXERCISE 29, p. 268. Review: comparatives and superlatives. (Charts 9-1 → 9-11)

It is hoped students will engage in informal conversation as they work through this exercise.

☐ EXERCISE 30, p. 268. Review: comparatives and superlatives. (Charts 9-1 → 9-11)

This exercise can be done in small groups to maximize each student's opportunity to speak. It can also be assigned as written homework. Or you can lead an open discussion and have students call out any comparisons they can think of. Also possible is to assign each student or each group of students only one item and then ask for oral reports of the comparisons they create.

POSSIBLE RESPONSES:

1. An orange is **sweeter** than a grapefruit. A lemon is **sourer/more sour** than a grapefruit. A grapefruit is **larger** than a lemon or an orange. A grapefruit is **the largest** of the three. Etc.
2. [Perhaps ask the students to compare three of their textbooks.] That book is **thinner** than this book. This book is **fatter** than that book. This book is **more interesting** than that book. The information in this book is **more useful** than the information in that book. This book is **better** than this book. That book is **worse** than this book. It isn't **as good as** the other one. Etc.
3. A kitten is **weaker** than a cheetah or a lion. A lion is **more powerful** than a cheetah. The cheetah is **the fastest** animal in the world. [Note: But a cheetah can maintain its speed for only short distances. It can run 70mph/110kph for only a few hundred yards or meters.] A lion is just **as wild as** a cheetah. A kitten is **gentler/more gentle** than a lion or a cheetah. Etc.
4. Air and water are **more important** to human life than wood. Wood is **heavier** than air but **lighter** than water. Etc.
5. Boxing is **more dangerous** than golf. Of the three sports, golf is **the safest**. Golf is **less exciting** to watch than soccer. Soccer is **more boring** than golf for some people. Etc.
6. The food at X is **more delicious** than the food at Y. Etc.

☐ EXERCISE 31, p. 269. Review of comparatives and superlatives. (Charts 9-1 → 9-11)

ANSWERS: **2.** friendlier/more friendly than **3.** the most famous . . . in **4.** more wheels than **5.** easier . . . than **6.** larger than . . . darker . . . than **7.** the loudest . . . in **8.** The most important **9.** more education than **10.** the longest **11.** the most delightful **12.** The harder . . . the more impossible **13.** the most common/commonest . . . in **14.** the biggest . . . in . . . more people than **15.** The greatest **16.** shorter **17.** The easiest **18.** the highest . . . of **19.** thicker than **20.** more words . . . than **21.** The longer . . . the more difficult **22.** faster than . . . the fastest . . . of **23.** larger than **24.** The greatest . . . in **25.** More houseplants . . . than from

9-12: USING *THE SAME, SIMILAR, DIFFERENT, LIKE, ALIKE*

- Typical errors in the use of *the same as:*
  - —omission of *the* with *same:*
    INCORRECT: *All of the students in our class use same book.*
  - —the use of *a* instead of *the:*
    INCORRECT: *Tom and Anna have a same book.*
  - —the use of *like, from,* or *than* instead of *as:*
    INCORRECT: *Tom's book is the same like Anna's.*
    INCORRECT: *Tom's book is the same from Anna's.*
    INCORRECT: *Tom's book is the same than Anna's.*

- Typical errors in the use of *similar:*
  INCORRECT: *My book is similar with Anna's.*
  INCORRECT: *My book is similar from Anna's.*

- Some grammars claim that only *from* should follow *different.* Students at this level don't need to be concerned with the debate over *than* vs. *from.* In almost all the situations in which they will use *different* in their own production, *from* will be correct. It should also be noted that in British English, *to* may follow *different: Although they are brothers, Bob is different to Tom in many ways.*

Just as a background note: in actual usage, both *from* and *than* have been used following *different* in American English for more than 300 years. There seems to be a clear preference for *from* when the next sentence element is a noun or pronoun: *Men are different from women.* As noted in the footnote to this chart, *than* is preferable when the next element is a clause: *Living on my own for the first time, I look at my life in a different way than I ever have (looked at it) before.* The understood subject and verb from the clause may be omitted: *I look at my life in a different way than ever before.*

☐ EXERCISE 32, p. 272. THE SAME, SIMILAR, DIFFERENT, LIKE, and ALIKE. (Chart 9-12)

EXPECTED RESPONSES: **5.** to **6.** as **7.** from **8.** Ø . . . Ø **9.** to . . . Ø . . . as . . . from **10.** Ø . . . as . . . Ø . . . to . . . from

☐ EXERCISE 33, p. 273. THE SAME, SIMILAR, DIFFERENT, LIKE, and ALIKE. (Chart 9-12)

Students could make up a similar exercise for each other by drawing their own geometric figures and asking their classmates to find the differences.

EXPECTED RESPONSES:

2. different from
3. different
4. the same/alike
5. different from
6. the same as
7. the same as

☐ EXERCISE 34, p. 273. THE SAME, SIMILAR, DIFFERENT, LIKE, and ALIKE. (Chart 9-12)

NOTE: The differences lie in the eyes and the eyebrows.

EXPECTED RESPONSES:

All the figures are similar.
Figures B and F are the same/alike.
Figure A is different from all the others.
Figures C, D, and E are the same.
Figure C is the same as Figures D and E.
Figure A is different from Figure B.
Figure C is different from Figure F.
Figures E and F are similar.

☐ EXERCISE 35, p. 274. THE SAME, SIMILAR, DIFFERENT, LIKE, and ALIKE. (Chart 9-12)

POSSIBLE COMPLETIONS:

3. different from / not the same as
4. the same
5. like/similar to
6. like . . . alike
7. the same . . . as
8. like
9. the same
10. different from / similar to
11. the same . . . as
12. different from / the same as
13. like
14. similar
15. like . . . like . . . like

☐ EXERCISE 36, p. 275. Making comparisons. (Chapter 9)

The emphasis in this exercise is on acquainting the students with some common English proverbs as a focus for conversation. In addition, the students are likely to use the target structures as they compare proverbs in their own languages to the ones given here.

These proverbs need to be explained and the vocabulary discussed.

☐ EXERCISE 37, p. 275. Making comparisons. (Chapter 9)

The topics are intended for a written composition. In English rhetoric, the ways of organizing comparison and contrast compositions are somewhat complex. The text intends the topics to be only prompts for the expression of casual opinions in a conversational tone. It is hoped that the writers will correctly use many of the comparison structures they have been working with in this chapter.

EXPANSION ACTIVITY: Following is a summary review exercise for Chapter 9 that combines both speaking and writing.

Directions: Ask three (or more) classmates four (or more) questions.

1. First, decide what you want to ask your classmates. Below are some suggestions.
2. Next, fill out the chart with the subjects of the questions.
3. Then, write in the names of the classmates you talk to and ask them the questions.
4. After you have all of your information, compare the answers using ***same, different, similar, like, alike, as . . . as, more/-er,*** and ***most/-est.***

Example:

Student	***Eye color***	***Favorite sport***	***Length of time at this school***	***Educational goals***	***Size of family***
Hamid	brown	soccer	3 mo.	engineering degree	5
Po	brown	baseball	3 mo.	business degree	4
Maria	brown	baseball	4 mo.	journalism degree	7

Possible comparisons:
I'm comparing three people: Hamid, Po, and Maria.

- All three have **the same** eye color.
- Po and Maria like **the same** sport, baseball. Hamid's favorite sport is **different from** theirs. He likes soccer.
- Maria has been at this school **longer than** Hamid and Po.
- Their educational goals are **similar**. All of them want to get university degrees.
- Maria has **the largest** family. Po's immediate family is **the smallest**.

Suggestions for questions to ask your classmates:

1. How long have you been at this school?
2. What color are your eyes?
3. What is your favorite kind of music?
4. What is your favorite sport?
5. What do you usually like to wear to class?
6. What are your educational goals?
7. How many people are there in your immediate family?*
8. How big is your hometown?
9. What kind of books do you like to read?
10. What kind of movies do you prefer?
11. What country would you most like to visit?
12. What is your favorite food?
13. When did you last visit home?
14. What kind of vacation do you prefer?
15. How tall are you?

Use this chart to record your information. Write in the topics of your questions, the names of the people you interview, and then their answers.

Student	***Eye color***	***Favorite sport***	***Length of time at this school***	***Educational goals***	***Size of family***

**Immediate family* = mother, father, and children (but not cousins, aunts, uncles, grandparents, etc.)

Chapter 10: THE PASSIVE

ORDER OF CHAPTER	CHARTS	EXERCISES	WORKBOOK
Active vs. passive	10-1 → 10-2	Ex. 1 → 6	Pr. 1 → 8
Transitive vs. intransitive	10-3	Ex. 7	Pr. 9
Summary review			Pr. 10 → 11
The *by*-phrase	10-4	Ex. 8 → 9	Pr. 12 → 14
Summary review		Ex. 10 → 11	Pr. 15
Passive forms of the present and past progressive	10-5	Ex. 12	Pr. 16 → 18
Summary review			Pr. 19
Passive modal auxiliaries	10-6	Ex. 13	Pr. 20 → 22
Summary review		Ex. 14 → 15	Pr. 23 → 25
Stative passive	10-7	Ex. 16 → 20	Pr. 26 → 27
Participial adjectives	10-8	Ex. 21 → 23	Pr. 28 → 31
Get + adjective/past participle	10-9	Ex. 24 → 25	Pr. 32 → 33
Be/get used/accustomed to	10-10	Ex. 26 → 29	Pr. 34
Used to vs. *be used to*	10-11	Ex. 30 → 32	Pr. 35 → 36
Be supposed to	10-12	Ex. 33 → 37	Pr. 37 → 38
Cumulative review		Ex. 38 → 39	Pr. 39

General Notes on Chapter 10

• Learners need to understand and be able to use the passive. It is a frequently used and important structure in English.

• This chapter begins by showing the relationship between active and passive sentences. After a brief explanation of transitive and intransitive verbs, focus shifts to the omission of the *by*-phrase in passive sentences. Next, the passive is used with progressive verbs and modal auxiliaries. A section of the chapter deals with other uses of past and present participles, concluding with some idiomatic expressions containing participles.

• TERMINOLOGY: The term "passive" is used here without the additional term "voice." The term used for explicit identification of the agent in a passive structure is "the *by*-phrase" because the preposition *by* is its first element.

10-1: ACTIVE SENTENCES AND PASSIVE SENTENCES

• The emphasis in this introductory chart is on the form of the passive as well as its meaning in equivalent active sentences.

• The passive is most commonly used without a *by*-phrase. All the example sentences in the initial charts and exercises, however, include a *by*-phrase as an aid to understanding the form and meaning of the passive. The omission of the *by*-phrase is discussed in Chart 10-4.

• GENERAL COMMENTS: The text concentrates on the form of the passive and its basic use, i.e., to express the accomplishment of an action when it is not known or not important to know exactly who performed it—for example, *Corn is grown in Iowa.* The passive performs a legitimate function in English rhetoric, especially in scientific and technical writing. For example, in the sentence "Energy can be changed from one form to another, but it cannot be destroyed," the passive describes a situation in which there is no particular actor nor any need to identify an actor. In such situations, the passive is a common and useful structure.

The passive does, however, lend itself to misuse: as a rhetorical device, it can be used to hide the perpetrators of actions. For example, in the sentence "When a husband died, his widow was burned alive on his funeral pyre," the use of the passive allows both the writer and the reader to distance themselves from this cruel behavior by not having to ask <u>who</u> burned widows to death. The use of the passive almost makes it seem as though no one was really responsible for killing a widowed woman. Sometimes the passive obfuscates and interferes with crisp analytical thought.

• Languages differ on passivization. English is rather flexible in attributing actions and volition to inanimate objects. For example, it accepts as grammatical *My shoe fell off.* Other languages insist that that sentence must always be in a passive form; a shoe could never will or cause itself to fall off. Students from such language backgrounds may attempt to "stretch" the grammar of English to conform to the "logic" of their grammars; no language has any more claim to logic than any other!

10-2: FORM OF THE PASSIVE

• The exercises contain only four tenses until Chart 10-5, which introduces passive progressives, and Chart 10-6, which introduces passive modals other than *will.* In the initial stages of the chapter, examples that you make up for the class should contain only the four tenses in this chart.

☐ EXERCISE 1, p. 277. Active vs. passive. (Charts 10-1 and 10-2)

Students have to transform not only verb forms but also pronouns. In addition, they need to pay attention to subject–verb agreement.

ANSWERS:

1. a. I am helped
   b. Jane is helped
   c. We are helped

2. a. I was helped
   b. They were helped

3. a. Joe has been helped
   b. We have been helped

4. a. I will be helped
   b. Tim is going to be helped

☐ EXERCISE 2, p. 278. Form of the passive. (Charts 10-1 and 10-2)

This exercise emphasizes that every passive verb has a form of *be,* and it is *be* that expresses tense and number. The main verb is always in the past participle form.

ANSWERS:

2. are employed
3. has been hired
4. are going to be faxed
5. was bought
6. will be done
7. were washed

☐ EXERCISE 3, p. 278. Active vs. passive. (Charts 10-1 and 10-2)

Tell the students not to change the tense. The emphasis here is still on basic form and meaning of the passive. The text teaches the meaning of the passive by showing the relationship to the active. The situations in which the passive is typically used are not addressed until Chart 10-4.

This exercise contains some words that may be new to your students *(phonograph, leaky, faucet, plumber, fascinate, helicopter, amaze)*. Discuss their meanings in the context provided by the sentences. Draw a picture of a leaky faucet on the board.

ANSWERS: **2.** The phonograph was invented by Thomas Edison. **3.** An island is surrounded by water. **4.** The leaky faucet is going to be fixed by a plumber. **5.** The sick child was examined by a doctor. **6.** Spanish is spoken by a large number of people. **7.** Children are fascinated by helicopters. **8.** *Hamlet* was written by Shakespeare. **9.** You will be amazed by this news.

☐ EXERCISE 4, p. 279. Active vs. passive: question forms. (Charts 10-1 and 10-2)

This exercise deals with the negative and question forms of the passive. It may help to write both the active and passive forms on the chalkboard and show their relationship. Sometimes, making changes such as *didn't surprise* to *wasn't surprised* confuses students until they review what they already know about the form of the negative in the active simple past and the use of *be* in questions and negatives. You should go through this exercise slowly, carefully explaining that the question and negative forms of *be* underlie the question and negative forms in the passive.

ANSWERS:

2. (a) Erin is surprised
   (b) Are you surprised

3. (a) Steve will be shocked
   (b) Will Pat be shocked

4. (a) The petition was signed
   (b) Was it signed

5. (a) The petition has been signed
   (b) Has it been signed

6. (a) It is going to be signed
   (b) Is it going to be signed

☐ EXERCISE 5, p. 279. Active vs. passive. (Charts 10-1 and 10-2)

This exercise asks the students to practice what they learned in Exercise 4 about forming questions and negatives in the passive.

ANSWERS: **2.** Was the bird killed by a cat? **3.** The bird wasn't killed by my cat. **4.** Is French spoken by a large number of people? **5.** Is the window going to be fixed by the janitor? **6.** Will our hotel room be cleaned by a maid? **7.** Are clean towels provided by the hotel? **8.** Sometimes I am frustrated by my inability to understand spoken English.

☐ EXERCISE 6, p. 280. Active vs. passive. (Charts 10-1 and 10-2)

Practice in changing passive to active clarifies the meaning of passive sentences.

ANSWERS: **2.** A customs officer inspected my suitcase. **3.** All children need love and understanding. **4.** Did your parents teach you to read? **5.** My parents taught me to read. **6.** Is your cousin going to meet us at the train station? **7.** Has the architect already drawn the plans for the new hospital? **8.** A dog chased the bear up a tree.

10-3: TRANSITIVE AND INTRANSITIVE VERBS

• Not infrequently, learners try to use intransitive verbs in a passive form. Examples of common errors: *I am agreed with you. He was died five years ago. An interesting event was happened to me when I was a child.* The intention of this short unit is to explain why some verbs cannot be used in the passive.

• Point out that information about whether a verb is transitive or intransitive can be found in a dictionary. Some common abbreviations are **v.t.** and **v.i.**, or **T** and **I**, or **V** and **V+O**. Perhaps you can help your students find this information in their dictionaries.

• To help the students understand the grammar terminology, relate the word *transitive* to other words with *trans- (transportation, translate, transfer, transform),* explaining that *trans-* means "across" or "carrying over to the other side." A transitive verb "connects or bridges" the subject and object; it "carries the meaning across" from the subject to the object. By contrast, an intransitive verb does not connect to an object. An adverbial usually completes a clause with an intransitive verb by giving information about place, time, or manner. Point out that the prefix *in-* is negative *(intransitive = not transitive),* as in words like *inactive, inexpensive, incapable.*

• Some verbs have both transitive and intransitive uses. Examples:

Everyone ***eats*** (v.i.) *and* ***sleeps*** (v.i.) *every day.* vs. *I* ***eat*** (v.t.) *breakfast every day. Flowers* ***grow*** (v.i.) *in every country in the world.* vs. *My mother* ***grows*** (v.t.) *flowers in her garden.*

☐ EXERCISE 7, p. 281. Transitive vs. intransitive verbs. (Chart 10-3)

As a way of aiding identification of transitive vs. intransitive verbs, ask the students to look for objects (i.e., direct objects) of the verbs. Make clear that if there is no object, the verb is intransitive.

ANSWERS:

3. stayed = v.i. *(no change)*
4. fell = v.i. *(no change)*
5. slept = v.i. *(no change)*
6. happened = v.i. *(no change)*

7. saw = v.t. → The accident was seen by many people.
8. existed = v.i. *(no change)*
9. agree = v.i. *(no change)*
10. die = v.i. *(no change)*
11. doesn't occur = v.i. *(no change)*
12. will discover = v.t. → A cure for AIDS will be discovered
13. appeared = v.i. *(no change)*
14. Did . . . invent = v.t. → Was gunpowder invented by the Koreans?
15. kissed = v.t. → A frog was kissed by a princess.

10-4: USING THE *BY*-PHRASE

- It is frequently not necessary or not possible to identify the exact performers (agents) of an action. In this situation, the passive is a very useful structure. The students should understand that usually the passive occurs without a stated *by*-phrase.

- It is beyond the scope of this text to deal with the various rhetorical or stylistic reasons for using the passive with a *by*-phrase.* The focus remains on a basic introduction to the form and meaning of the passive, with the goal being the ability to use the passive in typical situations (e.g., *Spanish is spoken in Mexico.* OR *Tom and Ann are married.)* and comprehend its meaning in written passages.

☐ EXERCISE 8, p. 282. The BY-phrase. (Chart 10-4)

The point of this exercise is to illustrate that usually a *by*-phrase is unnecessary.

ANSWERS: **3.** Rice is grown in India. **4.** Is Spanish spoken in Peru? **5.** The telephone was invented by Alexander Graham Bell. **6.** When was the first computer invented? **7.** Hammers are sold at a hardware store. They are used to pound nails. **8.** My name will be listed in the new telephone directory. **9.** *The Origin of Species* was written by Charles Darwin. **10.** *The Origin of Species* was published in 1859. **11.** Have you ever been hypnotized? **12.** The name of this street has been changed from Bay Avenue to Martin Luther King Way.

☐ EXERCISE 9, p. 283. The BY-phrase. (Chart 10-4)

This exercise can be discussed in small groups.

ANSWERS:

3. was built [The passive is used because it is unknown and unimportant to know exactly who built our classroom building.]
4. is grown [The passive is used because it is unknown and unimportant to know exactly who grows coffee in Brazil.]
5. were grown [The *by*-phrase is used because it is important to identify who grew the tomatoes. The passive keeps the focus on the tomatoes, while the *by*-phrase identifies the grower. The active could also be used: *My uncle grew these tomatoes . . . .*]

---

*For example, sometimes the passive (with a *by*-phrase) is used as a connective device between sentences, often allowing a pronoun to be near its antecedent: *He showed me* ***a beautiful wooden chest****.* ***It*** *had been made by his grandfather at least seventy-five years ago.* In another instance, the passive might be used when the writer/speaker is seeking to distinguish between two similar items, allowing the focus to be placed on the items in question by mentioning them first: *Look at these two pictures. Aren't they wonderful?* ***This picture*** *was drawn by Susie.* ***That one*** *was drawn by Michael.*

6. **was delayed** [What or who delayed the flight is not specifically known, so the passive is used.]
7. **have . . . been sold** [It's not known or not important to know exactly who sold the tickets, so the passive is used.]
8. **has . . . been ruled** [The *by*-phrase is used because it supplies important information. The active could also be used: *A foreign power has never ruled Thailand.* By using the passive, the focus stays on Thailand.]
9. **was invented** [It is not known who invented the wheel. This sentence is a clear example of why and how the passive is useful.]
10. **was invented** [The *by*-phrase is included because the name of the inventor is important information. The active could also be used: *Johannes Gutenberg invented it . . .*] . . . **were copied** [This is a little tricky—*by hand* is not a *by*-phrase that conveys the doer of an action in a passive sentence; it is an idiomatic prepositional phrase with *by (by hand, by machine)* that expresses how something is done. The understood *by*-phrase is *by people.* The equivalent active sentence would not be *Hand copied books,* but rather *People copied books by hand.* This item is included in the text in order to challenge better students.] [You might ask your students if they can imagine a world without books so that they can contemplate the significance of the invention of the printing press.]

☐ EXERCISE 10, p. 284. Active vs. passive. (Charts 10-1 → 10-4)

Some learners may have difficulty accepting some of the correct answers because their native languages allow more verbs to be passivized. Discuss the problem items.

ANSWERS: **2.** is read **3.** was interrupted **4.** belongs **5.** is delivered **6.** is not pronounced **7.** happened **8.** arrived . . . was met **9.** heard . . . was surprised . . . was shocked **10.** will be built / is going to be built **11.** wrote . . . was written **12.** was discovered **13.** was kicked . . . attended **14.** am confused **15.** have been accepted **16.** agree . . . prefer **17.** was your bike stolen **18.** Have you paid . . . will be / is going to be shut off **19.** happened . . . was hit . . . Was the bicyclist injured . . . called . . . was taken . . . (was) treated . . . happened . . . was arrested . . . wasn't killed **20.** is . . . is visited . . . was designed . . . was erected . . . has been . . . is recognized

☐ EXERCISE 11, p. 286. Active vs. passive. (Charts 10-1 → 10-4)

ANSWERS:

2. was established
3. established
4. were established
5. were disgusted
6. were replaced
7. were studied
8. (were) kept
9. became
10. understood
11. have been trying / have tried
12. was reduced
13. were killed
14. died
15. is
16. were
17. were saved *(also possible:* have been saved)
18. will become
19. believe
20. are put
21. are watched
22. are fed
23. have
24. is prepared
25. is designed
26. are fed
27. are fed
28. are treated

10-5: THE PASSIVE FORMS OF THE PRESENT AND PAST PROGRESSIVE

• The text intends only a brief introduction to these forms. Passive progressives are relatively infrequent. The goal is simply recognition of these forms and their meanings.

☐ EXERCISE 12, p. 288. Passive forms. (Chart 10-5)

ANSWERS:

2. is being built
3. is being built
4. was being painted
5. is being organized
6. are being petted
7. were being grown
8. are being lost

10-6: PASSIVE MODAL AUXILIARIES

• Emphasize again that every passive has a form of *be* as the auxiliary to the main verb.

• This text does not present the past forms of modals, so past forms in the passive are not found here either (e.g., *should have been mailed).* Instead, see *Understanding and Using English Grammar, Third Edition,* for past modal auxiliaries.

☐ EXERCISE 13, p. 289. Passive modals. (Chart 10-6)

ANSWERS:

2. should be planted
3. can't be controlled
4. had to be fixed
5. can be reached
6. can be found
7. ought to be washed
8. may be cooked . . . eaten
9. could be destroyed
10. must be kept
11. shouldn't be pronounced
12. can be worn

☐ EXERCISE 14, p. 290. Active vs. passive. (Charts 10-1 → 10-6)

ANSWERS:

2. disappeared
3. died
4. survived
5. were domesticated
6. were used
7. were used
8. became
9. were reintroduced
10. came
11. returned
12. left
13. developed
14. began
15. were captured
16. (were) tamed
17. were hunted
18. (were) killed
19. are protected
20. cannot be killed
21. Should wild horses be protected

☐ EXERCISE 15, p. 291. Active vs. passive. (Charts 10-1 → 10-6)

The focus of this exercise is on analyzing when the passive is or is not used and why. In general, the passive is used when there is no need or way to identify the actual performers of an action. In English rhetoric, the passive is used in preference to active sentences with subjects like *someone, people, you* (used as an impersonal pronoun meaning "anyone in general"), or *cheesemakers* (i.e., nonspecific people who make cheese).

Paragraphs one, two, and three discuss cheese and cheesemaking in general. These generalizations about what people in general do or can do and the technical descriptions of the cheesemaking process are typical situations in which the passive is used.

Paragraph four changes the approach to the topic from the general to the specific. The fourth paragraph, beginning with sentence (18), is made specific by the inclusion of a first-person narrator *("I")*. It is important for the writer to identify the performer of the actions as herself through the use of "*I*," so the passive is not used. In sentence (18), the information expressed by the pronoun "*I*" is important, so the actor is identified and the active is used.

ANSWERS: **(3)** Today it is eaten in almost all the countries of the world. **(4)** It can be eaten alone, or it may be eaten with bread. **(5)** It can be melted and added to noodles or vegetables. **(6)** It can be used as part of a main course or as a snack. **(7)** *(no change)* **(8)** *(no change)* **(9)** Most cheese is made from cow's milk, but it can be made from **(10)** . . . but other kinds can be found only in small geographical areas. **(11)** Cheese is produced in factories. **(12)** The milk has to be treated in special ways. **(13)** It must be heated **(14)** At the end, salt is added, and it is packed into molds. **(15)** Most cheese is aged for weeks **(16)** Cheese is usually sold to stores **(17)** These big rounds of cheese can be seen **(18)–(24)** *(no change)*

10-7: USING PAST PARTICIPLES AS ADJECTIVES (STATIVE PASSIVE)

• The stative passive is common in English. The text intends for the listed expressions to become familiar enough that the students begin to use them comfortably and correctly. Time needs to be spent discussing vocabulary and creating examples.

• The use of incorrect forms is a common problem with this structure. Typical mistakes include wrong form of the past participle and omission of *be*.

INCORRECT: *We were very frighten.*
INCORRECT: *My briefcase made of leather.*

Another common problem is misuse of prepositions.

INCORRECT: *Tom is married with Alice.*

See Chart 10-8 for a discussion of the problem of confusing present and past participles used as adjectives, e.g. *interesting* vs. *interested.*

• Stative = describing a state or status of existence. (The stative passive has also been termed the "finished-result passive.") In the stative passive, usually any action took place earlier than the situation which is being described. For example, *I am acquainted with Tom* means we became acquainted at an earlier time. *My watch is broken* means something happened to my watch earlier. *They are married* means that they married earlier.

• *Stative* is pronounced with a long *a,* as in *state + ive:* /steytiv/.

☐ EXERCISE 16, p. 293. Stative passive. (Chart 10-7)

ANSWERS:

2. is interested in
3. are disappointed in
4. is pleased with
5. am satisfied with
6. is married to
7. is related to
8. are done with

☐ EXERCISE 17, p. 293. Stative passive. (Chart 10-7)

ANSWERS:

2. is made
3. is crowded
4. is located
5. am exhausted
6. am lost
7. is broken
8. are related
9. is scared
10. is (not) satisfied
11. are disappointed
12. Are (you) acquainted
13. am (not) qualified
14. is spoiled
15. is composed

☐ EXERCISE 18, p. 294. Stative passive. (Chart 10-7)

Prepositions are always hard for students—such little words that cause so much trouble!
Review this exercise orally to give the students extra practice. For example:

TEACHER: If a store is full of shoppers, we say that it is crowded . . .
SPEAKER: with shoppers.
TEACHER: If Ali has good qualifications for a job, we say he is qualified . . .
SPEAKER: for the job.

ANSWERS:

2. for
3. to
4. of
5. to
6. for
7. with
8. about
9. to
10. with
11. about
12. of
13. to
14. in
15. with
16. with
17. in
18. with
19. to
20. of
21. with

☐ EXERCISE 19, p. 295. Stative passive. (Chart 10-7)

ANSWERS:

1. in
2. to
3. of
4. to
5. in/with
6. for
7. with
8. for
9. with
10. to
11. of
12. about
13. to *(also possible:* in)
14. from
15. of/from
16. with
17. with
18. in

☐ EXERCISE 20, p. 296. Stative passive. (Chart 10-7)

Learners must remember to indicate tenses and singular/plural agreement in the form of *be* they use.

ANSWERS:

3. are divorced
4. Are (you) related to
5. is spoiled
6. was exhausted
7. was involved in
8. is located in
9. is drunk
10. am interested in
11. is devoted to
12. Are . . . lost
13. were terrified
14. Are (you) acquainted with
15. was (not) qualified for
16. am disappointed in/with
17. am done with
18. is crowded
19. Are . . . shut
20. is gone

10-8: PARTICIPIAL ADJECTIVES: *-ED* vs. *-ING*

• The present participle conveys an active meaning. The past participle conveys a passive meaning. The text seeks to make the distinction clear by saying that the past participle describes a feeling that was caused by something, and that the present participle describes the cause of the feeling. The author has not yet found an easy way to explain the difference in meaning between these two forms. It is hoped that the exercises serve to clarify this grammar. [Perhaps refer to the explanation of transitive ("transfer" of action) given for Chart 10-3.]

• In (b) and (d), the form may look like a progressive verb tense, but it is not. Perhaps you could explain that these sentences consist of the main verb *be* followed by an adjective (that happens to be a present participle). In other words, *is interesting* and *was surprising* are not the present and past progressive tenses, respectively; they are ***be*** + *adjective,* like *is good* or *was happy.*

• Some grammars analyze some *-ing* adjectives as gerunds rather than present participles:

(a) *a chair that is rocking* = *a rocking chair,* in which *rocking* is a present participle
(b) *a chair that is designed for rocking* = *a rocking chair,* in which *rocking* is a gerund, used as a noun adjunct

This text designates all *-ing* adjectives as participial.

☐ EXERCISE 21, p. 297. Participial adjectives. (Chart 10-8)

These contrasting participles are always difficult for learners to understand and control. Take time to discuss any misunderstood items in this exercise.

ANSWERS:

2. a. excited
b. exciting
3. a. fascinated
b. fascinating
4. a. depressed
b. depressing
5. a. interested
b. interesting
6. a. shocking
b. shocked
7. a. confused
b. confusing
8. a. embarrassed
b. embarrassing
9. a. boring
b. bored
10. a. surprising
b. surprised
11. a. frightening
b. frightened

☐ EXERCISE 22, p. 299. Participial adjectives. (Chart 10-8)

ANSWERS:

3. shocked
4. shocking
5. surprised
6. surprising
7. depressed
8. depressing
9. interesting
10. interested

☐ EXERCISE 23, p. 300. Participial adjectives. (Charts 10-7 and 10-8)

The text has chosen examples for this exercise that will help communicate the idea that *-ing* participial adjectives convey an active meaning, while *-ed* participial adjectives convey a passive meaning. You might transform the items with past participles into equivalent passive sentences. For example, in item 1, spoiled children are children who are spoiled by their parents. In item 2, a stolen car is a car that was stolen by someone.

ANSWERS:

3.	stolen car	**9.**	planning committee
4.	crowded room	**10.**	boiling water
5.	rising costs	**11.**	missing person
6.	existing danger	**12.**	frozen vegetables
7.	dried fruit	**13.**	freezing weather
8.	planned event	**14.**	broken pencil

10-9: *GET* + ADJECTIVE; *GET* + PAST PARTICIPLE

- *Get* expresses the idea of *become* when it is followed by an adjective or past participle.
- The passive with *get* is common, especially in spoken English. It is a somewhat informal structure, although it is sometimes found in formal writing.
- The text intends for the students to become familiar enough with the listed expressions to use them easily in creative production. These expressions can be quite useful.

☐ EXERCISE 24, p. 301. GET + adjective/past participle. (Chart 10-9)

ANSWERS:

2.	hot	**7.**	busy	**12.**	hurt
3.	full	**8.**	lost	**13.**	angry
4.	sleepy	**9.**	dirty	**14.**	dizzy
5.	tired	**10.**	rich	**15.**	sick
6.	dressed	**11.**	bald	**16.**	drunk

☐ EXERCISE 25, p. 302. GET + adjective/past participle. (Chart 10-9)

This is a review exercise on verb forms as well as on stative *get.* The verb forms the students need to choose from are *get, gets, getting,* and *got.*

ANSWERS:

2.	get well	**7.**	getting tired	**12.**	get lost
3.	get married	**8.**	getting worried	**13.**	get excited
4.	gets hungry	**9.**	gets thirsty	**14.**	get crowded
5.	gets dark	**10.**	got killed	**15.**	got hungry
6.	get dry	**11.**	getting cold	**16.**	get involved

10-10: USING *BE USED / ACCUSTOMED TO* AND *GET USED / ACCUSTOMED TO*

- The structures in this chart are common and useful, but learners frequently have some difficulty with them. Common errors: *I'm use to living here. I'm used to live here.* Also, *accustomed* is often misspelled as *acustomed, acustommed,* or *accustommed.*
- In British English, *to* may be considered part of an infinitive phrase in the expression *be accustomed to,* allowing the simple form of a verb to follow: *I'm accustomed to* ***live*** *in a warm climate.* In American English, *to* is considered a preposition, requiring that a gerund follow: *I'm accustomed to* ***living*** *in a warm climate.*

☐ EXERCISE 26, p. 303. BE USED/ACCUSTOMED TO. (Chart 10-10)

ANSWERS: **2.** is used to **3.** am not used to . . . am used to **4.** are used to **5.** is accustomed to . . . isn't accustomed to **6.** am accustomed to . . . am not accustomed to **7.** are accustomed to **8.** are not accustomed to

☐ EXERCISE 27, p. 304. BE USED/ACCUSTOMED TO. (Chart 10-10)

Encourage the students to contrast their former habits (perhaps in their home countries) with their present way of doing things. The students should not think that *I am used to* is the same as *I usually.*

☐ EXERCISE 28, p. 304. BE USED/ACCUSTOMED TO. (Chart 10-10)

Encourage the questioners to pursue this as a natural conversation in which they are genuinely curious about their partner's answers.

☐ EXERCISE 29, p. 305. GET USED/ACCUSTOMED TO. (Chart 10-10)

SAMPLE RESPONSES: **1.** He had to get used to having a full-time job, to being married, to not going to school, etc. **2.** She's going to have to get used to paying all her own bills, to living in an apartment with other people, to being responsible for herself, etc. **3.** I wasn't used to the weather and the food. I got used to the weather, but I never got used to the food. **4.** I wasn't used to working in a small cubicle under fluorescent lights. I wasn't used to being at work at seven o'clock. I got used to the cubicle after a while.

10-11: ***USED TO*** **vs.** ***BE USED TO***
• *Used to* and *be used to* are often confusing for students. This chart seeks to clarify their differences in form and meaning.

☐ EXERCISE 30, p. 305. USED TO vs. BE USED TO. (Chart 10-11)

ANSWERS: **3.** am **4.** Ø **5.** Ø **6.** are **7.** is **8.** Ø

☐ EXERCISE 31, p. 306. USED TO vs. BE USED TO. (Chart 10-11)

ANSWERS:
3. used to eat
4. is used to growing
5. is used to eating
6. used to have
7. am used to taking
8. used to go

☐ EXERCISE 32, p. 306. USED TO vs. BE USED TO. (Charts 2-9 and 10-11)

Encourage students to write about their actual experiences.

10-12: USING *BE SUPPOSED TO*

- *Be supposed to* is included in this chapter because its form is passive. In meaning, it is related to the modals *should/ought to.* (See Chart 9-9 in *Understanding and Using English Grammar, Third Edition,* for a comparison of the meanings of *should* and *be supposed to.)* This text emphasizes that the idea of expectation is included in the meaning of *be supposed to:* it communicates the idea that somebody expects something.

☐ EXERCISES 33 → 36, pp. 307–308. BE SUPPOSED TO. (Chart 10-12)

EX. 33 ANSWERS: **2.** The weather is supposed to be cold tomorrow **3.** The plane is supposed to arrive at 6:00 **4.** I am supposed to work late tonight **5.** The mail was supposed to arrive

EX. 34 ANSWERS: **2.** We're not **supposed** to tell **3.** You **aren't** supposed to talk **4.** My friend was **supposed** to call **5.** Children **are** supposed to respect **6.** **Weren't** you supposed **to** be

EX. 35 ANSWERS: **2.** Ann is supposed to call Mary at nine. **3.** Johnny is supposed to make his bed **4.** Susie is supposed to put her dirty clothes **5.** Bobby is supposed to pick up his toys . . . . Annie is supposed to hang up her coat. **6.** The patient is supposed to take one pill every eight hours and drink plenty of fluids. **7.** The students are supposed to read the directions carefully and raise their hand(s)

EX. 36 ANSWERS: **2.** Doctors are supposed to care for their patients. **3.** Employees are supposed to be on time for work. **4.** Air passengers are supposed to buckle their seatbelts before takeoff. **5.** Theatergoers are not supposed to talk during a performance. **6.** Soldiers on sentry duty are not supposed to fall asleep. **7.** Children are supposed to listen to their parents. **8.** Heads of state are supposed to be diplomatic. **9.** A dog is supposed to obey its trainer. **10.** People who live in apartments are supposed to pay their rent on time.

☐ EXERCISE 38, p. 309. Written. (Chapters 1 → 10)

This is a general topic that should, with any luck, produce some appropriately used passive sentences. You may want the students to underline their passive sentences. Alternatively, students could exchange papers and identify each other's passive sentences.

☐ EXERCISE 39, p. 309. Error analysis. (Chapter 10)

ANSWERS: **1.** An accident ~~was~~ happened at the corner yesterday. **2.** This pen ~~is~~ **belongs** to me. **3.** I am very **surprised** by the news. **4.** I'm **interested** in that subject. **5.** He is **married to** my cousin. **6.** Thailand is **located** in Southeast Asia. **7.** Mary's dog ~~was~~ died last week. **8.** Were you **surprised** when you saw him? **9.** When I went (go) downtown, I **got** (get) lost. **10.** Last night I **was** very **tired**. **11.** The bus ~~was~~ arrived ten minutes late. **12.** I ~~am~~ disagree(d) with that statement. **13.** Our class is **composed of** immigrants. **14.** I am not **accustomed** to cold weather. **15.** We're not **supposed** to have pets in our apartment.

Chapter 11: COUNT/NONCOUNT NOUNS AND ARTICLES

ORDER OF CHAPTER	CHARTS	EXERCISES	WORKBOOK
A vs. *an*	11-1	Ex. 1 → 3	Pr. 1
Preview			Pr. 2
Count and noncount nouns	11-2 → 11-4	Ex. 4 → 10	Pr. 3 → 6
Several, a lot of, many/much, a few, a little	11-5	Ex. 11 → 14	Pr. 7 → 11
Nouns that can be count or noncount	11-6	Ex. 15	Pr. 12
Units of measure with noncount nouns	11-7	Ex. 16 → 17	Pr. 13 → 15
Article usage	11-8	Ex. 18 → 23	Pr. 16 → 22
Summary review: articles		Ex. 24	Pr. 22
Using *the* or Ø with nouns	11-9	Ex. 25 → 26	Pr. 23 → 24
Capitalization	11-10	Ex. 27 → 28	Pr. 25 → 26
Cumulative review		Ex. 29	Pr. 27

General Notes on Chapter 11

• The concept of count vs. noncount nouns is often quite difficult for students to understand. Some students find it illogical. Many find it a confusing nuisance. Nevertheless, just as students need to gain understanding and usage ability of verb forms, they need to understand and be able to use noun forms if they want to communicate competently and correctly in English.

• In addition, article usage in English cannot make sense unless the students understand the distinction between count and noncount nouns. In many ways, the first half of the chapter seeks to lay the groundwork for the presentation of the bare-bones basics of article use in Chart 11-8.

• TERMINOLOGY: "Count" and "noncount" may also appear in some texts as "countable" and "uncountable." A noncount noun is sometimes called a "mass" noun.

☐ EXERCISE 1, p. 311. Preview: using A and AN. (Charts 11-1 and 11-2)

This previews not only ***a*** and ***an*** but count and noncount nouns.

ANSWERS: **4.** Jack has **a** wallet in his back pocket. **5.** *(no change)* **6.** There was **an** earthquake in Turkey last week. **7. A** ball is **a** round object. **8.** *(no change)* **9.** Anna is wearing **a** ring on her fourth finger. **10.** *(no change)* **11.** Simon Bolivar is **a** hero to many people. **12.** . . . It was **an** honest mistake. **13.** I had **an** unusual experience yesterday. **14.** Ann had **a** unique experience yesterday. **15.** *(no change)*

CHART 11-1: *A* vs. *AN*
• Discuss the pronunciation of ***a*** and ***an***. When unstressed, they are pronounced as weak vowel sounds: /ə/ and /ə+n/. Only when they are emphasized are they pronounced /ey/ and /æn/.

☐ EXERCISE 2, p. 312. A vs. AN. (Chart 11-1)

ANSWERS:

2. an	**8.** a	**14.** a
3. a	**9.** an	**15.** a
4. an	**10.** an	**16.** a
5. an	**11.** a	**17.** an
6. a	**12.** an	**18.** an
7. a	**13.** an	

☐ EXERCISE 3, p. 312. A vs. AN. (Chart 11-1)

Students needn't produce dictionary-quality definitions. Students find their own creative ways of giving meanings. Keep the emphasis on article usage.

POSSIBLE DEFINITIONS:

1. **An astronaut** is a person who travels in outer space.
2. **A microscope** is an instrument that magnifies very small things.
3. **An enemy** is a person you fight against.
4. **A ferry** is a boat that carries people between short distances.
5. **An absent-minded person** is someone who is very forgetful.
6. **A camel** is a large animal that lives in desert regions and carries people and things.
7. **An umbrella** is something that people carry to protect themselves from rain.
8. **A unicorn** is a mythical animal with one horn.
9. **An onion** is a root vegetable.
10. **A honeymoon trip** is a trip newly married couples take.
11. **An hourly wage** is the amount of money a worker earns per hour.
12. **A horn** is something that grows on the heads of goats or cows.
    A horn is also a musical instrument.
13. **An unlit hallway** is a passageway without lights.
14. **A utensil** is a tool you use in the kitchen or the house.
15. **An orchard** is a field where fruit trees grow.

CHART 11-2: COUNT AND NONCOUNT NOUNS

• To make the initial distinction between count and noncount, concentrate on the examples in Chart 11-2 *(chair* vs. *furniture)* and in Exercise 5 *(banana* vs. *fruit; letter* vs. *mail;* and *question* vs. *information)*. Point out which ones can take a final *-s* and which "count or amount" words (i.e., quantifiers or expressions of quantity) can be used. Try to get across the concept that noncount nouns represent "masses" or "whole categories." (See Chart 11-3.)

• Typical mistakes involve using final *-s* at the end of noncount nouns and using improper expressions of quantity (e.g., *too many homeworks)*.

• Most nouns are used as count nouns. Some nouns are used only as noncount nouns. Many nouns have both count and noncount uses (see Chart 11-6). *Fruit* is an example of a noun that can be used as either, but for pedagogical purposes it is presented as a noncount noun throughout this chapter. (When some nouns that are used predominantly or typically as noncount are used as count nouns, they may refer to "different kinds of." For example: *Apples, bananas,* and *pears* are fruits, not vegetables. Other examples would be different kinds of *breads, foods, teas, soups, world Englishes.)* It is the text's view that students at this level of language study would find these subtleties confusing and disruptive rather than beneficial.

• A good ESL/EFL dictionary will indicate a noun's count and/or noncount status and usages.

☐ EXERCISE 4, p. 313. Count and noncount nouns. (Chart 11-2)

The purpose of Exercises 4 and 5 is to clarify Chart 11-2 by comparing "individual parts" to "wholes." At the same time, the students are focusing on the troublesome final *-s/-es.*

Usual problems in the usage of nouns are that the learners don't use final *-s/-es* with count nouns when they should and do use it with noncount nouns when they shouldn't. Tell your students you sympathize with them. It's not easy.

ANSWERS:

3. *(no change)*
4. four chairs / some furniture
5. *(no change)*
6. some furniture / a chair
7. a chair / some chairs / some furniture
8. some furniture

☐ EXERCISE 5, p. 314. Preview: count and noncount nouns. (Charts 11-2 and 11-3)

First the students learn which nouns are count and which are noncount. Once this information is known, they then (in the following exercises) decide which expressions of quantity they can use with these nouns. The purpose of these exercises is to clarify the use of indefinite articles, final *-s/-es,* and expressions of quantity used with two different kinds of nouns.

ANSWERS:

3. a *(count)*
4. some *(noncount)*
5. a *(count)*
6. some *(noncount)*
7. some *(noncount)*
8. an *(count)*
9. some *(noncount)*
10. a *(count)*

CHART 11-3: NONCOUNT NOUNS

• It is important for students to understand the concept of a noncount noun. That is the purpose of this chart. Discuss the concept in relation to some of the words listed at the bottom of this page, all of which are "wholes."

• In addition to understanding the concept of a noncount noun, it helps if students simply become aware of some of the common nouns that are usually noncount. That is the purpose of the lists at the bottom of this chart and in the subsequent chart (11-4).

• It is strongly suggested that you wait until Chart 11-5 to discuss possible count usages of any of the words in this chart (e.g., ***works*** *of art, the* ***literatures*** *of France and England, green* ***peppers,*** *the* ***sands*** *of time)*. Chart 11-5 deals briefly with that type of usage in a way appropriate to the students' level.

☐ EXERCISE 6, p. 315. Count and noncount nouns. (Charts 11-2 and 11-3)

The troublesome final *-s/-es* is revisited. You might want to use this practice in class discussion to review pronunciation of final *-s/-es.* (See Chapter 6, Chart 6-1, p. 157, for information about pronunciation.) Omission of final *-s/-es* in speech and writing, even when the students understand the grammar thoroughly, may often be due to the fact that the learners don't hear it clearly. Extra work on production of *-s/-es* can help reinforce habits of correct usage.

ANSWERS:

3. traffic **/**
4. automobiles
5. scenery **/**
6. mountains
7. information **/**
8. facts
9. words
10. vocabulary **/**
11. songs
12. music **/**
13. suggestions
14. advice **/**
15. literature **/**
16. novels
17. sand **/**
18. beaches

CHART 11-4: MORE NONCOUNT NOUNS

• This chart provides information for the students to use if and as they can; this information will have varying degrees of usefulness. The students do not need to memorize these noncount nouns, but the information can be quite useful for learners who already know and use many of these words. Students to whom much of the vocabulary is new may not benefit a great deal immediately in terms of appropriate use of noncount nouns in their own speech and writing. For them, it can serve principally as a reference when they attempt these exercises and the *Workbook* practices.

☐ EXERCISE 7, p. 316. Count and noncount nouns. (Charts 11-2 → 11-4)

ANSWERS: **3.** weather **/** **4.** storms **5.** is . . . chalk **/** **6.** wishes **7.** luck **/** **8.** Thunder **/** . . . lightning **/** **9.** Gold **/** . . . is . . . Diamonds . . . are **10.** knowledge **/** **11.** ideas . . . opinions **12.** patience **/** **13.** patients **14.** progress **/** **15.** pollution **/** **16.** bridges . . . rivers . . . bodies . . . water **/**

☐ EXERCISE 8, p. 316. Noncount abstractions. (Chart 11-4)

This practice presents a few common sayings in English that the students might find interesting. These sayings illustrate the use of abstractions as noncount nouns. There is no reason to expect the students to know the proper completions; they may not have encountered these expressions before. Tell your students just to guess if they have never heard them. Use the practice as a springboard for a discussion of the students' interpretations of and reactions to these sayings. Do they have similar sayings in their languages?

ANSWERS: **2.** G **3.** F **4.** B **5.** E **6.** C **7.** A

☐ EXERCISE 9, p. 317. Noncount abstractions. (Chart 11-4)

The purpose here is for the students to reach for nouns that are abstractions. Most of the noncount nouns given in the answers below can be found in the list in Chart 11-4. Suggest that the students consult this chart.

SAMPLE ANSWERS:

a. 1. patience
2. honesty
3. courage
4. reliability
5. compassion
6. gentleness

b. 1. greed
2. ignorance
3. jealousy
4. dishonesty
5. laziness
6. cowardice

c. 1. good health
2. peace
3. prosperity
4. literacy
5. justice
6. freedom
7. progress

d. 1. hunger
2. poverty
3. disease
4. homelessness
5. violence

☐ EXERCISE 10, p. 317. Count and noncount nouns. (Charts 11-1 → 11-4)

This exercise is intended to elicit nouns and quantifiers. Tell the students to complete the sentence "I see . . . ." when making their lists.

CHART 11-5: USING *SEVERAL, A LOT OF, MANY/MUCH,* AND *A FEW/A LITTLE*

- Using the classroom as your context, ask the students how many desks is "several desks." How many desks is "a lot of desks"?
- You might mention that *a lot of* occurs principally in informal English. You might also mention that *lots of* is the even more informal equivalent of *a lot of.*

☐ EXERCISE 11, p. 318. SEVERAL, A LOT OF, and MANY/MUCH. (Charts 11-1 → 11-5)

The sentence with the spelling error is number 11. Spelling "a lot" as one word is a common error.

ANSWERS: **3.–5.** *(no change)* **6.** too **many** chairs **7.** a **little** furniture **8.** *(no change)* **9.** **some** new furniture~~s~~ **10.** *(no change)* **11.** are **a lot** *(spelled as two words)* of **desks** **12.** **is** a lot of furniture~~s~~

☐ EXERCISE 12, p. 319. HOW MANY and HOW MUCH. (Charts 11-1 → 11-5)

ANSWERS: **3.** many players are there **4.** much homework do you have **5.** many apples are there **6.** much fruit is there **7.** many provinces are there **8.** much Japanese did you know **9.** many kinds of fish are there **10.** much cheese should I buy **11.** much coffee / many cups of coffee do you drink **12.** much chalk is there / many pieces of chalk are there

☐ EXERCISE 13, p. 320. MANY vs. MUCH. (Charts 11-1 → 11-5)

EXPECTED QUESTIONS: **1.** How much tea do you usually drink every day? **2.** How many words are there . . . ? **3.** How much (money) does a pencil cost? **4.** How many bones are there . . . ? **5.** How many teeth does the average person have? **6.** How much mail did you get yesterday? **7.** How much sugar do you put in your tea? **8.** How many languages can you speak? **9.** How much English had you studied . . . ? **10.** How many people were there . . . ? **11.** How many human beings are there . . . . ? **12.** How many butterflies can you see . . . ?

☐ EXERCISE 14, p. 320. A FEW vs. A LITTLE. (Charts 11-1 → 11-5)

NOTE: This text does not deal with the difference between *a few* vs. *few* or *a little* vs. *little*. See Chart 7-10 in *Understanding and Using English Grammar, Third Edition.*

ANSWERS:

3. a little help
4. a little pepper
5. a few things
6. a few apples
7. a little fruit
8. a little advice
9. a little more money
10. a few coins
11. A few friends
12. a little rain
13. a little French
14. a few more hours
15. a little toothpaste
16. a little more chicken
17. a few chickens

CHART 11-6: NOUNS THAT CAN BE COUNT OR NONCOUNT

• The nouns presented here are but a drop in the bucket of those that have dual count-noncount usages. The intention is simply to introduce the students to the idea that such a possibility exists in English. Point out that they may find count vs. noncount information in their dictionaries. Again, the purpose in this text is to get across the concept of a noncount noun, for it is this concept that will serve the students well as they gain experience with English and expand their usage ability. The ultimate goal is for learners to use nouns as count or noncount as unthinkingly as a native speaker does. In the meantime, it helps them to pay a little special attention to this phenomenon in English. In this chart, discuss how the noncount usages deal with "wholes" and the count usages with individual items.

☐ EXERCISE 15, p. 322. Nouns that can be count or noncount. (Chart 11-6)

ANSWERS:

3. time
4. times
5. papers
6. paper
7. a famous paper
8. works
9. work
10. light . . . gets . . . it
11. are . . . lights
12. hair . . . hair
13. hairs
14. glasses
15. glasses
16. glass
17. Iron is
18. Irons are
19. experiences
20. experience

CHART 11-7: USING UNITS OF MEASURE WITH NONCOUNT NOUNS

- These units of measure are also called "partitives."
- Some other units of measure not introduced in the text are *carton, dozen, head* (of lettuce or cabbage), *pack, package, roll* (of film or paper towels), *tablespoon, teaspoon, tub* (of butter or margarine). Additional nonmetric terms not in the text are *ounce, pint, inch, foot, yard.*
- The United States is the only major country that does not use the metric system. Nonmetric terms have little meaning to most students and little use unless the students are living in the United States and have to do their own food or gas shopping.
- Nonmetric terms originated in English in the 1200s and are called "English" or "British units." The metric system was created by French scientists late in the eighteenth century. At that time, each country had its own system of measurements that had developed from local traditions. By late in the nineteenth century, most major countries had recognized the need for an international system of measurements and had adopted the metric system. Great Britain, Canada, and Australia began converting to it in the 1960s. The United States government is still wrestling with the problem of if and how to convert to metric.
- The spellings "metre" and "litre" are chiefly British. The spellings "meter" and "liter" are used in American English.

☐ EXERCISE 16, p. 324. Units of measure with noncount nouns. (Chart 11-7)

There may easily be more than one possible completion. Often only one is idiomatic (i.e., the expression a native speaker would typically use) or culturally appropriate in most English-speaking countries. For example, in item 1 it would be grammatically correct to say "a bag of olives" or "a box of olives," but "can" and "jar" are the words idiomatically and culturally appropriate for quantifying olives.

USUAL COMPLETIONS *(others are possible):*

PART I.

3. bottle
4. jar
5. can
6. can
7. bag/box
8. bottle
9. can
10. can
11. bag
12. bottle/can
13. can
14. box

PART II.

17. piece
18. slice/piece
19. slice/piece
20. glass/cup
21. bowl/cup
22. slice/piece
23. glass
24. bowl/cup
25. glass
26. bowl
27. slice/piece
28. bowl/cup
29. bowl

☐ EXERCISE 17, p. 325. Writing activity: count and noncount nouns. (Charts 11-1 → 11-7)

The intention here is directed writing practice. Writing about food requires both count and noncount nouns.

CHART 11-8: GUIDELINES FOR ARTICLE USAGE

- This chart presents the basics of article usage. It by no means covers the myriad uses of articles in English. Almost all students find article usage difficult to learn, and many teachers and textbook authors find articles difficult to teach. There are many idiomatic uses, complex patterns, intricate variations, and subtleties. Proficient use of articles can only come with experience over time. Tell your students not to get frustrated. Articles are just one small part of English.
- Most students need help with this chart; it contains too much information to be grasped independently. It is suggested that you combine an explanation of this chart with a discussion of the illustrations in Exercise 18, or even do Exercise 18 first, before looking at the chart.
- For more information about articles, see Charts 7-7 and 7-8 in the third edition of *Understanding and Using English Grammar.*

☐ EXERCISE 18, p. 328. Count and noncount nouns. (Chart 11-8)

The key point the students need to understand from this exercise is that article usage often depends upon what the speaker assumes the listener is familiar with and is thinking about. If they have shared knowledge and are thinking about the same object or person, the speaker uses *the*.

☐ EXERCISE 19, p. 330. THE vs. A/AN. (Chart 11-8)

Again the key point is what the speaker assumes the listener is familiar with and thinking about.

ANSWERS:

3. a . . . a
4. the . . . the
5. a
6. the . . . the
7. a . . . a
8. the
9. the
10. a
11. the
12. a . . . a
13. the . . . the . . . the . . . the . . . the
14. the
15. a

☐ EXERCISE 20, p. 331. Using A or Ø for generalizations. (Chart 11-8)

ANSWERS:

3. Ø **M**ilk . . . Ø *(none possible)*
4. **A** . . . **F**lowers are beautiful.
5. Ø **W**ater . . . Ø *(none possible)*
6. **A** . . . **H**orses are strong.
7. Ø **J**ewelry . . . Ø *(none possible)*
8. Ø **S**oap . . . Ø *(none possible)*
9. **A** . . . **S**hirts **have** sleeves.
10. Ø **H**oney . . . Ø *(none possible)*

☐ EXERCISE 21, p. 332. Using THE for specific statements. (Chart 11-8)

Students can discuss this exercise in groups or pairs prior to class discussion.

ANSWERS:

2. a. **M**ountains
   b. **The** mountains
3. a. **W**ater
   b. **The** water
4. a. **The** information
   b. information
5. a. **H**ealth
   b. **the** health
6. a. **M**en . . . women
   b. **the** men . . . **the** women
7. a. problems
   b. **the** problems
8. a. **the** happiness
   b. happiness
9. a. **V**egetables
   b. **The** vegetables
10. a. **G**old
    b. **The** gold

☐ EXERCISE 22, p. 333. Using THE for specific statements. (Chart 11-8)

ANSWERS: **3.** Ø **Air** **4. The** air **5. The** windows **6.** Ø **Windows** . . . Ø glass **7.** Ø children **8. the** children **9.** Ø **Paper** . . . Ø trees **10. The** paper **11.** Ø **Nurses** **12. the** nurses **13.** Ø English . . . Ø grammar **14. The** grammar **15.** Ø plants . . . Ø fruit . . . Ø vegetables . . . Ø plants . . . Ø meat . . . Ø plants **16. The** plants

☐ EXERCISE 23, p. 333. Using THE for second mention. (Chart 11-8)

ANSWERS:

3. **a** desk . . . **a** bed . . . **The** desk . . . **The** bed
4. **a** pen . . . **some** paper . . . **the** pen . . . **the** paper
5. **a** picnic . . . **a** movie . . . **The** picnic . . . **the** movie
6. **a** dog . . . **a** cat . . . **The** dog . . . **the** cat . . . **The** cat was chasing **a** mouse. **The** mouse . . . **a** hole . . . but **the** hole . . . **The** cat . . . **the** hole . . . **a** tree. **The** dog . . . **the** tree
7. **a** bag . . . **some** sugar . . . **some** cookies . . . **The** sugar . . . **the** flour . . . **the** flour . . . **some** little bugs . . . **the** little bugs . . . **a** new bag . . . **The** new bag
8. **a** princess . . . **a** prince . . . **The** princess . . . **the** prince . . . **a** distant land . . . **a** messenger . . . **some** things . . . **the** prince . . . **The** messenger . . . **some** jewels . . . **a** robe . . . **the** prince . . . **The** princess . . . **the** messenger's . . . **the** prince . . . **some** tokens . . . **the** messenger . . . **the** jewels . . . **the** beautiful silk robe . . . **the** princess . . . **the** messenger . . . **the** prince . . . **a** wife

☐ EXERCISE 24, p. 335. Summary: A/AN vs. Ø vs. THE. (Charts 11-1 → 11-8)

ANSWERS:

2. **a** radio . . . Ø music (*also possible:* some music)
3. **the** radio . . . **The** music
4. **A** good book . . . **a** friend . . . Ø life
5. **a** book . . . **the** life
6. **the** lake . . . **a** good idea
7. **A** lake . . . Ø water . . . **a** sea . . . **a** pond . . . **An** ocean . . . **a** sea
8. **the** beach . . . **the** ocean
9. Ø **Water** . . . **the** water . . . **The** pollution
10. Ø fresh water . . . Ø seawater . . . Ø salt
11. **the** salt . . . **the** pepper
12. Ø different countries . . . Ø different geography . . . **a** peninsula . . . **an** island nation
13. **a** taxi
14. Ø fresh fish
15. Ø **Good** food . . . Ø pleasure
16. **The** food . . . **the** fish . . . **the** service . . . **the** waitress . . . **a** good tip
17. **the** car . . . **the** kids . . . **the** car
18. Ø coins . . . Ø shells . . . Ø beads . . . Ø salt . . . Ø paper . . . Ø plastic cards
19. Ø **Money** . . . Ø trees
20. Ø sick people . . . **A** farmer . . . Ø crops . . . **An** architect . . . Ø buildings . . . **An** artist . . . Ø new ways . . . **the** world . . . Ø life
21. Ø **Earthquakes** are Ø rare events
22. **an** earthquake . . . **the** earthquake . . . **The** ground
23. **a** good program . . . **a** documentary . . . **an** old movie . . . **the** documentary
24. Ø **Modern** people . . . **the** universe . . . **the** moon . . . Ø life . . . **a** star . . . **the** universe . . . **the** sun

☐ EXERCISE 25, p. 337. Preview: using THE or Ø with names. (Chart 11-9)

Suggestion: Bring a world map to class.

ANSWERS:

3. Ø
4. the
5. the
6. Ø
7. the
8. the
9. Ø
10. Ø

CHART 11-9: USING *THE* OR Ø WITH NAMES

- Using a world map, point to places and ask the students to identify them: *That is **the** Nile River. That is Ø Brazil. That is Ø Beijing. Those are **the** Alps.* Etc.
- American English uses a period at the end of abbreviated titles:

  Mr. Wang, Mrs. Doe, Ms. Jackson, Dr. Singh.

  British English does not use a period:

  Mr Wang, Mrs Doe, Ms Jackson, Dr Singh

☐ EXERCISE 26, p. 338. Using THE or Ø with names. (Chart 11-9)

Refer students to the *Workbook* for practice with a wider variety of place names.

ANSWERS:

3. Ø . . . Ø
4. The
5. The . . . the
6. The . . . Ø . . . the
7. Ø
8. Ø . . . Ø

CHART 11-10: CAPITALIZATION

- One of the principal ideas for the students to understand from this chart is that nouns are capitalized when they are part of a name (i.e., a proper noun). The text does not use the term "proper noun." You may decide to use it if it helps your class.
- This is a reference chart. You might want to proceed directly to the exercises, then refer to the chart as questions arise.
- Correct capitalization can be a problem in student writing. Some language groups, such as Spanish speakers, have different rules for capitalizing words; for example, words related to nationality are not capitalized in Spanish, but are in English. Some students from other language groups don't consider capitalization important. It may be necessary to emphasize that proper capitalization is a value in English rhetoric, for it signals a writer's competent, educated use of the language.

☐ **EXERCISE 27, p. 340. Capitalization. (Chart 11-10)**

ANSWERS: **2.** Do you know **R**ichard **S**mith? **H**e is a professor at this university. **3.** I know that **P**rofessor **S**mith teaches at the **U**niversity of **A**rizona. **4.** The **N**ile **R**iver flows into the **M**editerranean **S**ea. **5.** John is a **C**atholic. **A**li is a **M**oslem. **6.** Anna speaks **F**rench. **S**he studied in **F**rance for two years. **7.** *(no change)* **8.** I'm taking **M**odern **E**uropean **H**istory 101 this semester. **9.** We went to **V**ancouver, **B**ritish **C**olumbia, for our vacation last summer. **10.** Venezuela is a **S**panish-speaking country. **11.** Canada is in **N**orth **A**merica. **12.** Canada is north of the **U**nited **S**tates. **13.** *(no change)* **14.** The **M**ississippi **R**iver flows south. **15.** The **A**mazon is a river in **S**outh **A**merica. **16.** We went to **B**rookfield **Z**oo in **C**hicago. **17.** The title of this book is ***F**undamentals of **E**nglish **G**rammar.* **18.** I enjoy studying **E**nglish grammar. **19.** On **V**alentine's **D**ay (**F**ebruary 14), sweethearts give each other presents. **20.** I read a book entitled ***T**he **C**at and the **M**ouse in **M**y **A**unt's **H**ouse.*

☐ **EXERCISE 28, p. 341. Capitalization. (Chart 11-10)**

ANSWERS: **(1)** Jane **G**oodall is . . . in **T**anzania. **(2)** . . . heart of **L**ondon, **E**ngland, as . . . books were ***T**he **J**ungle **B**ook,* by **R**udyard **K**ipling, and books about **T**arzan, a fictional . . . . **(3)** . . . go to **A**frica . . . and **E**nglish literature . . . poets was **T. S. E**liot . . . passage to **A**frica. **(4)** . . . the **R**ed **S**ea and southward down the **A**frican coast to **M**ombasa in **K**enya . . . in **N**airobi with a **B**ritish company . . . she met **L**ouis **L**eakey, a famous . . . shore of **L**ake **T**anganyika. **(5)** Jane **G**oodall lived . . . . **(6)** . . . **J**ane couldn't afford . . . a Ph.D. from **C**ambridge **U**niversity and became a professor at **S**tanford **U**niversity . . . of them is ***M**y **F**riends, the **W**ild **C**himpanzees.*

☐ **EXERCISE 29, p. 342. Error analysis. (Chapter 11)**

ANSWERS: **2.** There **is** a lot of **information** in that book. **3.** ~~The~~ **O**il is a natural resource. **4.** . . . there **was** too **much traffic**. **5.** I drank two **glasses of water**. **6.** Our teacher gives us too **much homework**. **7.** Nadia knows a lot of **vocabulary**. **8.** I had **an** egg for breakfast. **9.** There **are** many **kinds** of trees in the world. **10.** I'm studying ~~the~~ **English**. **11.** My cousin **is** living/**lives** in **the** United **States**. **12.** Only twelve **students** were in class yesterday. **13.** I need some **advice**. **14.** We all have a few **problems** in ~~the~~ life. **15.** There were no **jobs**, and . . . much **money**. **16.** . . . animals except for **chickens**. **17.** When I **was** a **child**, . . . with ~~the~~ **horses**. **18.** I live with two **friends**. One is from ~~the~~ **Chile** . . . from ~~the~~ Saudi Arabia. **19.** I think ~~the~~ **English** is **a** difficult language. **20.** When people use a lot of **slang**, I can't understand them.

Chapter 12: ADJECTIVE CLAUSES

ORDER OF CHAPTER	CHARTS	EXERCISES	WORKBOOK
Introduction	12-1		
Who, whom, which, and *that* in adjective clauses	12-2 → 12-4	Ex. 1 → 12	Pr. 1 → 14
Summary review		Ex. 13	
Subject–verb agreement in adjective clauses	12-5	Ex. 14	Pr. 15
Prepositions in adjective clauses	12-6	Ex. 15 → 16	Pr. 16 → 18
Summary review		Ex. 17 → 18	
Whose in adjective clauses	12-7	Ex. 19 → 20	Pr. 19 → 20
Cumulative review		Ex. 21 → 30	Pr. 21 → 24

General Notes on Chapter 12

• By learning to use adjective clauses, students will greatly expand their ability to communicate and comprehend complex descriptions, definitions, contrasts, etc.

• To keep the focus on the main patterns, the text presents only restrictive (identifying) adjective clauses. These include fundamental structures with subject and object relative pronouns, omission of the object pronoun from an adjective clause, the placement of prepositions within a clause, and the use of *whose*. The text is designed so that the students first gain control of the basic patterns; they can wrestle with the punctuation of nonrestrictive (vs. restrictive) clauses at a later stage in their study of English (see *Understanding and Using English Grammar, Third Edition,* Chart 13-10).

• TERMINOLOGY: Minimal terminology to describe dependent (subordinate) clauses is introduced in the extensive footnote to Chart 12-1. Some books use the term "relative clause" instead of "adjective clause" and "relative pronoun" instead of "adjective clause pronoun." Some students may find the terminology helpful; others will understand and gain control of the structures in this chapter without paying much attention to the terminology of grammar descriptions.

The extent to which you emphasize terminology in your teaching is your decision and in large part depends on the predominant learning styles of your students. Academically oriented students often like and need descriptive labels for grammar structures. Students interested in conversational English often concentrate more on understanding the examples than trying to grasp the grammar explanations. There is no "right" way to incorporate terminology in the teaching of grammar. The intention of the text is to offer just enough so that teacher and students can communicate about the structures.

• SUGGESTION: Before beginning the chapter in class, ask your students to turn to page 366 and write out Exercise 27 (or make up a similar exercise yourself with the same structures but different words). Collect the papers. You will be able to judge the ability levels of your class in using adjective clauses, and the students will have a preview of the grammar in this chapter. When the class is at the end of the chapter, return the papers and have the students correct their own errors, or have them write the exercise again and compare their two papers.

CHART 12-1: ADJECTIVE CLAUSES: INTRODUCTION

• There are three principal kinds of dependent clauses in English: (1) an adverb clause, (2) an adjective clause, and (3) a noun clause. The text presents the fundamentals of all three kinds.

The concept of a dependent clause (e.g., a "time clause" or an "*if*-clause") is presented first in Chapters 2 and 3 in conjunction with the study of verb tenses. The terminology "adverb clause" is first used in Charts 8-6 and 8-7 in connection with the use of *because* and *even though*.

This chapter presents adjective clauses.

The third type of dependent clause, the noun clause, is introduced in Chapter 14.

• The approach in this chart is to connect the function of adjectives to the function of adjective clauses as a way of helping the students understand the purposes and uses of adjective clauses. One problem in examples (a) through (d) in the chart is that some students may think an adjective clause needs to have an adjective in it. That is not true. Ask students to note that example (e) contains no adjective; the information in the clause itself serves to describe the noun; i.e., the function of the clause is the same as the function of an adjective, and that's why these clauses are called adjective clauses. The real point here is that adjectives in a noun phrase <u>precede</u> the noun, whereas adjective clauses <u>follow</u> the noun.

• The approach of the text is to connect the use of personal pronouns and relative pronouns. In a simple sentence or main clause, *he, she, it, they, him, her, them, his,* and *their* are used. Their counterparts in an adjective clause are *who, whom, that, which,* and *whose*. The object of this chapter is to show how these relative pronouns are used.

CHART 12-2: USING *WHO* AND *WHOM* IN ADJECTIVE CLAUSES

- The text presents a little information at a time about the patterns of adjective clauses, beginning here with a presentation of the subject pronoun *who* vs. the object pronoun *whom.*
- Review the terms "subject" and "object" as needed.
- Typical mistakes include the use of both an adjective clause pronoun and a personal pronoun:

  INCORRECT: *The man who **he** lives next to me is friendly.*
  INCORRECT: *The man whom I met **him** was friendly.*

  Learners need to understand that *who* and *whom* are used instead of personal pronouns. The two kinds of pronouns have the same meaning (e.g., in the examples, *he* and *who* as well as *him* and *whom* refer to *the man),* but they are not used together. (Some languages do require both kinds of pronouns, but standard English does not accept both.)

- A few notes on *whom:* It is used infrequently in adjective clauses (and questions and noun clauses as well). It is presented here as a device to help students distinguish between subject and object relative pronouns in adjective clause patterns. The students will not be wrong if they use *whom* in object pronoun adjective clause patterns, but this usage may seem a bit stilted or old-fashioned. Later charts and exercises encourage them to use *that* or *who* or to omit the pronoun if possible.

  The situations in which *whom* must be used instead of *who* or *that* are
  (1) following a preposition (e.g., *The man about whom I told you.* See Chart 12-6); and
  (2) in formal written English in a nonrestrictive clause (e.g., *The Prime Minister, whom no one dared interrupt, spoke for two hours on the need for trade restrictions).*

  This text does not present nonrestrictive relative clauses. (Instead, see *Understanding and Using English Grammar, Third Edition,* Chart 13-10.) *Whom* is also used in what the *Longman Dictionary of Contemporary English* calls "careful speech." Otherwise, the use of *whom* is disappearing from contemporary English usage, especially in spoken language.

☐ EXERCISE 1, p. 344. Adjective clauses with WHO and WHOM. (Charts 12-1 and 12-2)

Constructing these sentences, especially with *whom,* can be quite challenging. Give students time to work out the answers, then discuss any problems or alternatives.

ANSWERS:

3. The police officer who gave me directions was friendly.
4. The waiter who served us dinner was friendly.
5. The people whom I met at the party last night were very nice.
6. The people who live next to me have three cars.
7. The man whom I met on the plane talked a lot.
8. The man who sat next to me talked a lot.
9. Three women whom I didn't know walked into my office.
10. I talked to the women who walked into my office.

☐ EXERCISE 2, p. 345. Adjective clauses with WHO and WHOM. (Charts 12-1 and 12-2)

ANSWERS:

		S	V	
3.	**(whom**	**we**	**visited)**	
4.		**(who**	**live**	on a boat)
5.		**(who**	**was sitting**	next to me)
6.		**(who**	**were playing**	football at the park)
7.	**(whom**	**I**	**admire**	tremendously)
8.	**(whom**	**they**	**met**	in their English class)
9.		**(who**	**listen**	to very loud music)
10.		**(who**	**had put**	a beefsteak . . . without paying)
11.	**(whom**	**I**	**invited**	to dinner at my home)

☐ EXERCISE 3, p. 346. Adjective clauses with WHO. (Charts 12-1 and 12-2)

You might also ask the students to divide the sentences into two simple sentences. Item 1: *The man answered the phone. He was polite.*

ANSWERS: **2.** I liked the people **who** sat **3.** People **who** paint **4.** . . . married couples **who** argue **5.** . . . gentleman **who** started

☐ EXERCISE 4, p. 346. Adjective clauses with WHO. (Charts 12-1 and 12-2)

Adjective clauses are commonly used in definitions. Students are introduced to this typical use in this and the next exercise. Exercises 4 and 5 work well as group activities. Students will need to consult their dictionaries.

ANSWERS:

2. C	**5.** A	**8.** D
3. G	**6.** B	**9.** H
4. J	**7.** F	**10.** I

☐ EXERCISE 5, p. 346. Adjective clauses with WHO. (Charts 12-1 and 12-2)

POSSIBLE COMPLETIONS: **1.** . . . makes bread, cakes, pies, etc. **2.** . . . fixes cars. **3.** . . . serves drinks. **4.** . . . collects stamps. **5.** . . . spends money unwisely. **6.** . . . studies outer space. **7.** . . . makes things from wood. **8.** . . . hoards his money.

CHART 12-3: USING *WHO, WHO(M),* AND *THAT* IN ADJECTIVE CLAUSES

• This chart expands upon what the students learned in Chart 12-2 by presenting the other possible patterns: those with *that* or with Ø (nothing).

• In actual usage, *who* is preferred to *that* as a subject pronoun, *that* is preferred to *whom* as an object pronoun, and in everyday use, omission of the object pronoun is usually preferred to the use of either *whom* or *that.* The text does not give the students this information. Rather, it aims to help the students gain control of a few basic patterns.

At this stage in language study, the learners generally still do not use adjective clauses idiomatically and may even avoid them altogether. Assure them that their idiomatic usage ability will grow as they gain experience with the language. As the English saying goes, from a small acorn the great oak grows. It is counterproductive for the grammar teacher or text to present the whole oak tree at the beginning.

☐ EXERCISE 6, p. 347. Adjective clauses with WHO, WHO(M), and THAT. (Chart 12-3)

ANSWERS:

3. who(m)/that/Ø
4. who/that
5. who/that
6. who(m)/that/Ø
7. who/that
8. who(m)/that/Ø
9. who(m)/that/Ø
10. who/that

CHART 12-4: USING *WHICH* AND *THAT* IN ADJECTIVE CLAUSES

- *Which* is also used in questions to ask for a choice between known items (i.e., *Which book is yours?*). Students are learning a different use of *which* in this chart.
- A fairly common error is the use of *what* in place of *which:*

  INCORRECT: *The book **what** I read was very interesting.*

What is never used as an adjective clause pronoun.

☐ EXERCISE 7, p. 348. Adjective clauses with WHO, WHO(M), WHICH, and THAT. (Charts 12-3 and 12-4)

Two or three students can respond to each item, each student giving a different form of the answer. Or the sentences can be written on the board by the students.

ANSWERS: **2.** The soup which/that/Ø I had for lunch was too salty. **3.** I have a class which/that begins at 8:00 A.M. **4.** I know a man who/that doesn't have to work for a living. **5.** The information which/that/Ø I found on the Internet helped me a lot. **6.** The people whom/that/Ø we saw on the bridge waved at us. **7.** My daughter asked me a question which/that/Ø I couldn't answer. **8.** The woman who/that read my palm predicted my future. **9.** Where can I catch the bus which/that goes downtown? **10.** All of the people who(m)/that/Ø I asked to my party can come.

☐ EXERCISE 8, p. 349. Adjective clauses with WHO and THAT. (Charts 12-3 and 12-4)

These items are in the form of simple definitions, a useful structure for language learners.

The information about preferred patterns is in a footnote so that it can be emphasized or not as you see fit. The preferred patterns are given in the answers below, but any correct pattern a student uses is fine. The text seeks to give students initial familiarity with the meaning and structure of adjective clauses, but not to overburden them, especially at this level, with too many usage refinements concerning pattern frequency, variations in formal vs. informal registers, or restrictive vs. nonrestrictive clauses and their punctuation.

ANSWERS:

2. F that measures air pressure.
3. G that can be shaped
4. E who designs buildings.
5. H that is difficult to solve.
6. I who doesn't eat meat.
7. C that forms when water boils.
8. J that has a hard shell
9. A who leaves society
10. D that is square

☐ **EXERCISE 9, p. 350. Adjective clauses. (Charts 12-1 → 12-3)**

The directions do not specify that students must use adjective clauses in their definitions. When a good definition is given that does not contain an adjective clause, accept it and then ask for a definition with an adjective clause. For example, item 3: *Birds are creatures with wings.* OR *Birds are creatures that have wings and can fly.*

POSSIBLE COMPLETIONS: **1.** . . . that defines words. **2.** . . . who takes care of sick people. **3.** . . . that can fly. **4.** . . . that we use to open locks. **5.** . . . who is in jail. **6.** . . . that has a very long neck. **7.** . . . who take pictures with cameras. **8.** . . . (whom) many people admire. **9.** . . . that modifies a noun. **10.** . . . (whom) we can trust.

☐ **EXERCISE 10, p. 350. Object pronouns in adjective clauses. (Charts 12-3 and 12-4)**

ANSWERS: **2.** . . . you wore ~~it~~ to class yesterday. **3.** . . . you to meet ~~her.~~ **4.** . . . to rent ~~it~~ had two bedrooms. **5.** . . . we bought ~~it~~ for ourselves last week. **6.** . . . you met ~~her~~ at **7.** . . . cat that ~~it~~ likes to catch birds. **8.** . . . cat catches ~~them~~ are very frightened. **9.** . . . had brought ~~it~~ into the house.

☐ **EXERCISE 11, p. 351. Adjective clauses with WHO, WHO(M), WHICH, THAT, and Ø. (Charts 12-3 and 12-4)**

The boxed answers could advantageously be written on the chalkboard.

ANSWERS:

1. which, that, Ø
2. who, that
3. which, that
4. which, that, Ø
5. who(m), that, Ø
6. which, that

☐ **EXERCISE 12, p. 351. Identifying adjective clauses. (Charts 12-3 and 12-4)**

ANSWERS: **2.** The (food) we ate at the sidewalk cafe was delicious. **3.** . . . a (person) who owns or operates a store. **4.** The (bus) I take to school every morning is **5.** (Pizza) that is sold by the piece is **6.** . . . (pirates) who sailed the South China Sea and the Gulf of Thailand. **7.** . . . (heat) the sun produces. **8.** . . . (fish) that can tear the flesh off an animal as large as a horse in a few minutes. **9.** . . . (People) who read gain . . . A (person) who does not read is . . . (person) who cannot read. **10.** . . . (birds) that live in most parts of North America . . . a (bird) that is a little larger than a sparrow and has a band of yellow across the end of its tail, it

☐ **EXERCISE 13, p. 352. Review: adjective clauses. (Charts 12-1 → 12-4)**

ANSWERS: **3. The** student who raised her hand in class asked the teacher a question. **The** student who sat quietly in his seat didn't. **4. The** girl who won the foot race is happy. **The** girl who lost the foot race isn't happy. **5. The** man who was listening to the radio heard the news bulletin . . . **The** man who was sleeping didn't hear it. **6. The** person who bought a *(make of car)* probably spent more money that the person who bought a *(make of car)*. **7. The** vegetables Tom picked from his grandfather's garden probably tasted fresher than **the** vegetables (OR: **the** ones) Amanda bought at a supermarket. **8. The** young musicians who practiced hours and hours every day showed a great deal of improvement . . . **The** one who had a regular job and practiced only in the evenings and on the weekends didn't show as much improvement. **9. The** city that uses its rivers and streams as both a source of water and a sewer has a high death rate from infections diseases such as typhoid and cholera. **The** city that provides clean water and a modern sewer system for its citizens doesn't.

CHART 12-5: SINGULAR AND PLURAL VERBS IN ADJECTIVE CLAUSES

- Relative pronouns in English have the same forms in singular as in plural, but they carry the same number as their antecedents; verbs must agree with that number.
- Special attention is paid to subject–verb agreement in adjective clauses because it is a common source of errors. (Indeed, subject–verb agreement even in simple sentences remains a problem for learners at this level and beyond.)

INCORRECT: *My brother knows several people who* ***is*** *from Lebanon.*
INCORRECT: *I know a woman who* ***live*** *in the Courtyard Apartments.*

☐ EXERCISE 14, p. 354. Subject-verb agreement in adjective clauses. (Chart 12-5)

ANSWERS:

2. tools . . . are
3. woman . . . lives
4. people . . . live
5. cousin . . . works
6. miners . . . work
7. athlete . . . plays
8. athletes . . . play
9. books . . . tell
10. book . . . tells
11. men . . . were
12. woman . . . was

CHART 12-6: USING PREPOSITIONS IN ADJECTIVE CLAUSES

- The pattern in example (b) is uncommon and very formal ("careful English"). A native speaker might use *who* instead of *whom* but would be more likely to use the patterns in (c) and (d). The pattern in (e) is formal written English.
- Discuss the concept of formal vs. informal English. Formal English is found, for example, in academic journals, a school or business report, official correspondence, nonfiction books. Informal English occurs in everyday conversation, a letter to a friend or family member, a relaxed classroom, e-mail.

☐ EXERCISE 15, p. 355. Prepositions in adjective clauses. (Chart 12-6)

Students could write these and then correct each other's papers, or they could be written on the board by the students.

ANSWERS:

2. The man who(m)/that/Ø I told you **about** is over there.
   The man **about** whom I told you is over there.
3. The woman who(m)/that/Ø I work **for** pays me a fair salary.
   The woman **for** whom I work pays me a fair salary.
4. . . . the family who(m)/that/Ø she is living **with**.
   . . . the family **with** whom she is living.

5. The picture which/that/Ø Tom is looking **at** is beautiful.
The picture **at** which Tom is looking is beautiful.
6. . . . the music which/that/Ø we listened **to** after dinner.
. . . the music **to** which we listened after dinner.

☐ EXERCISE 16, p. 356. Prepositions in adjective clauses. (Chart 12-6)

Students sometimes ask how they are supposed to know which preposition they need to use. This exercise consists of preposition combinations with verbs, as listed in Appendix 2. Preposition combinations can be memorized, but principally, at least in the author's teaching experience, they need to be practiced until they "sound right." Appendix 2 contains preposition exercises, as does the Appendix section in the *Workbook*. The intention of the text is that the teacher intersperse work on prepositions throughout the teaching term, using the material in the Appendix as it best fits in with her/his syllabus.

ANSWERS: **2.** to . . . (we went **to**) **3.** in/at . . . (we stayed **in/at**) **4.** to . . . (we listened **to**) **5.** for . . . (Sally was waiting **for**) **6.** to . . . (**to** whom I talked) **7.** (that I was looking **for**) **8.** (I borrowed money **from**) **9.** (we talked **about** in class) **10.** (I've been interested **in** for a long time) **11.** (I had graduated **from**) **12.** (**with** whom he is living) **13.** (I was staring **at**) **14.** (that I'm not familiar **with**) **15.** (**with** whom I almost always agree) **16.** (**to/with** whom you speak at the airline counter) **17.** (you introduced me **to** at the restaurant last night) **18.** (I've always been able to depend **on**) **19.** (you waved **at**) **20.** (**to** whom you should complain)

☐ EXERCISE 17, p. 357. Review: adjective clauses. (Charts 12-1 → 12-6)

The directions ask the students to practice omitting the pronoun. If they do, that's good. If they don't, that's fine too.

ANSWERS: **1.** The plane you're taking to Denver leaves . . . . **2.** The university you want to go to is . . . . **3.** You met the people I told you about. **4.** The bananas your husband/wife bought were . . . . **5.** The shirt/blouse the teacher is wearing is . . . . [Clarify that shirts are worn by both males and females, but blouses by females only.] **6.** The market you usually go to has . . . . **7.** You couldn't understand the woman you talked to . . . . **8.** The scrambled eggs you had . . . cafeteria were cold. **9.** You had a good time on the trip you took to Hawaii. **10.** The doctor you went to yesterday prescribed some medicine . . . . **11.** The cream you put in your coffee was . . . . **12.** The . . . recorder you bought last month doesn't . . . . **13.** You're going to call about the want ad you saw in . . . . [*Want ad* = an ad in a special section of a newspaper.]

☐ EXERCISE 18, p. 357. Review: adjective clauses. (Charts 12-1 → 12-6)

Being able to recognize complex structures in their reading can help students decipher meanings of sentences.

ANSWERS: **2.** (Flowers) that bloom year after year are . . . (Flowers) that bloom only one season are . . . **3.** . . . (birds) that have long legs and curved bills. [Ask a student to draw a flamingo on the board, or draw one yourself.] **4.** . . . an (animal or plant) that lived in the past. [*Remains,* as a noun, is always in the plural form and refers to the parts that are left after most other parts have been destroyed.] **5.** . . . the (boy) who's wearing the striped shirt or the (boy) who has on the T-shirt? . . . the (boy) who just waved at us . . . the (kid) that has the red baseball cap? **6.** . . . a (family) who lived near Quito, Ecuador . . . the (things) they did and said seemed . . . (people) who were like him in their customs and habits . . . the (way) of life that his host family followed . . . the (things) he did with his host family began . . . the (things) that were different between his host family and himself . . . (things) they had in common as human beings despite their differences in cultural background. **7.** . . . the (problems) that exist today have existed . . . (people) who come from different geographical areas or cultural backgrounds . . . group of (people) who are different from themselves in language, customs, politics, religion, and/or appearance . . . the (violence) that has occurred throughout the history of the world.

CHART 12-7: USING *WHOSE* IN ADJECTIVE CLAUSES

- The use of *whose* in adjective clauses is difficult for most learners. It occurs relatively infrequently. The text presents only a brief introduction and does not anticipate any degree of usage mastery by the learners.
- Pronounce *whose* and *who's* for the students, pointing out that they sound identical. One can discern the meaning (as a possessive or as a contraction of *who* and *is*) from the sentence structure and context.
- Point out that *whose* always accompanies a noun in an adjective clause; it does not stand alone as a pronoun as do *who, which,* and *that. Whose* functions as a possessive adjective, grammatically equivalent to the personal possessive adjectives *their, her, his.* (*Whose* can also be the equivalent to the possessive adjective *its,* but the text does not introduce the use of *whose* to modify "things" as well as "people," e.g., *an organization whose membership exceeds a thousand people.* See *Understanding and Using English Grammar, Third Edition,* Chart 13-6.)

☐ EXERCISE 19, p. 359. WHOSE in adjective clauses. (Chart 12-7)

First ask the students to find the possessive adjective for each item in the given sentences. For example, in item 1, the possessive adjective is *his.* Then have them change *his* to *whose.* Ask them to identify to whom *his* and *whose* refer. (Point out that *his* and *whose* have an identical meaning.) They refer to *the man. His* = *the man's* and *whose* = *the man's.* The man in sentence (a) lost his car to thieves. Tell them to keep *whose* with the noun that immediately follows *(car)* and move the phrase *whose car* immediately after the noun it modifies. That's how an adjective clause with *whose* is formed. Some students find these clauses confusing, especially in a case such as item 4 in which the word order changes from simple sentence to adjective clause, with the object (in this case *husband)* preceding the subject and verb.

ANSWERS: **2.** There is the woman whose cat died. **3.** Over there is the man whose daughter is in my English class. **4.** Over there is the woman whose husband you met yesterday. **5.** There is the professor whose course I'm taking. **6.** That is the man whose daughter is an astronaut. **7.** That is the girl whose camera I borrowed. **8.** There is the boy whose mother is a famous musician. **9.** They are the people whose house we visited last month. **10.** That is the couple whose apartment was burglarized.

☐ EXERCISE 20, p. 360. WHOSE in adjective clauses. (Chart 12-7)

This exercise repeats some of sentences from the previous exercise.

ANSWERS: **1.** The man whose car was stolen called the police. **2.** The woman whose cat died was sad. **3.** The man whose daughter is in my English class is friendly. **4.** The professor whose course I'm taking gives hard tests. **5.** The man whose daughter is an astronaut is very proud. **6.** The girl whose camera I borrowed is a good friend of mine. **7.** The people whose house I visited were very nice. **8.** I have a friend whose brother is a police officer. **9.** I have a neighbor whose dog barks all day long. **10.** I like the people whose house we went to. *(Also possible, in very formal English:* to whose house we went) **11.** I thanked the woman whose dictionary I borrowed. **12.** The woman whose purse was stolen shouted "Stop! Thief!" **13.** The man whose picture is in the newspaper is famous. **14.** I know a girl whose family never eats dinner together.

☐ EXERCISE 21, p. 360. Review: adjective clauses. (Chapter 12)

ANSWERS: *(Usual usage is in* ***boldface****.)*

3. **who**/that
4. **whose**
5. which/**that**
6. who(m)/that/**Ø**
7. **whom**
8. **whose**
9. which/that/**Ø**
10. **who**/that
11. **whom**
12. which/**that**
13. **whose**
14. which/that/**Ø**
15. A: which/that/**Ø** . . . which/that/**Ø**
    B: which/**that**
    B: which/that/**Ø**
    A: **whose**

☐ EXERCISE 22, p. 362. Written: adjective clauses. (Chapter 12)

When making this assignment, ask your students to come up with some possible sentences they could write. Encourage imaginative and colorful descriptions.

☐ EXERCISE 23, p. 362. Review: adjective clauses. (Chapter 12)

This probably works best teacher-led. You might want to do this exercise with books open first, then books closed the next day to build fluency in the use of basic adjective clause structures. As another possibility, you could have the students work the answers out in groups one day, and then you could lead an oral (books closed) review the next day.

Accept any correct structure, but encourage the learners to omit object pronouns.

It is important to write the main clause on the board so that the students can concentrate on forming the adjective clause. Substitute your students' names in the blanks between parentheses.

☐ EXERCISE 24, p. 363. Review: adjective clauses. (Chapter 12)

ANSWERS: **2.** whose son was in an accident **3.** (that/which/Ø) I slept on in a hotel last night **4.** (that/which) erupted in Indonesia recently **5.** whose specialty [BrE: speciality] is heart surgery **6.** (that/which) lived in the jungles of Southeast Asia **7.** whose mouth was big enough to swallow a whole cow in one gulp **8.** (that/which/Ø) you drink . . . (that/which) have been used

☐ EXERCISE 25, p. 364. Review: adjective clauses. (Chapter 12)

ANSWERS:

(1) . . . are (people) who provide love, care, and education for children.
Parents . . . (people) who raise a child . . . .

(2) . . . one (adult) with whom they can form a loving, trusting relationship.
A strong . . . (babies) who are not picked up frequently and held lovingly may . . .
(Youngsters) who are raised in an institution without bonding with an older (person) who functions as a parent often . . . .

(3) . . . safety. Children who are denied such basics in their early lives may . . . . One of the greatest responsibilities that parents have is . . . .

(4) . . . The lessons that parents teach their children are . . . the education that young people need in order to become independent, productive members of society.

☐ EXERCISE 26, p. 365. Adjective clauses. (Chapter 12)

This exercise presents a typical pattern in which adjective clauses are used and also draws attention to problems of number when *one of* and *some of* are part of the subject of a sentence.

The pattern with *one of* seems to be a particular source of errors. It is a useful pattern. Perhaps you could follow this exercise with oral practice. You give a noun + "*I*" and have the students complete this pattern: *One of the + plural noun + adjective clause + singular verb + rest of sentence*. For example:

TEACHER: cities I
SPEAKER: One of the cities I like best is Bangkok.

TEACHER: books I
SPEAKER: One of the books I use in my English classes is *(name of a book)*.

Topics for oral practice: *places I, people I, women I, men I, problems I, buildings I, classes I, colors I, countries I, movies I, holidays I, restaurants I, students I, teachers I, animals I.*

☐ EXERCISE 27, p. 366. Written: adjective clauses. (Chapter 12)

These sentence completions should be easily accomplished by the students at this point in the chapter. If you have the students write their sentences, return their papers with lots of praise.

☐ EXERCISE 28, p. 366. Error analysis: adjective clauses. (Chapter 12)

ANSWERS: **2.** The woman that/**whom/Ø** I met yesterday **was nice**. **3.** The people **who** live next to me are friendly. **4.** I met a woman **whose** ~~her~~ husband is a famous lawyer. **5.** Do you know the people who **live** in that house? **6.** The professor **who** teaches Chemistry 101 is **7.** . . . the people who/**whom/Ø** I visited ~~their house~~ on Thanksgiving Day. (OR: . . . the people **whose** ~~their~~ house I visited on Thanksgiving Day.) **8.** The people who/**Ø** I met ~~them~~ at the party **9.** . . . that/**Ø** we listened to ~~it.~~ **10.** The man **whose** bicycle was stolen was very angry. **11.** . . . an instrument **that** measures time. **12.** The apple tree that we planted ~~it~~ last year is **13.** . . . I **didn't** have . . . people **whose** ~~their~~ native tongue is English. **14.** One of the **things** I need to get **is** a new alarm clock. **15.** The people who **were** waiting in line for tickets to the game ~~they~~ were

☐ EXERCISES 29 and 30, p. 367. Adjective clauses. (Chapter 12)

The topics for speaking and writing are designed to be conducive to the use of adjective clauses. Some of the students' adjective clauses may be "forced," which is understandable and even appropriate for learners who are trying out a new tool. Encourage your students to experiment.

Chapter 13: GERUNDS AND INFINITIVES

ORDER OF CHAPTER	CHARTS	EXERCISES	WORKBOOK
Verbs + gerunds and infinitives	13-1 → 13-4	Ex. 1 → 12	Pr. 1 → 7
Preposition + gerund	13-5	Ex. 13 → 16	Pr. 8 → 9
Summary review			Pr. 10 → 12
By vs. *with*	13-6	Ex. 17 → 19	Pr. 13 → 15
Using gerunds as subjects; using *it* + infinitive	13-7 → 13-8	Ex. 20 → 27	Pr. 16 → 17
In order to and *for*	13-9	Ex. 28 → 31	Pr. 18 → 20
Too and *enough* + infinitive	13-10	Ex. 32 → 35	Pr. 21 → 22
Cumulative review		Ex. 36 → 39	Pr. 23 → 25
Review of verb forms		Ex. 40 → 41	

General Notes on Chapter 13

• To this point in the text, the learners have focused on the forms of verbs used as the main verb of a sentence or clause. In this chapter, students will learn other forms and uses of verbs: gerunds and infinitives. The ability to use these verbals and their associated verbs is indispensable; they are exceedingly common and very useful for students in expressing their wants, needs, likes, dislikes, hopes, plans, attitudes, and activities.

• TERMINOLOGY: A **gerund** is sometimes called a "verbal noun." Calling it merely "the *-ing* form of a verb" invites confusion with the present participle, which has different grammatical functions.

In this text, an **infinitive** is defined as ***to*** + *the simple form of a verb.* The text does not use the terms "*to*-less infinitive" or "base infinitive" or "the infinitive form without *to*" to describe the verb form that follows, for example, modal auxiliaries (as in *must* ***go***) or *let's* (as in *let's* ***go***). Rather, the text simply calls those **the simple form of a verb**. For students' purposes, **the simple form of the verb** is defined as the form found in a dictionary listing (Chart 2-6, p. 32).

CHART 13-1: VERB + GERUND

• The *verb + gerund phrase* is a source of errors for many students. Although relatively few verbs are followed by gerunds, those phrases occur with some frequency in both spoken and written English. It is easy for learners to confuse *verb + gerund phrases* with *verb + infinitive phrases*. For example: *I want* ***to watch*** *TV. I enjoy* ***watching*** *TV*. Learners commonly mix these elements and make errors such as the following:

INCORRECT: *I enjoy to watch TV.*

• The text presents a few common verbs and verb phrases followed by gerunds that students might find useful. As their vocabularies grow, they will encounter other verbs followed by gerunds, such as *risk, resist, deny, delay*. (See *Understanding and Using English Grammar, Third Edition*, Chart 14-9, for a longer list of verbs followed by gerunds.) Here, however, the focus is on only a few phrases as a starting point.

• You might want to note for the class that not all *-ing* verbs are gerunds; some are present participles.

I enjoy ***working*** = gerund, used as a noun, in this case as the object of the verb.
(*I* = subject; *enjoy* = verb; *working* = object)

I am ***working*** = present participle.
(*I* = subject; *am working* = verb)

• Notes on the verbs listed in this chapter:

- ***stop*** can also be followed by an infinitive of purpose (see footnote p. 370 in the text): *Jane was walking home. When she saw a coin on the sidewalk, she* ***stopped (in order) to pick*** *it* ***up***.
- ***keep*** and ***keep on*** have the same meaning when followed by a gerund.
- ***consider*** is followed by a gerund when it means "think about," as in the example in the text; it is followed by a *(pro)noun object + infinitive* when it means "believe" *(We consider him to be our closest friend)*.

☐ EXERCISE 1, p. 369. Verb + gerund. (Chart 13-1)

This exercise can be done without the students preparing it. Just ask them to call out possible completions. Its intention is to get across the idea that one verb can immediately follow another verb: i.e., that an *-ing* verb (a gerund) can follow a main verb.

You might also note for the students that gerunds, as verb forms, can be followed by objects. In *We postponed visiting the zoo, zoo* is the object of the gerund *visiting*.

EXPECTED RESPONSES: **3.** going to / driving to / flying to **4.** washing / sweeping / vacuuming / mopping / cleaning **5.** doing / finishing / studying **6.** snowing **7.** reading / buying **8.** taking / signing up for / registering for **9.** looking for / changing to **10.** watching / playing / taking part in / reading about **11.** visiting / moving to / moving out of / traveling to **12.** talking **13.** working / painting / playing **14.** closing / shutting / opening **15.** attending / going to

☐ EXERCISE 2, p. 370. Verb + gerund. (Chart 13-1)

You might ask the students to do both: complete the dialogues by choosing from the given phrases and also by using their own words.

ANSWERS: **2.** buying a new car . . . getting a Toyota **3.** reading a good book **4.** smoking **5.** trying **6.** doing things . . . doing my homework **7.** helping him **8.** tapping your fingernails on the table **9.** going to the zoo on Saturday **10.** repeating that

☐ EXERCISE 3, p. 371. Verb + gerund. (Chart 13-1)

Students can prepare their completions as homework or in groups or pairs. Elicit two or three completions in class discussion: e.g., *I enjoy buying clothes. I enjoy doing homework. I enjoy eating chocolate. I enjoy exercising at the gym.* Etc.

CHART 13-2: *GO* + *-ING*

- Definitions of some vocabulary items in the chart:
  - *bowling* = a game in which a heavy ball is rolled down a wooden alley at wooden pins
  - *camping* = living outdoors in a tent or trailer
  - *hiking* = walking a great distance through rural areas
  - *sailing* = a voyage on water in a vessel with sails
  - *window shopping* = looking at articles in store windows without making a purchase
  - *sightseeing* = looking at the sights when visiting places of interest
  - *ice skating* = gliding (moving or sliding smoothly) on ice, wearing special shoes with blades on the bottom
  - *skiing* = the sport of gliding on skis (NOTE: Double "i" is rare in English spelling. Indeed, *skiing* may be the only word spelled with a double "i.")
  - *water-skiing* = gliding on water wearing water skis
  - *skydiving* = jumping from an airplane and opening a parachute
- The illustrations below the chart show, starting in the upper left and going clockwise: hiking, bowling, sailing, skiing, ice skating, and in the center, jogging/running. This might be a good opportunity for you to teach your students "clockwise" and "counterclockwise."
- A typical error in using this structure is the addition of *to* after *go:*

  INCORRECT: *Did you go to shopping?*
  CORRECT: *Did you go shopping?*
- The list in the chart presents only some of the more common expressions with *go* + *-ing*. See *Understanding and Using English Grammar, Third Edition,* Chart 14-5, for additional items.

☐ EXERCISE 4, p. 372. GO + -ING. (Chart 13-2)

The purpose here is to discuss the meaning of the *go* + *-ing* expressions listed in Chart 13-2.

ANSWERS:

2. Nancy and Frank like to go fishing.
3. Adam went camping.
4. Tim likes to go shopping.
5. Laura goes jogging/running.
6. Fred and Jean like to go skiing.
7. Joe likes to go hiking.
8. Sara often goes bowling.
9. Liz and Greg probably go dancing a lot.
10. The Taylors are going to go (ice) skating.
11. Alex and Barbara like to go sailing/boating.
12. Tourists go sightseeing on buses.
13. Colette and Ben like to go skydiving.
14. *(free response)*

CHART 13-3: VERB + INFINITIVE

- In this text, an infinitive is defined as a verb form that consists of ***to*** + *the simple form;* "*to*-less infinitives" such as those used following modal auxiliaries *(must* ***go****)* are simply called "the simple form" in this text.
- *To* is simply a marker; it has no meaning in and of itself in an infinitive structure.
- The *to* in an infinitive is normally unstressed in speech. It is usually pronounced /tə/ instead of /tu/.
- The text presents just a few of the common verbs followed by infinitives. See *Understanding and Using English Grammar, Third Edition,* Chart 14-7, for a more complete reference list.
- *Forget* and *try* are listed in this text as being followed by infinitives, for that is how they are most commonly used. They can, however, be followed by gerunds—with a change of meaning. See *Understanding and Using English Grammar, Third Edition,* Chart 14-8. As mentioned in an earlier chapter in this Teacher's Guide, the text is planting acorns from which the tree will grow, not presenting the whole tree—but that means teachers might get asked questions about branches the text does not cover. Hence, these notes and references to a higher level textbook.

☐ EXERCISE 5, p. 373. Verb + infinitive. (Chart 13-3)

Some items have only one possible completion. For others, elicit a variety of completions in class discussion.

EXPECTED ANSWERS: **2.** to find / to rent **3.** to be **4.** to buy / to get **5.** to visit / to go to / to see **6.** to go to / to visit / to live in **7.** to do / to finish **8.** to get to / to arrive in **9.** to watch **10.** to be **11.** to be **12.** to be . . . to hear **13.** to buy **14.** to become / to be **15.** to lend / to loan / to give **16.** to eat **17.** to go to . . . to attend **18.** to pass **19.** to get to / to be in **20.** to see / to be with **21.** to hurt / to offend / to ignore / to interrupt / to embarrass **22.** to swim / to read / to answer the phone / to tell time

CHART 13-4: VERB + GERUND OR INFINITIVE

- In using the main verbs listed in this chart, native speakers may have a preference for either a gerund or an infinitive in certain instances, or there may be a difference in preferences in AmE and BrE. However, the learners will be grammatically correct if they use either form following the common verbs listed here.

  There is usually no substantial difference in meaning between one form or the other following these verbs, but there may be some subtle differences that learners at this stage would have trouble discerning. (A common example used to illustrate this is *I hate singing* vs. *I hate to sing. I hate singing* can mean the speaker hates it when other people sing or hates it when he sings. *I hate to sing* means the speaker hates it when he sings. In other instances, however, there is only a very small and very subtle difference between a gerund or an infinitive following *hate: I hate being late for appointments* and *I hate to be late for appointments.* This is generally too much information for students at this level.)
- This might be a good opportunity to discuss the difference between *like* and *would like: Do you like to dance?* (Do you enjoy this?) vs. *Would you like to dance?* (an invitation)
- *Can't stand* (meaning "hate") may be new for your students. It is used principally in informal spoken English. It isn't quite as strong as the word *hate,* but is stronger than *do not like.*

☐ **EXERCISE 6, p. 375. Verb + gerund or infinitive. (Chart 13-4)**

This exercise seeks to make clear that either form is correct after certain verbs.

☐ **EXERCISE 7, p. 375. Verb + gerund or infinitive. (Chart 13-4)**

This practice encourages students to discuss their likes and dislikes. The class can work in small groups. The goal is meaningful communication in direct conversation that employs the target structures.

SAMPLE RESPONSES:

2. I don't like to live/living in this city.
3. I can't stand to wash/washing dishes.
4. I love to fly/flying.
5. I don't mind waiting in airports.
6. I enjoy reading novels in my spare time.
7. I enjoy eating a delicious meal slowly.
8. I don't mind speaking in front of a large group.
9. I enjoy playing cards for money.
10. I hate to drive/driving on city streets during rush hour.
11. I don't like to go/going to parties where I don't know a single person.
12. I like to listen/listening to the sounds of the city while I'm trying to get to sleep.
13. I love to visit/visiting with friends I haven't seen in a long time.
14. I don't like to get/getting in between two friends who are having an argument.
15. I enjoy travel(l)ing to strange and exotic places. [spelling: AmE prefers *traveling;* BrE prefers *travelling.*]

☐ **EXERCISE 8, p. 375. Gerunds vs. infinitives. (Charts 13-1 → 13-4)**

Some students may want to try to memorize the lists in the charts, but the intention of the text is to supply plenty of practice to help the students become comfortable and familiar with common verbs followed by gerunds and infinitives.

ANSWERS:

4. to get
5. eating
6. to meet/meeting
7. to help
8. to watch/watching
9. cracking
10. to feed
11. to be
12. moving
13. to go/going
14. to lock
15. living
16. to take
17. to give
18. to hire/hiring . . . coming
19. to say
20. to go shopping
21. to want to go sailing
22. sleeping
23. trying to grow
24. being

☐ **EXERCISE 9, p. 377. Gerunds vs. infinitives. (Charts 13-1 → 13-4)**

Encourage the students to use a variety of place names by telling them they can say a place name only one time.

Student A needs to monitor B's responses for correct usage of gerunds and infinitives. Student A can look in the charts, if necessary, to ascertain whether B's response is correct, or ask the teacher.

☐ **EXERCISE 10, p. 377. Gerunds vs. infinitives. (Charts 13-1 → 13-4)**

The purpose of this exercise is to illustrate parallel usage of gerunds and infinitives. Lack of parallelism is a common problem; e.g., *INCORRECT: I enjoy getting up early and watch the sunrise.* (NOTE: Without *and,* the sentence *I enjoy getting up early (in order) to watch the sunrise* is also possible.)

ANSWERS:

2. to relax
3. to stay . . . relax
4. to stay . . . relax . . . go
5. getting
6. watching
7. getting . . . watching
8. getting . . . watching . . . listening
9. selling . . . buying
10. to move . . . find . . . start
11. painting
12. to go . . . buy
13. going . . . having
14. to be/being
15. going
16. to stop making
17. quitting . . . going
18. to leave . . . return
19. washing
20. to unplug . . . turn off . . . lock
21. to understand
22. to stop driving
23. to reach . . . to keep trying

□ EXERCISE 11, p. 379. Gerunds vs. infinitives. (Charts 13-1 → 13-4)

ANSWERS:

1. plan to go
2. consider going
3. offer to lend
4. like to visit / like visiting
5. enjoy reading
6. intend to get
7. decide to get
8. seem to be
9. put off writing
10. forget to go
11. can't afford to buy
12. try to learn
13. need to learn
14. would love to take
15. would like to go swimming
16. promise to come
17. finish studying
18. would mind helping
19. hope to go
20. think about going
21. quit trying
22. expect to stay
23. stop eating (OR: stop in order to eat)
24. refuse to lend
25. agree to lend
26. postpone going
27. begin to study / begin studying
28. continue to walk / continue walking
29. talk about going
30. keep trying to improve

□ EXERCISE 12, p. 379. Gerunds vs. infinitives. (Charts 13-1 → 13-4)

This passage was written specifically to include a number of gerunds and infinitives, but it nonetheless illustrates how useful and common these verbals are.

ANSWERS:

2. to drive
3. to compromise
4. to find
5. to go
6. going
7. fishing
8. taking
9. renting
10. going
11. sailing
12. staying
13. relaxing
14. doing
15. to visit/visiting
16. to do/doing
17. seeing
18. to visit
19. to go
20. camping
21. camping/to camp
22. to go
23. to spend/spending
24. to say
25. to like
26. thinking
27. thinking
28. to find
29. to go
30. to hear
31. to call
32. skiing
33. waterskiing
34. hiking
35. swimming
36. exploring
37. to climb
38. look

CHART 13-5: PREPOSITION + GERUND

• A gerund, not an infinitive, immediately follows a preposition. (In the idiomatic expression *to be **about to do** something, about* functions as an adjective, not a preposition. It means "just ready." See Chart 3-9.)

• The text does not introduce gerunds that have their own "subjects" that can occur between a preposition and the gerund: *Kate insisted on Jake('s) coming with us.* (See *Understanding and Using English Grammar, Third Edition,* Chart 15-6.)

☐ EXERCISE 13, p. 381. Preposition + gerund. (Chart 13-5 and Appendix 2)

Students can look up the correct prepositions by referring to Appendix 2, Chart A2-2, p. 463. More efficiently, the teacher can supply the correct prepositions when there is a question.

ANSWERS:

2. for opening
3. about being
4. in going
5. for being
6. of flying
7. about taking
8. about going
9. on paying
10. of/about being
11. like eating
12. for not calling
13. of living
14. in being
15. on meeting/to meet
16. for cleaning
17. from entering
18. at cutting

☐ EXERCISE 14, p. 382. Preposition + gerund. (Chart 13-5 and Appendix 2)

Item 9 might cause confusion. *Plan* can be followed immediately by an infinitive, or by a preposition and gerund: *I'm planning **to go** to a movie tonight.* OR *I'm planning **on going** to a movie tonight.*

SAMPLE ANSWERS: **1.** I'm interested in going swimming. **2.** I'm worried about failing my exams. **3.** I thanked my friend for watering my plants. **4.** I apologized for interrupting the teacher. **5.** I'm afraid of walking home alone at night. **6.** I'm nervous about taking final exams. **7.** I'm excited about going to the opera. **8.** I feel like cutting class today. **9.** I'm planning on visiting my relatives in Miami. **10.** I'm tired of doing grammar exercises.

☐ EXERCISE 15, p. 382. Preposition + gerund. (Chart 13-5)

You could make up a quick oral exercise to help the students learn the preposition combinations in this exercise: start a sentence and have the students call out the correct preposition. For example:

TEACHER: *I don't like big dogs. I'm afraid . . .*
CLASS: ***of***
TEACHER: *Right! . . . afraid **of** them.*

ANSWERS:

3. of drowning
4. about meeting
5. for helping
6. in going
7. about visiting
8. about pleasing
9. to taking
10. like telling
11. for lying
12. on paying
13. for causing
14. at remembering
15. about/of quitting
16. from doing
17. on eating
18. for spilling
19. of losing

☐ EXERCISE 16, p. 384. Preposition + gerund. (Chart 13-5)

Having students make up quizzes for each other is a good technique for reviewing grammar. Students who teach other students learn a lot themselves.

This is the only example of this type of exercise in the text, but you can use this technique in almost every chapter. One suggestion is to have students make up preposition quizzes for each other based on the groups of phrasal verbs and preposition combinations in the appendices.

SAMPLE ITEMS:

1. I thanked Mustafa ________ (open) ________________ the door.
2. I feel ________ (take) ________________ a trip.
3. Ana is worried ________ (not have) ________________ a valid passport.
4. Jack insisted ________ (drive) ________________ the car.
5. I don't believe ________ (trust) ________________ other people with my money.
6. Sam is nervous ________ (speak) ________________ in front of the class.
7. I look forward ________ (do) ________________ my workout at the gym.
8. Nadia apologized to her roommate ________ (sell) ________________ her radio.
9. Please forgive me ________ (lie) ________________ to you.
10. Are you excited ________ (move) ________________ to Los Angeles?

CHART 13-6: USING *BY* AND *WITH* TO EXPRESS HOW SOMETHING IS DONE
• In general, *by* is used with means of transportation or communication, and *with* is used with tools or parts of the body. (EXCEPTION: *by hand*)

☐ EXERCISE 17, p. 385. BY + gerund. (Chart 13-6)

Some of the vocabulary might require explanation and discussion.

POSSIBLE ANSWERS: **2.** by washing **3.** by watching **4.** by smiling **5.** by eating **6.** by drinking **7.** by guessing **8.** by waving **9.** by wagging **10.** by staying . . . taking **11.** by cooking / by freezing **12.** by frying . . . boiling . . . poaching **13.** by reading a lot / speaking only English / etc. **14.** by recycling glass (newspapers, aluminum, etc.) / by not wasting water (oil, electricity, etc.) / by turning off the electricity when we leave a room / etc. **15.** by asking knowledgeable questions **16.** by exercising **17.** by reading aloud to them from a very young age **18.** by conserving the earth's resources / by working for peace / etc.

☐ EXERCISE 18, p. 386. Using WITH. (Chart 13-6)

ANSWERS:

2. with a needle and thread
3. with a saw
4. with a thermometer
5. with a spoon
6. with a shovel
7. with a hammer
8. with a pair of scissors

☐ **EXERCISE 19, p. 386. Using BY or WITH. (Chart 13-6)**

ANSWERS:

3. with
4. by
5. with
6. with
7. by
8. with
9. by
10. by
11. with
12. by
13. with
14. by

CHART 13-7: USING GERUNDS AS SUBJECTS; USING *IT* + INFINITIVE

• Point out that a gerund phrase as subject is singular and takes a singular verb, even if the gerund is followed by a plural noun: ***Reading*** *books* ***is*** *fun.* In this sentence, *reading,* not *books,* determines the verb.

• Confusion may arise in cases where the *-ing* word is used as an adjective to modify a noun: *Reading* **books** (i.e., books that teach reading skills) ***are*** *usually collections of essays and stories.* (Some grammars analyze this use of *reading* as a gerund used as a noun adjunct; others view it as a present participle used as an adjective.)

Other examples:

Washing (gerund) *dishes* ***isn't*** *much fun.* vs. *Washing* (adjectival) ***machines are*** *expensive.*
Helping (gerund) *other people* ***is*** *important.* vs. *Helping* (adjectival) ***verbs are*** *also called auxiliary verbs.*

The text does not address these grammar points, but questions may arise.

• Keep the students' focus on the two patterns presented in examples (a) and (b). Infinitives can, of course, be used as the subject of a sentence: *To ride horses is fun.* The text chooses to emphasize the more common pattern that uses a gerund as the subject. It is also possible for a gerund to follow *it: It is fun riding horses.* Again the text chooses to emphasize the more common pattern of ***it*** + *infinitive.*

☐ **EXERCISE 20, p. 387. Gerunds as subjects. (Chart 13-7)**

ANSWERS:

2. Making friends isn't hard.
3. Cooking rice is easy.
4. Taking a long walk is relaxing.
5. Is learning a second language difficult?
6. Cheating during a test is wrong.
7. Is living in an apartment expensive?
8. Living in a foreign country isn't easy.
9. Making new friends takes time.

☐ **EXERCISE 21, p. 387. IT + infinitive. (Chart 13-7)**

ANSWERS:

2. It's fun to play tennis. **3.** It's important to be polite to other people. **4.** It's interesting to learn about other cultures. **5.** It's dangerous to walk alone at night **6.** Is it easy to ride a motorcycle? **7.** It isn't much fun to have a cold. **8.** It takes a long time to learn a second language. **9.** It takes three minutes to cook

☐ **EXERCISE 22, p. 387. Gerunds as subjects; IT + infinitive. (Chart 13-7)**

Responding students may need to leave their books open for this exercise.

SAMPLE ANSWER:

1. B: It's more fun to go to a movie than (to) study at the library.
A: I agree. Going to a movie is more fun than studying at the library.

CHART 13-8: *IT* + INFINITIVE: USING *FOR (SOMEONE)*

- This chart expands the ***it*** + *infinitive* pattern by adding *for (someone)*. This is a frequent and productive sentence type, especially in spoken English.

☐ EXERCISE 23, p. 388. Using FOR (SOMEONE). (Chart 13-8)

ANSWERS:

2. for teachers to speak clearly
3. for us to hurry
4. for a fish to live out of water
5. for students to budget their time carefully
6. for a child to sit still for a long time
7. for my family to eat turkey on Thanksgiving Day [Thanksgiving occurs on the fourth Thursday in November in the U.S. and on the second Monday of October in Canada.]
8. for people to take trips to the moon
9. for me to understand Mr. Alvarez
10. for guests to wait until the hostess begins to eat
11. for the bride to feed the groom the first piece of wedding cake
12. for me to understand our teacher

☐ EXERCISE 24, p. 390. Gerunds as subjects; IT + infinitive. (Charts 13-7 and 13-8)

ANSWERS:

2. Reading newspapers is important/fun/educational/relaxing. OR
   It is important/fun/educational/relaxing to read newspapers.
3. Studying grammar is easy/hard/important. OR
   It is easy/hard/important to study grammar.
4. Playing tennis is easy/hard/exciting/fun/relaxing. OR
   It is easy/hard/exciting/fun/relaxing to play tennis.
5. Stealing cars is against the law/dangerous. OR
   It is against the law/dangerous to steal cars.
6. Listening to a two-hour speech is boring/hard/impossible/a waste of time. OR
   It is boring/hard/impossible/a waste of time to listen to a two-hour speech.
7. Predicting the exact time of an earthquake is impossible. OR
   It is impossible to predict the exact time of an earthquake.
8. Forgetting someone's name is embarrassing. OR
   It is embarrassing to forget someone's name.
9. Walking alone through a dark forest at night is dangerous/frightening. OR
   It is dangerous/frightening to walk alone through a dark forest at night.
10. Going fishing with your friends is fun/relaxing. OR
    It is fun/relaxing to go fishing with your friends.
11. Knowing the meaning of every word in a dictionary is impossible. OR
    It is impossible to know the meaning of every word in a dictionary.
12. Being honest with yourself at all times is hard/important. OR
    It is hard/important to be honest with yourself at all times.
13. Changing a flat tire is easy/hard. OR
    It is easy/hard to change a flat tire.
14. Visiting museums is boring/educational/exciting/fun/relaxing. OR
    It is boring/educational/exciting/fun/relaxing to visit museums.
15. Logging on to the Internet is easy/fun/exciting/educational/relaxing. OR
    It is boring/a waste of time to log on to the Internet.

☐ EXERCISE 25, p. 390. IT + FOR (SOMEONE) + infinitive. (Charts 13-7 and 13-8)

One of the main points of this exercise is to show how the *for (someone)* phrase qualifies generalizations, i.e., limits them.

SAMPLE RESPONSES: **2.** It's easy for children to learn how to swim. It's easy for some people to change a flat tire. **3.** It's fun for most people to visit new places. It's fun for most people to learn how to swim. It's fun for most people to spend time with friends. **4.** It's important for students to be on time for class. It's important for children to obey their parents. It is important for anyone to spend time with friends. **5.** It's impossible for anyone to live on the planet Mars. It's impossible for some people to learn how to swim. It is impossible for some people to change a flat tire. It's impossible for anyone to predict the exact time of an earthquake. **6.** It's enjoyable for anyone to spend time with friends. It's enjoyable for most people to visit new places. It's enjoyable for children to learn how to swim. **7.** It's interesting for most people to observe animals in their wild habitat. It's interesting for most people to visit new places. **8.** It's possible for most people to change a flat tire. It's possible for most people to learn how to swim.

☐ EXERCISE 26, p. 391. IT + FOR (SOMEONE) + infinitive. (Charts 13-7 and 13-8)

SAMPLE RESPONSES:

1. It is easy for David to build a chair.
2. It's traditional for the man to ask the woman to marry him.
3. It's impossible for me to read your mind. [*to read your mind* = to guess your thoughts]
4. It takes an hour for Guido to deliver the morning newspapers.
5. It's sensible for people to exercise each day.
6. Is it necessary for you to play the stereo so loudly?
7. It's important for children to go to bed early.
8. It's difficult for me to call you during the day.

☐ EXERCISE 27, p. 391. IT + TAKE + infinitive. (Charts 5-13 and 13-8)

The pattern with ***it*** + ***take*** + *infinitive* is introduced in Chapter 5 in connection with questions with *how long.* The pattern is reviewed and expanded upon here to include ***take*** + *time* (or an expression of time, e.g., *days, years, months*), *money, patience, courage, skill, hard work, stamina,* and *determination* + *(for someone)* + *infinitive phrase.* In other words, this exercise presents information not covered in a chart by teaching vocabulary used in the pattern with ***it*** + ***take***. You might want to make special note for your students of the common words used in this pattern.

SAMPLE RESPONSES:

1. It takes time for young adults to decide what career to follow.
2. It takes a lot of money to build a house.
3. It takes three minutes to poach an egg.
4. How long does it take to cross the English Channel?
5. It will take many years for nations to learn to live together in peace.
6. It takes patience to learn to knit. It takes courage to live by your principles. It takes skill to ride a horse.
7. It takes hard work for construction workers to erect a building.
8. It takes stamina and determination to compete in the Olympic Games.

CHART 13-9: EXPRESSING PURPOSE WITH *IN ORDER TO* AND *FOR*

- Common mistakes are:

  INCORRECT: *She came here for studying English.*
  INCORRECT: *She came here for to study English.*
  INCORRECT: *She came here for study English.*

- There is an exception in which *for* is followed by a gerund to express purpose. The phrase *be used for* expresses the typical or general purpose of a thing. In this case, the preposition *for* is followed by a gerund: *A saw is used for cutting wood.* Also possible: *A saw is used (in order) to cut wood.*

- This might be a good place to review the information in the footnote on p. 370 regarding ***stop*** + *gerund* compared to ***stop*** + *infinitive of purpose.*

  COMPARE: *I **stopped reading** and took a walk.*
  *I was reading, but around three o'clock I **stopped (in order) to take** a walk.*

☐ EXERCISE 28, p. 392. Using IN ORDER TO. (Chart 13-9)

ANSWERS:

3. . . . hospital **in order** to visit
4. *(no change)*
5. . . . today **in order** to deposit
6. . . . drugstore **in order** to buy
7. . . . dictionary **in order** to find
8. . . . cafeteria **in order** to eat
9. *(no change)*
10. . . . TV **in order** to improve
11. *(no change)*
12. . . . university **in order** to ask
13. . . . shoulder **in order** to get
14. *(no change)*
15. . . . bookstore **in order** to buy

☐ EXERCISE 29, p. 392. Using (IN ORDER) TO. (Chart 13-9)

ANSWERS:

2. C (in order) to listen
3. D (in order) to find
4. A (in order) to keep
5. I (in order) to see
6. B (in order) to reach
7. J (in order) to look
8. F (in order) to chase
9. H (in order) to get
10. G (in order) to help

☐ EXERCISE 30, p. 393. Expressing purpose with TO and FOR. (Chart 13-9)

ANSWERS:

3. to
4. for
5. for
6. to
7. to
8. for
9. to
10. for
11. to
12. to
13. for
14. for
15. to

☐ EXERCISE 31, p. 393. Expressing purpose with TO and FOR. (Chart 13-9)

Whichever pattern students use is fine: infinitives or *for*-phrases.

SAMPLE ANSWERS: **1.** I went to the supermarket for some bread / to get some bread. **2.** I need to go to the bookstore for some notebook paper / to get some notebook paper. **3.** I went to the post office for some stamps / to get some stamps. **4.** I went to the health clinic for an appointment with a dermatologist / to see a dermatologist. **5.** I reached into my pocket/purse for some change / to get some change for the candy machine. **6.** I came to this school to study English / for the Intensive English Program.

7. I borrowed some money from (. . .) for gas [BrE: petrol] for my car / to buy gas for my car. **8.** I stopped at the service station for gas / to get gas. **9.** I play tennis for exercise / to get exercise. **10.** I had to go out last night for a meeting / to go to a meeting.

CHART 13-10: USING INFINITIVES WITH *TOO* AND *ENOUGH*

- Review the meanings and spellings of *to, too,* and *two,* all of which have the same pronunciation.

  to = a preposition or part of an infinitive.
  too = (1) an adverb meaning "also" that comes at the end of a sentence; or
  (2) as in this chart, a modifier that means "excessive."
  two = the number 2.

- Note that *too* is not used before adjectives immediately followed by nouns:

  CORRECT: *We didn't go swimming because the water was* ***too cold.***
  INCORRECT: *We didn't go swimming because of the* ***too cold water.***

There is another possible but infrequent pattern with *too* and a singular count noun:

too + *adjective* + **a** + *noun.*

Example: *It was* ***too hot a day*** *for hard work in the sun.*

- A common problem results from learners attempting to use *too* as an intensifier meaning "very, very."

  INCORRECT: *We all enjoyed the scenery a lot. It was too beautiful!*

Explain that the use of *too* implies a negative result (i.e., something can't happen, as in *This ring is too expensive. I can't buy it.)* and does not mean "very, very." (In a negative sentence, of course, the opposite is true and *too* implies a positive result: *The ring wasn't too expensive. I could buy it.)*

- *Enough* means "sufficient or sufficiently." It conveys the presence of the necessary extent, amount, or degree of something to produce a certain result. The result is expressed in the infinitive phrase: *I'm tall enough to touch the ceiling.* = *My being able to touch the ceiling is the result of the fact that I have the necessary height.*

  Explaining the meaning of *enough* by using synonyms or definitions is not easy. Usually students can understand its meaning simply from the examples in the charts and exercises.

- Perhaps you can think of a way to illustrate *too* and *enough* in the classroom. One idea would be to pick a high spot in the room, maybe the top of a window. Who is tall enough to touch it? Who isn't tall enough? Who is too short? Is anyone too short to touch the top of the window?

☐ EXERCISE 32, p. 394. TOO and ENOUGH + infinitive. (Chart 13-10)

Note the instructions to use *too* in items 1–6 and *enough* in 7–10.

PART I. ANSWERS: **2.** I was too sleepy to finish my homework last night. **3.** This jacket is too small for me to wear. **4.** Mike was too busy to go to his aunt's housewarming party. **5.** I live too far from school to walk there. **6.** Some movies are too violent for children to watch.

PART II. ANSWERS: **8.** I'm not strong enough to lift a horse. **9.** It's not warm enough today for us to go outside in shorts and sandals. **10.** I wasn't sick enough to stay home and miss work, but I didn't feel good all day.

☐ EXERCISE 33, p. 394. TOO and ENOUGH + infinitive. (Chart 13-10)

ANSWERS:

3. too busy to answer
4. early enough to get
5. too full to hold
6. large enough to hold
7. too big to get
8. big enough to hold

☐ EXERCISE 34, p. 395. TOO and ENOUGH + infinitive. (Chart 13-10)

ANSWERS:

3. Ø . . . enough
4. too . . . Ø
5. too . . . Ø
6. too . . . Ø
7. Ø . . . enough
8. Ø . . . enough
9. too . . . Ø

☐ EXERCISE 35, p. 396. TOO and ENOUGH + infinitive. (Chart 13-10)

POSSIBLE COMPLETIONS:

1. . . . to touch the ceiling.
2. . . . to touch the ceiling.
3. . . . to lift a horse.
4. . . . to do my homework.
5. . . . to call my mother.
6. . . . for me to buy.
7. . . . to buy a Mercedes.
8. . . . to finish my homework.
9. . . . to stay home alone . . . to have his or her own apartment.
10. . . . to have conversations about the weather . . . to understand everything I hear

☐ EXERCISE 36, p. 396. Review: gerunds vs. infinitives. (Chapter 13)

ANSWERS:

3. (in order) to look
4. to go/going swimming
5. (in order) to invite
6. going
7. listening
8. drawing
9. to understand . . . to improve . . . to be . . . Lecturing
10. to feed
11. to feed . . . getting
12. feeding
13. (in order) to earn . . . to take
14. to take
15. to get . . . sleep
16. staring . . . thinking . . . to be
17. to work . . . going/to go . . . looking . . . doing
18. Asking . . . getting . . . to make . . . keep . . . to be
19. forgetting to call
20. to travel/traveling . . . to go/going
21. (in order) to make
22. taking
23. cracking . . . to be
24. to shake . . . looking *(also possible:* to look)
25. to stand/standing . . . to move/moving
26. Smiling

☐ EXERCISE 37, p. 398. Error analysis. (Chapter 13)

As in other error-analysis exercises, almost all the entries are adapted from actual student writing. Students might like to know that students before them made the same errors they make but have gone on to successful second-language acquisition. Making errors is just part of the process—you could compare it to learning a musical instrument. No one can sit down and play perfectly from the beginning or just from studying a manual. It takes practice, practice, practice (mistakes and all)—as does language learning.

ANSWERS: **2.** I went to the store **to get** some toothpaste. **3.** Did you go ~~to~~ shopping yesterday? **4.** I usually go to the cafeteria ~~for~~ to get a cup of coffee in the morning. (OR: . . . to the cafeteria for ~~to get~~ a cup of coffee) **5.** Bob needed to **go** downtown yesterday. **6.** I cut the rope **with** a knife. **7.** I thanked him for **driving** me to the airport. **8.** **It is** difficult to learn a second language. **9.** It is important **to get** an education. **10.** Timmy isn't **old** enough **to** get married. **11.** Do you want **to** go ~~to~~ swimming tomorrow? **12.** I went to the bank **to cash** a check. **13.** I was **too** sleepy to finish my homework last night. **14.** **It is easy to do** this exercise. / **This exercise is** easy to do. **15.** Last night **I was** too tired **to** do my homework. **16.** I've never gone ~~to~~ sailing, but I would like to. **17.** Reading ~~it~~ is one of my **hobbies**. **18.** The man began to **build** a wall around his garden. **19.** . . . you learn **a lot** about other countries and cultures. **20.** Instead of **settling** down in one place **21.** My grandmother likes to **fish** / likes ~~to~~ fishing / likes to **go** fishing. **22.** Mary would like to **have** a big family.

☐ EXERCISE 38, p. 399. Speaking. (Chapter 13)

Brainstorm ideas for topics before dividing the class into groups. In organizing the groups, make one student the time-keeper.

☐ EXERCISE 39, p. 399. Writing. (Chapter 13)

As a preliminary to the assignment, ask students what activities they enjoy and discuss what they could write about them. Help the students get started on this assignment by showing a lot of interest in their activities and asking a lot of questions about them.

☐ EXERCISE 40, p. 400. Review: verb forms. (Chapters 1 → 13)

This practice contains almost all of the verb forms introduced from the beginning of the text through this chapter.

ANSWERS:

2. went
3. is
4. manufactures
5. are made
6. has
7. needs
8. to meet
9. travels
10. went
11. (in order) to meet
12. speaks
13. knows
14. doesn't know
15. was staying
16. had
17. was staying
18. was getting
19. heard
20. walked
21. opened
22. found
23. took
24. looked
25. saw
26. turned
27. to go
28. was closed/had closed
29. was locked
30. didn't have
31. wasn't dressed
32. was wearing
33. am I going to do / will I do / should I do / can I do
34. standing
35. decided
36. to get
37. started
38. walking/to walk
39. knocking
40. (in order) to ask
41. to ask
42. reached
43. pushed
44. waited
45. came
46. took
47. got
48. were surprised

49. saw
50. was wrapped
51. thought
52. trying
53. to explain
54. didn't know
55. nodded
56. didn't smile / wasn't smiling
57. looked
58. smiled
59. reached
60. walked
61. looked
62. didn't have to understand
63. (in order) to figure
64. didn't have to say
65. grabbed
66. took
67. led
68. is still embarrassed
69. laughs
70. tells

☐ EXERCISE 41, p. 402. Review of verb forms: writing. (Chapters 1 → 13)

Students can model their composition on the passage in Exercise 40. Discuss embarrassing experiences with your class to help them get started on this assignment. Think of an embarrassing experience you have had and share that. You could also volunteer to write a composition yourself and bring it to class to share with the students. Students often like the idea that the teacher is doing the same writing assignment. It also helps the teacher understand writing assignments from the students' perspective and how s/he can best help students produce good compositions.

Chapter 14: NOUN CLAUSES

ORDER OF CHAPTER	CHARTS	EXERCISES	WORKBOOK
Introduction	14-1		
Noun clauses that begin with a question word	14-2 → 14-3	Ex. 1 → 7	Pr. 1 → 10
Noun clauses that begin with *if* or *whether*	14-4	Ex. 8 → 9	Pr. 11 → 14
Summary review		Ex. 10 → 14	
That-clauses	14-5 → 14-6	Ex. 15 → 20	Pr. 15 → 18
Substituting *so* for a *that*-clause	14-7	Ex. 21 → 22	Pr. 19
Quoted vs. reported speech	14-8 → 14-9	Ex. 23 → 27	Pr. 20 → 24
Reported speech	14-10 → 14-11	Ex. 28 → 31	Pr. 25 → 31
Cumulative review		Ex. 32 → 38	Pr. 32 → 36

General Notes on Chapter 14

• The first part of the chapter is organized around the three types of noun clauses: those introduced by (1) question words, (2) *if/whether,* and (3) *that.* In the first two sections, noun clauses are presented as transformations of information questions and yes/no questions.

In the second part of the chapter, students also learn to report the words of another person. This is useful in situations ranging from informal conversation to formal academic writing.

• TERMINOLOGY: Other terms for some types of noun clauses are "nominal clause," "WH-clause," "that-clause," and "included, embedded or indirect questions." In this text, subordinating conjunctions (e.g., *who, what, if, that)* are simply called "words that introduce noun clauses." *Quoted speech* is also called "direct speech" or "direct discourse." *Reported speech* is also called "indirect speech" or "indirect discourse."

CHART 14-1: NOUN CLAUSES: INTRODUCTION

- The principal problem learners have with noun clauses is correct word order. Students may use question word order (i.e., inverted subject and verb) in noun clauses introduced by a question word:

  INCORRECT: *I wanted to know why did Ann leave early.*

Similarly, students may use noun clause word order in questions:

  INCORRECT: *Why you left early?*

- Another difficulty stems from tense changes in noun clauses. For example, the spoken question *Why* ***is*** *Tom absent?* sometimes changes tense if the reporting verb is past: *The teacher* ***wanted*** *to know why Tom* ***was*** *absent.*

  The formal sequence of tenses in noun clauses is presented in Chart 14-10. Until that point in the chapter (i.e., until all three forms of noun clauses have been introduced and practiced), no introductory verbs are past tense if the student is required to supply the noun clause verb. In this way, students can avoid the complicating problem of changing noun clause verbs to past forms. You should remember to use only present introductory verbs such as *I don't know* when making up your own examples or quizzes.

CHART 14-2: NOUN CLAUSES THAT BEGIN WITH A QUESTION WORD

- The focus in this chart and the accompanying exercises is on word order in noun clauses that begin with question words. A quick review of question forms at this point is helpful for students.

☐ EXERCISE 1, p. 404. Information questions and noun clauses. (Charts 5-2 and 14-2)

The difference between a question and a noun clause lies in word order. That's what students are being asked to recognize here. The exception, of course, is that the word order is the same in the two when the question word is the subject, as in items 11 and 12.

ANSWERS:

3. I don't know . . . living**.** *(noun clause)*
4. **W**here is she living**?** *(information question)*
5. **W**here did Paul go**?** *(information question)*
6. I don't know . . . went**.** *(noun clause)*
7. I don't know . . . begins**.** *(noun clause)*
8. **W**hat time . . . begin**?** *(information question)*
9. **H**ow old is Kate**?** *(information question)*
10. I don't know . . . angry**.** *(noun clause)*
11. **W**hat happened**?** I don't know what happened**.** *(both)*
12. **W**ho came to the party**?** I don't know who came to the party**.** *(both)*
13. **W**ho(m) did . . . party**?** *(information question)*
14. **W**hat did Sue say**?** *(information question)*
15. I don't know . . . about**.** *(noun clause)*

☐ **EXERCISE 2, p. 405. Noun clauses that begin with a question word. (Chart 14-2)**

This exercise attempts to give students an idea of how noun clauses are typically used in conversation. Speaker B could, of course, simply stop after saying "I don't know," but often a speaker will repeat what has been asked, often repeating nouns and proper names instead of substituting pronouns.

ANSWERS: **2.** where Natasha went **3.** why Maria is laughing **4.** why fire is **5.** how much a new Honda costs **6.** why Mike is always **7.** how long birds live **8.** when the first wheel was invented **9.** how many hours a light bulb burns **10.** where Emily bought **11.** who lives **12.** who(m) Julie talked

☐ **EXERCISE 3, p. 406. Information questions and noun clauses. (Charts 5-2 and 14-2)**

In the example, Student A is "Marco" and Student B is "Ingrid." This exercise should probably be teacher-led due to its somewhat complicated format. You could change the content of some items to reflect your students' habits and interests.

☐ **EXERCISE 4, p. 406. Information questions and noun clauses. (Charts 5-2 and 14-2)**

In this practice, students have to produce correct word order for both noun clauses and information questions.

ANSWERS:
2. Jason works / is working . . . does he work / is he working
3. does that camera cost . . . this camera costs
4. can you run . . . I can run
5. did you see . . . I saw
6. did she get . . . she got
7. is it . . . it is
8. Who invented . . . who invented
9. are some people . . . some people are
10. will you spend / are you going to spend . . . you will spend / you are going to spend

CHART 14-3: NOUN CLAUSES WITH *WHO, WHAT, WHOSE* + *BE*

• Incorrect word order is a common problem in these clauses.

INCORRECT: *Do you know what is a wrench?*

• In these questions and clauses, the text defines *subject* as "the word that determines the number of the verb." You might discuss the words that determine the number of the verb in the following examples: *Who IS **that boy**? Who ARE **those boys**?*

When the subject follows *be*, the verb can be either singular or plural. However, when *who* is the subject of the question, the verb is almost always singular: *Who is in the office?* (not *Who are in the office?*)

• Students may find the grammar in this chart somewhat confusing. Use Exercise 5 to point out again and again when the question word is the subject and when it's not, discussing throughout how that affects the word order in the noun clause.

☐ EXERCISE 5, p. 408. Noun clauses with WHO, WHAT, WHOSE + BE. (Chart 14-3)

ANSWERS:

3. is = (V); a crow = (S) . . . what a crow is
4. What = (S); is = (V) . . . what is in that bag
5. cat = (S); is = (V) . . . whose cat is in the driveway
6. that = (S); is = (V) . . . whose car that is
7. is = (V); violin = (S) . . . what a violin is
8. Who = (S); is = (V) . . . who is in the doctor's office
9. this = (S); is = (V) . . . whose hammer this is . . . whose hammer this is
10. is = (V); doctor = (S) . . . who Bob's doctor is
11. What = (S); is = (V) . . . what is at the end of a rainbow

☐ EXERCISE 6, p. 409. Noun clauses. (Charts 14-2 and 14-3)

Tell the students to substitute their classmates' or friends' names between parentheses. In Items 11, 17, and 18, they can substitute other appropriate words between parentheses.

ANSWERS: I don't know . . .

1. where (. . .) went yesterday.
2. how old (. . .) is.
3. where (. . .) eats lunch.
4. what (. . .)'s name is.
5. what time (. . .) usually gets up.
6. when (. . .) got home last night.
7. what time (. . .) went to bed last night.
8. who (. . .)'s best friend is.
9. who (. . .) called last night.
10. how long (. . .) has been living here.
11. who wrote *(Tales of the South Pacific)*.
12. what happened in Alaska yesterday.
13. what (. . .) did yesterday.
14. who that girl is.
15. who those people are.
16. what kind of tree that is.
17. whose (backpack) that is.
18. whose (gloves) those are.

☐ EXERCISE 7, p. 409. Information questions and noun clauses. (Charts 5-2, 14-2, and 14-3)

Tell the student pairs to pay attention to each other's word order in questions and noun clauses. Students generally have fun thinking of questions their partners don't know the answer to.

SAMPLE ANSWERS: **1.** Where was Mahatma Gandhi born? I don't know for sure where Mahatma Gandhi was born. Was it India? **2.** Who invented the flashlight? I don't know who invented the flashlight. Maybe Thomas Edison? **3.** How far is it from Madrid to Barcelona? I don't know exactly how far it is from Madrid to Barcelona. About 500 kilometres? **4.** What kind of technology is needed to launch a space shuttle? I don't know what specific kind of technology is needed to launch a space shuttle. Perhaps the most up-to-date aerospace technology. **5.** What time do you think you'll get home tonight? I don't know exactly when I'll get home tonight. Probably ten o'clock. **6.** Whose book is that? I don't know whose book that is. Maybe it's Yoko's. **7.** When does the library open in the morning? I don't know exactly when the library opens in the morning. Probably eight o'clock. **8.** Why are some people afraid of snakes? I don't know why some people are afraid of snakes. **9.** What do you think is the greatest virtue? I don't know what the greatest virtue is. Probably charity.

CHART 14-4: NOUN CLAUSES THAT BEGIN WITH *IF* OR *WHETHER*

- In everyday usage, native speakers generally prefer *if* to *whether* to introduce noun clauses. The text emphasizes the use of *if* while acquainting the students with the use of *whether.*
- Point out that *weather* and *whether* have the same pronunciation but different meanings and spellings (i.e., are homophones).
- All possible patterns with *whether* and *or not* are not presented here. See *Understanding and Using English Grammar, Third Edition,* Chart 12-3.

☐ EXERCISE 8, p. 410. Noun clauses that begin with IF or WHETHER. (Chart 14-4)

ANSWERS: **2.** if (whether) Mr. Pips will be at the meeting **3.** if (whether) Paulo went to work yesterday **4.** if (whether) Barcelona is a coastal town **5.** if (whether) I still have Yung Soo's address

☐ EXERCISE 9, p. 410. Noun clauses that begin with IF or WHETHER. (Chart 14-4)

Ask the students to identify the yes/no question that they are transforming to a noun clause. Point out that these dialogues illustrate a typical pattern of usage: one speaker asks a yes/no question, and another restates or reports it using a noun clause.

ANSWERS:

2. if you are going to be
3. if all birds have
4. if she took
5. if he can babysit
6. if you have
7. if you should take

☐ EXERCISE 10, p. 411. Noun clauses. (Charts 14-2 → 14-4)

Note that some of the sentences are questions, so the main subject and verb are in inverted word order (e.g., *Do you know . . . ?*). The word order of the noun clause that follows is not inverted (e.g., . . . *what an amphibian is?)* even though the sentence ends in a question mark. Some students may find this momentarily confusing.

ANSWERS: **2.** what time it is. **3.** what an amphibian is? **4.** if a frog is an amphibian? **5.** what's on TV tonight. **6.** what the speed of sound is? **7.** if sound travels faster than light? **8.** if dogs are colorblind? **9.** why the sky is blue. **10.** if insects have ears. **11.** if beings from outer space have ever visited the earth. **12.** how dolphins communicate with each other? **13.** if people can communicate with dolphins.

☐ EXERCISE 11, p. 412. Noun clauses. (Charts 14-2 → 14-4)

This exercise is intended for pair work, but can be done in groups or be teacher-led. Real conversations do not include restatements of questions this consistently, but the format provides useful practice in noun clause formation.

☐ EXERCISE 12, p. 412. Noun clauses. (Charts 14-2 → 14-4)

Encourage imaginative responses by modeling your own curiosity about life. What do you know, not know, want to know, wonder?

☐ **EXERCISE 13, p. 413. Noun clauses. (Charts 14-1 → 14-4)**

This exercise is another approach to group work. Again, encourage imaginative responses. This practice can also be assigned as written homework.

☐ **EXERCISE 14, p. 413. Noun clauses and questions. (Charts 5-2 and 14-1 → 14-4)**

Some students may have difficulty understanding the somewhat algebraic use of "X" in this exercise. To help clarify the format, ask the class as a whole for sample questions for several of the items selected at random, or use these as introductory examples: the size of X (How big is a breadbasket?); the length of X (How long is a pencil? How long is a soccer game?); the height of X (How high is Mt. Everest?).

CHART 14-5: NOUN CLAUSES THAT BEGIN WITH *THAT*

• Write *I think that* . . . on the board. Ask the students to complete the sentence. They should find this task exceedingly simple; this pattern is surely already used by all your students. Now you are asking them to expand their usage ability by learning more words that introduce these clauses, such as *assume* and *realize*.

• Discuss the meaning of the verbs followed by *that*-clauses in this chart by eliciting examples from the class. If you have class time available, discuss the verbs in the footnote. They are useful, too. They are in a footnote because the chart itself lists only the verbs used in the exercises.

• The word *that* has no semantic meaning in this structure. It marks (i.e., signals) the beginning of a clause. Its omission does not affect the meaning of a sentence. In everyday English, especially spoken English, it is usually omitted. If it is not omitted, it is almost always unstressed and pronounced /thət/.

☐ **EXERCISE 15, p. 414. THAT-clauses. (Chart 14-5)**

ANSWERS: **2.** dreamed that I **3.** believe that we **4.** know that Matt . . . assume that he **5.** notice that Ji Ming . . . hope that he's **6.** believe that she **7.** read that half **8.** know that forty . . . believe that the immigrants **9.** think that a monster . . . says that some investigators say that they can prove that the Loch Ness

☐ **EXERCISE 16, p. 415. THAT-clauses. (Chart 14-5)**

This exercise can be done quickly, with students calling out completions. Its intention is to survey words other than *think* that introduce *that*-clauses and give the students some vocabulary practice.

CHART 14-6: OTHER USES OF *THAT*-CLAUSES

• This chart seeks to acquaint learners with common expressions in which *that*-clauses are used.

• Discuss the meaning of the expressions in this chart followed by *that*-clauses by eliciting examples from the class. If you have class time available, discuss the phrases in the footnote too.

☐ EXERCISE 17, p. 416. THAT-clauses. (Charts 14-5 and 14-6)

The ability to recognize when the clause marker *that* has been omitted can be important in reading comprehension. Whenever a reader (native or non-native speaker) is trying to figure out what a particularly confusing sentence means, an understanding of the underlying structure of the sentence is helpful if not essential. It's important for language users to know that optional parts of a structure (such as introductory *that)* might be omitted. It also explains to students why there is no period in a structure that contains two S–V combinations, as in item 1.

ANSWERS:

2. pleased that you
3. surprised that Ann . . . think that she
4. afraid that another . . . convinced that it
5. aware that you . . . certain that I'll
6. disappointed that my son . . . realize that young people . . . worried that my son's . . . forget that he's . . . think that he'll
7. a fact that some
8. aware that dinosaurs . . . true that human beings
9. a fact that blue whales . . . believe that they

☐ EXERCISE 18, p. 416. THAT-clauses. (Charts 14-5 and 14-6)

POSSIBLE ANSWERS: **2.** Mrs. Day is worried that Bobby is sick / might have the flu. Bobby is sure that he doesn't have the flu. **3.** Kim is surprised that Tina failed her chemistry course. Tina is disappointed that she failed her chemistry course. **4.** David is glad that Mike has come. Mike is happy that he's there. Mike is pleased that David invited him. **5.** Fred is upset that Susan's closet is empty. Fred is upset that Susan's suitcases are gone. Fred is afraid that Susan won't come back. Erica is sure that Susan will be back. **6.** John was shocked that Ed was in jail. Ed was shocked that he had been arrested. Ed was relieved that he didn't have to stay in jail long.

☐ EXERCISE 19, p. 417. THAT-clauses. (Charts 14-5 and 14-6)

This exercise can be accomplished quickly, with students calling out responses. Its purpose is to survey common phrases that introduce *that*-clauses.

☐ EXERCISE 20, p. 418. THAT-clauses. (Charts 14-5 and 14-6)

The opportunity for discussion is more important than the grammar. The exercise directions encourage noun clause usage, but if lively conversation begins, emphasis on the target structures can easily, and indeed should, be dropped.

You might ask students what topics they would like to discuss and use those instead of the ones in the text. Some classes like to discuss local issues like pesticide use on school grounds, or social issues like suicide, homelessness, or care of the mentally ill. Explore what your class is interested in talking about.

SAMPLE ANSWERS: **1.** I am convinced that cigarette smoking is harmful to your health. I have concluded that smoking a pipe is just as bad as smoking cigarettes. I hope that cigar smokers heed the warnings about smoking in general. I think that fewer people will smoke in the future. **2.–6.** *(free response)*

CHART 14-7: SUBSTITUTING *SO* FOR A *THAT*-CLAUSE IN CONVERSATIONAL RESPONSES

• This structure allows speakers to answer yes/no questions without committing themselves to a definite, black-and-white, yes-or-no answer. It allows for "gray areas" in speakers' knowledge.

• Focus the students' attention on the meaning of *so* in expressions such as *I think so.* In this structure, *so* functions as a substitute for a noun clause introduced by *that.*

• The word *so* has various uses. A dictionary will label it an adverb, adjective, pronoun, conjunction, and interjection. To the second language learner, *so* is probably one of the most confusing and unpredictable words in English. You could explain to your students that English has more than one *so,* each with a different function and meaning.

☐ EXERCISE 21, p. 419. Substituting SO for a THAT-clause. (Chart 14-7)

ANSWERS: **2.** I don't believe that we are going to have **3.** I hope that Margo will be **4.** I believe that cats can swim. **5.** I don't think that gorillas have tails. **6.** I suppose that Janet will be **7.** I hope that my / our flight won't be canceled

☐ EXERCISE 22, p. 419. Substituting SO for a THAT-clause. (Chart 14-7)

These short dialogues are typical of everyday conversations.

CHART 14-8: QUOTED SPEECH

• Using examples on the chalkboard, go through the punctuation and capitalization of quotations step by step. This information will probably be new to at least a few of the students.

• Learning how to use quotations in writing will help the students improve their narrative-descriptive writing as well as prepare them for academic writing in which they must cite sources (i.e., use the words of another writer). Students who are not interested in the conventions of written English could skip this unit.

• Information not included in the chart: When reporting words are not at the beginning of a quotation, the reporting phrase is sometimes inverted. For example: *"Cats are fun to watch,"* ***said Jane***. This inversion is used in writing rather than in speaking.
Also, reporting words can come in the middle of a quoted sentence: *"Cats," said Jane / Jane said, "are fun to watch."* Give your students as much information as will be useful to them without overloading them. Most students at this level don't require a survey of all the variations possible in writing quotations.

☐ EXERCISE 23, p. 420. Quoted speech. (Chart 14-8)

EXPANSION: Cut out comic strips from the newspaper and hand them out to the class. Tell the students to make up a story based on their comic strip. In their story, they should quote the speakers exactly.

ANSWERS:
2. Ann **asked,** "Is your brother a student?"
3. Rita **said,** "We're hungry."

4. "We're hungry," Rita **said** / **said** Rita. "Are you hungry too?" OR
"We're hungry. Are you hungry too?" Rita **said** / **said** Rita. [The possibility of inverted word order (e.g. *said Rita)* is not presented in Chart 14-8.]
5. Rita **said,** "We're hungry. Are you hungry too? Let's eat." [*Rita said* can be placed at the beginning, between sentences, or at the end, as in item 4.]
6. John F. Kennedy **said,** "Ask not . . . do for you. Ask what . . . for your country."
7. The fox **said,** "I'm going to eat you." The rabbit **said,** "You have to catch me first!"

☐ EXERCISE 24, p. 421. Quoted speech. (Chart 14-8)

ANSWERS:

"Both of your parents are deaf, aren't they?" I asked Roberto.

"Yes, they are," he replied.

"I'm looking for someone who knows sign language," I said. "Do you know sign language?" I asked.

He said, "**O**f course I do. I've been using sign language with my parents since I was a baby. It's a beautiful and expressive language. I often prefer it to spoken language."

"A deaf student is going to visit our class next Monday. Could you interpret for her?" I asked.

"I'd be delighted to," he answered. "I'm looking forward to meeting her. Can you tell me why she is coming?"

"She's interested in seeing what we do in our English classes," I said.

☐ EXERCISE 25, p. 422. Quoted speech. (Chart 14-8)

You should read all the cues to the students. However, between parentheses in item 1 are instructions to the teacher; only the examples or similar sentences should be spoken to the students.

After the students have written the quotations on their own paper, ask some of them to write the quotations on the chalkboard for all to see and discuss.

☐ EXERCISE 26, p. 422. Quoted speech. (Chart 14-8)

The purpose of this writing exercise is to practice using quoted material.

CHART 14-9: QUOTED SPEECH VS. REPORTED SPEECH

• The purposes of this chart are to introduce the concept of "reported speech" and to define terminology.

• Point out that "I" in quoted speech in (a) becomes "she" in (c) because the "I" in the quotation refers to Ann, the original speaker. You could illustrate this by using names of students and having them read short sentences from the board for other students to report.

Example:

SENTENCE ON BOARD: *I'm sleepy.*
SPEAKER A: *I'm sleepy.*
SPEAKER B: *Natasha said that* ***she*** *was sleepy.*
SPEAKER C: *I'm sleepy.*
SPEAKER B: *Po said that* ***he*** *was sleepy.*
Etc.

☐ EXERCISE 27, p. 423. Reported speech: pronoun usage. (Chart 14-9)

ANSWERS: **2.** she . . . her **3.** they . . . their **4.** he . . . me **5.** he . . . me . . . my . . . he . . . his . . . his

CHART 14-10: VERB FORMS IN REPORTED SPEECH

• Students will not control these patterns immediately, but the following exercises give lots of opportunity for practice.

• Some students might benefit from a quick reminder of names and meanings of the verb forms in Chapters 1, 2, 3, 4, and 7. Perhaps focus on the fact that auxiliaries carry most of the information about tense and number.

Following are the sequences of verb forms in the examples in the text:

simple present → simple past
present progressive → past progressive
present perfect → past perfect
simple past → past perfect
am, is, are going to → *was, were going to*
will → *would*
can → *could*

Other changes not introduced in this text (but covered in *Understanding and Using English Grammar, Third Edition,* Chart 12-7): *may* → *might; have to* → *had to; must* (meaning "necessity") → *had to; should* → *should* (no change); *ought to* → *ought to* (no change).

• In actual usage, there is no consistent rule for changing verb forms in noun clauses. The chart provides guidelines, but that's all they are.

• After discussing the verb changes shown in the chart, use a different verb and ask the class to change it appropriately. For example, conduct an oral exercise using the verb *watch:*

TEACHER: *I watch TV a lot.*
STUDENT: *You said you watched TV a lot.*
TEACHER: *I am not watching TV right now.*
STUDENT: *You said you weren't watching TV right now.*
Etc.

☐ EXERCISE 28, p. 424. Reported speech: formal verb forms. (Chart 14-10)

ANSWERS:

2. was meeting
3. had studied
4. had forgotten
5. was going to fly
6. would carry
7. could teach

☐ EXERCISE 29, p. 424. Quoted vs. reported speech. (Charts 14-9 and 14-10)

The focus is on tenses used to report a statement that was made in the past. Anticipate the exercise to proceed slowly and require a lot of discussion.

ANSWERS: **2.** Sally said (that) she didn't like chocolate. **3.** Mary said (that) she was planning . . . her family. **4.** Tom said (that) he had already eaten lunch. **5.** Kate said (that) she had called her doctor. **6.** Mr. Rice said (that) he was going to go to Chicago. **7.** Eric said (that) he would come to my house at ten. **8.** Jane said (that) she couldn't afford to buy a new car. **9.** Ann said (that) she can't afford to buy a new car. **10.** Ms. Topp said (that) she wanted to see me in her office after my meeting with my supervisor.

CHART 14-11: COMMON REPORTING VERBS: *TELL, ASK, ANSWER / REPLY*

• The main point the students need to understand from this chart is simply that *tell* is always followed by a (pro)noun object when used to report speech.

• Another pattern with *say* that is not mentioned in the chart is the use of *to* + a (pro)noun object: *Ann said* ***to me*** *that she was hungry.* Native speakers generally prefer *told me* to *said to me,* but both are correct.

• As a side note, the pattern *said . . . to me* is used idiomatically to report greetings and good-byes: *Tom said good morning to me. I said hello to him. We said good-bye to each other.*

INCORRECT: *Tom told me good morning. I told him hello. We told each other good-bye.*

☐ EXERCISE 30, p. 425. SAY vs. TELL vs. ASK. (Chart 14-11)

ANSWERS: **4.** said **5.** told **6.** asked **7.** told . . . said . . . asked . . . told . . . said **8.** said . . . asked . . . told . . . asked . . . said

☐ EXERCISE 31, p. 426. SAY vs. TELL vs. ASK. (Chart 14-11)

This is intended as a fun exercise. Student A is to whisper a sentence in the ear of Student B, who then reports aloud what Student A said. Students don't need to use only the sentences in the text.

Explain the meaning of "at random" in the directions, i.e., without a pattern or a plan.

☐ EXERCISE 32, p. 426. Noun clauses and questions. (Charts 5-2, 14-2 → 14-4, and 14-11)

Encourage interesting questions by coming up with some yourself as examples of what you want the students to do.

☐ EXERCISE 33, p. 427. Reported vs. quoted speech. (Charts 14-9 → 14-11)

ANSWERS:

1. In the middle of class yesterday, my friend tapped me on the shoulder. **"What** time is it?**"** she asked me.
"Two-thirty," I answered.

2. I met Mr. Redford at the reception for international students. **"Where** are you from?**"** he asked.
"I'm from Argentina," I told him.

3. When I was putting on my hat and coat, Robert asked me, **"Where** are you going?**"**
"I have a date with Anna," I told him.
"What are you going to do?" he wanted to know.
"We're going to a movie," I answered/replied.

☐ EXERCISE 34, p. 427. Reported speech. (Charts 14-9 → 14-11)

Students can use reporting verbs other than those in the quoted speech sentences, but the answers below use the same ones used in the text.

ANSWERS:
Conversation One: Susan asked me where Bill was. I told her (that) he was in the lunch room. She wanted to know when he would be back in his office. I said (that) he would be back around two.

Conversation Two: Mrs. Ball asked her husband if he could help her clean the hall closet. Mr. Ball told his wife (that) he was really busy. She wanted to know what he was doing. He replied (that) he was fixing the zipper on his winter jacket. Then she asked him if/whether he would have some time to help her after he fixed the zipper. He said (that) he couldn't because he had to watch a really important ball game on TV. With a note of exasperation in her voice, Mrs. Ball finally said (that) she would clean the closet herself.

☐ EXERCISE 35, p. 428. Reported speech. (Charts 14-9 → 14-11)

Make sure all the students understand the format of the cartoon, i.e., that the story should be read from top left to top right to bottom left to bottom right.

ANSWERS: (that) he wasn't going to have . . . wasn't hungry . . . had (already) eaten . . . he had come . . . he needed to talk to her about a problem he was having at work.

☐ EXERCISE 36, p. 428. Reported speech. (Charts 14-9 → 14-11)

Put the focus on the activity, not the grammar. This exercise requires fairly sophisticated use of a second language. Praise highly whatever target structures are used in the reports and let other errors go.

☐ EXERCISE 37, p. 429. Error analysis: noun clauses. (Chapter 14)

As in other error-analysis exercises, these sentences are adapted from actual student writing. Students often like to know that.

ANSWERS: **2.** I don't know what ~~is~~ your e-mail address **is**. **3.** I think ~~so~~ that Mr. Lee is out of town. **4.** Can you tell me ~~that~~ where Victor **5.** . . . what kind of movies ~~does~~ he **likes**. **6.** I think *(no comma)* that my English **7. It** is true that people are **8.** . . . **I didn't** know who **he was**. **9.** I want to know **if Pedro has** a laptop computer. **10.** . . . what ~~do~~ they say. **11.** . . . He told **me** / said that he **didn't** like *(also possible:* doesn't like) **12.** . . . and **asked me, "**Where is your brother?**"** **13.** . . . doctor said, **"**You will be fine. It's nothing serious.**"** **14.** . . . what ~~do~~ I read . . . what **he is** saying. **15.** . . . asked me ~~that~~, **"**When **will you be** home?**"** [Sometimes learners write quotation marks on the line rather than above the line.]

☐ EXERCISE 38, p. 430. Noun clauses and questions. (Charts 5-2 and 14-1 → 14-4)

Depending upon your students' purposes in studying English, this final exercise could be developed into a full-fledged composition that includes thoughtful argument for or against the views stated by John Newsom (a fictional person invented for the textbook). His views should appear in quotations in the students' compositions—much as is done in research papers. You could ask your students to agree or disagree with each of Mr. Newsom's statements, one at a time, in order to encourage ample opportunity to practice the mechanics of quoting from a source.

Appendix 1: PHRASAL VERBS

ORDER OF CHAPTER	CHARTS	EXERCISES	WORKBOOK
Preview		Ex. 1	
Introduction	A1-1	Ex. 2 → 4	
Phrasal verbs: separable and nonseparable (Groups A → E)		Ex. 5 → 15	Pr. 1 → 10
Phrasal verbs: intransitive (Group F)	A1-2	Ex. 16 → 17	Pr. 11 → 12
Three-word phrasal verbs (Groups G and H)	A1-3	Ex. 18 → 19	Pr. 13 → 16
Reference list of phrasal verbs	A1-4		
Cumulative review			Pr. 17

General Notes on Appendix 1

• Phrasal verbs are presented in an appendix so that the teacher may dip into its units when it best fits into her or his lesson plans.

The Appendix presents the phrasal verbs in groups so that students can concentrate on learning only a limited number at a time. In the previous edition, the phrasal verbs came at the ends of various chapters in order to intersperse them through the term. Now they are gathered in an appendix to allow the teacher flexibility in their use.

• TERMINOLOGY: A phrasal verb consists of a verb and a particle (or two particles) that in fixed combination have a single meaning. Phrasal verbs are also called "two-word / three-word verbs" or sometimes "prepositional verbs."

A particle (simply defined as a "small word" in the text) is either a preposition (e.g., *off, on)* or an adverb of direction or position (e.g., *away, back)*.

☐ EXERCISE 1, p. 431. Preview: phrasal verbs. (Chart A1-1)

This preview introduces the concept of what a phrasal verb is: two words with one meaning.

ANSWERS:

2. on
3. back *(also possible:* away)
4. off
5. up
6. on . . . off
7. back
8. on . . . off

CHART A1-1: PHRASAL VERBS: INTRODUCTION

• The text introduces the concept of phrasal verbs and explains the difference between separable and nonseparable. It is beyond the scope of this text to present more than just a few of the hundreds of phrasal verbs in English. Chart A1-4 contains an alphabetical list of the 109 phrasal verbs introduced in the text.

• To give students an overview of the many meanings phrasal verbs can express in English, you might present the example ***put*** + *particle.* All of the following have different meanings, and some of them (such as *put on)* have a variety of meanings: *put about, put across, put aside, put at, put away, put back, put down, put forth, put in, put off, put on, put out, put through, put to, put together, put under.* Students will understand this is an area of English that will take some time to master. The text offers them a starting point. Experience is the best teacher.

Dictionaries written for second language students are good sources of information about the meanings of phrasal verbs.

• Phrasal verbs are typical of informal usage. They are especially common in speech, but also find their way into many kinds of writing. In formal reporting or academic writing, phrasal verbs are used minimally.

☐ EXERCISE 2, p. 432. Phrasal verbs: separable vs. nonseparable. (Charts A1-1 and A1-4)

ANSWERS:

3. SEPARABLE
4. NONSEPARABLE
5. SEPARABLE
6. NONSEPARABLE
7. SEPARABLE
8. SEPARABLE

☐ EXERCISE 3, p. 433. Identifying phrasal verbs. (Chart A1-1)

ANSWERS:

3. up
4. over
5. in
6. up
7. up
8. on
9. up
10. up
11. down . . . off

☐ EXERCISE 4, p. 433. Phrasal verbs: separable vs. nonseparable. (Chart A1-1)

ANSWERS:

3. it off . . . SEP
4. them down . . . SEP
5. into him . . . NONSEP
6. it out . . . SEP
7. them off . . . SEP
8. over it . . . NONSEP
9. them off . . . SEP
10. it away . . . SEP

☐ EXERCISE 5, p. 434. Phrasal verbs. (Group A)

ANSWERS:

2. off
3. in
4. up
5. off
6. up
7. down
8. up
9. out
10. up
11. off
12. on
13. out
14. down
15. away/out

☐ EXERCISE 6, p. 435. Phrasal verbs. (Group A)

ANSWERS:

2. it up
3. her up
4. them away/out
5. it off
6. it up
7. them in
8. it down
9. it out
10. you down
11. it up
12. it on . . . it off
13. them out
14. it on

☐ EXERCISE 7, p. 436. Phrasal verbs. (Group B)

ANSWERS:

2. into
3. over
4. on . . . off
5. in . . . out of
6. on . . . off
7. into
8. from

☐ EXERCISE 8, p. 436. Review: phrasal verbs. (Groups A and B)

ANSWERS:

2. them off
3. it up . . . it down
4. it out
5. it on
6. into him
7. it away/out . . . on me . . . it up
8. into it

☐ EXERCISE 9, p. 437. Review: phrasal verbs. (Groups A and B)

ANSWERS:

1. it down
2. on me
3. it down
4. it up
5. it off
6. them on
7. it off
8. it up
9. into him/her
10. it off
11. it in
12. him/her up
13. it out
14. it away/out
15. over it
16. it up
17. a bus, a train, a plane
18. a car, a taxi
19. a bus, a train, a plane
20. a car, a taxi
21. a light, a radio, a computer
22. a light, a radio, a computer

☐ EXERCISE 10, p. 438. Phrasal verbs. (Group C)

ANSWERS:

2. it down
3. it up
4. him up
5. you back
6. it up
7. it off
8. it back
9. it out
10. me out
11. it back
12. them away (*also possible:* back)
13. it off
14. it on
15. it back

☐ EXERCISE 11, p. 439. Review: phrasal verbs. (Groups A, B, and C)

ANSWERS:

1. it up
2. it up
3. it out
4. them on
5. it in
6. her out
7. it off
8. it up
9. it off
10. it off
11. it down (*also possible:* off)
12. them out
13. it off
14. it up
15. it up
16. it on
17. him/her up
18. them away (*also possible:* back)
19. them away / out
20. it on

☐ EXERCISE 12, p. 440. Phrasal verbs. (Group D)

ANSWERS:

2. out
3. over . . . out
4. out
5. out . . . out
6. up
7. in
8. out
9. up
10. down
11. on
12. out
13. around/back

☐ EXERCISE 13, p. 441. Phrasal verbs. (Group D)

ANSWERS:

1. out
2. over
3. out
4. out
5. out
6. down
7. up
8. over
9. around/back
10. up
11. out
12. in
13. on
14. out

☐ EXERCISE 14, p. 442. Phrasal verbs. (Group E)

ANSWERS:

2. off
3. out
4. out
5. over
6. on
7. out
8. up
9. up
10. back
11. back
12. on
13. up
14. over
15. away
16. out

☐ EXERCISE 15, p. 443. Phrasal verbs. (Group E)

ANSWERS:

1. back
2. off
3. out
4. over
5. on
6. away
7. out
8. back
9. up
10. on
11. over
12. out
13. up
14. up
15. back
16. out

CHART A1-2: PHRASAL VERBS: INTRANSITIVE

• Some phrasal verbs that are commonly intransitive also have transitive uses and meanings: for example, *Digestive juices* ***break down food particles***. *The celebrants* ***broke out a bottle*** *of bubbly. The police* ***broke up the fight***. To simplify the students' learning task, the text limits the information presented about possible uses and meanings of phrasal verbs, in this instance presenting only the intransitive uses of this selected list.

☐ EXERCISE 16, p. 444. Phrasal verbs. (Group F)

ANSWERS:

2. on
3. out
4. up
5. up
6. in . . . in . . . down
7. down
8. up
9. up
10. out
11. out
12. down
13. up
14. up
15. up
16. out . . . in
17. up
18. up
19. over
20. off

☐ EXERCISE 17, p. 446. Phrasal verbs. (Group F)

ANSWERS:

1. up
2. out
3. up
4. up
5. down
6. down
7. down
8. back
9. up
10. up
11. on
12. out
13. in
14. out
15. up
16. up
17. up
18. off

CHART A1-3: THREE-WORD PHRASAL VERBS
• Some phrasal verbs expand into three words. The basic meaning doesn't change with the addition of the second particle, but an intransitive verb becomes transitive.

☐ EXERCISE 18, p. 447. Phrasal verbs. (Group G)

ANSWERS:

3. up
4. up in
5. out of
6. around
7. back from
8. out of
9. out for
10. done with
11. in on
12. along with
13. up for . . . up

☐ EXERCISE 19, p. 448. Phrasal verbs. (Group H)

ANSWERS:

2. together
3. around/out with
4. over to
5. out about
6. out
7. away from
8. over
9. out
10. back to
11. around

CHART A1-4: PHRASAL VERBS: A REFERENCE LIST
• This chart provides a list of the phrasal verbs used throughout Appendix 1. It's designed as a quick and easy reference for students. The principal criterion used in selecting which phrasal verbs to present in the text was their frequency of use.

Appendix 2: PREPOSITION COMBINATIONS

ORDER OF CHAPTER	CHARTS	EXERCISES	WORKBOOK
Introduction	A2-1		
Preview		Ex. 1	
Preposition combinations Groups A → G		Ex. 2 → 12	Pr. 1 → 14
Reference list of preposition combinations	A2-2		
Cumulative review			Pr. 15 → 16

General Notes on Appendix 2

• Prepositions can be humorously defined as "small words that cause second language learners a lot of trouble." Most students will smile at that definition. Students often ask how they can learn prepositions. Lots of practice and long-term experience with the language are the essentials.

General definitions of individual prepositions can be attempted, but overall there is usually no easy, logical explanation for why one preposition and not another is used in combination with a particular verb or adjective. To give students some sense of how varied and complex prepositions are, have them look up *at* or *in* in a dictionary: the listings are voluminous.

• The purpose of this Appendix is to give the students small chunks of preposition combinations to deal with at a time, manageable units to memorize (if that's their strategy), to practice, to review, and to practice again. The *Workbook* offers additional self-study practice.

• TERMINOLOGY: The text does not define *preposition* because it is very difficult to define, especially for the purposes of second language learners. Perhaps teachers who have found a definition of a preposition that works for their students could share it with the rest of us on the Azar Web site: **http://www.longman.com/azar**.

CHART A2-1: PREPOSITION COMBINATIONS: INTRODUCTION

• This chart introduces the content of this appendix: combinations of prepositions with adjectives and verbs. Sometimes preposition combinations correspond to those in a students' native language, but often they do not. Sometimes correct prepositions can be guessed, but often not. Sometimes English uses a preposition where another language does not, and vice versa. The approach in this textbook is for the students to learn only a few at a time, then move on to another group and learn those.

☐ EXERCISE 1, p. 453. Preview: preposition combinations. (Chart A2-2)

Ask the students to complete this exercise in their seats, then discuss the correct answers. The main purpose of this exercise is to make sure the students know what the term "preposition" refers to.

ANSWERS:

2. with	7. with	12. for
3. of	8. to	13. with
4. about	9. of	14. from
5. with	10. of	15. with
6. about	11. to	

☐ SELF-STUDY PRACTICE, p. 454. Group A.

Demonstrate what the student is supposed to do: cover the answers and complete the sentences first, then cover the answers and the sentences and complete the reference list.

Rather than simply giving a list, the text seeks to maximize student exposure and practice by involving them in the creation of the reference list. This approach allows quick self-testing and immediate reinforcement.

Some students probably won't follow the directions to cover the answers and will "cheat," thus depriving themselves of an opportunity to gain learning experience with preposition combinations. It's up to the student to take the responsibility.

The directions given in this practice are to be followed in all the self-study practices in this appendix.

☐ EXERCISE 2, p. 454. Preposition combinations. (Group A)

Follow class discussion of the correct answers with a quick oral drill in which you give the first part of the sentence and the students call out the preposition:

TEACHER: *Mr. Porter is nice . . . .*
STUDENTS: *to*
TEACHER: *to everyone.*

ANSWERS:

2. from	6. to	9. to	12. for
3. for	7. to	10. with	13. about
4. at/with	8. for	11. about	14. of
5. of			

☐ EXERCISE 3, p. 455. Review: preposition combinations. (Group A)

This technique of having students create quizzes (as yet another way of giving them practice) can be used for every group of preposition combinations. This exercise is an example of what you can have students do routinely.

☐ EXERCISE 4, p. 455. Review: preposition combinations. (Group B)

Again, as in Exercise 2, follow class discussion of the correct answers with a quick oral drill in which you give the first part of the sentence and the students call out the preposition. Use this oral drill technique for each group and for frequent oral reviews.

TEACHER: *I borrowed this dictionary . . .*
STUDENTS: *from*
TEACHER: *from Pedro.*

ANSWERS:

1. from
2. with
3. to
4. at
5. in
6. at
7. for
8. with . . . about/over
9. with
10. for
11. for
12. at

☐ EXERCISE 5, p. 456. Preposition combinations. (Group C)

ANSWERS:

1. to
2. for
3. for
4. of
5. for . . . for
6. for
7. to . . . from
8. to
9. about . . . in
10. of/about
11. of

☐ EXERCISE 6, p. 457. Preposition combinations. (Group D)

ANSWERS:

1. for
2. from
3. for
4. on
5. with
6. in
7. at
8. to
9. of
10. to
11. to . . . about
12. with
13. to . . . about

☐ EXERCISE 7, p. 458. Review: preposition combinations. (Groups A and B)

ANSWERS:

1. to
2. A: from
   B: for
3. A: to
   B: at
4. to
5. of
6. from . . . for
7. A: in
   B: with
8. A: for . . . with
   B: to

☐ EXERCISE 8, p. 458. Review: preposition combinations. (Groups A, B, C, and D)

ANSWERS:

1. about
2. from
3. of
4. to . . . with
5. to
6. for
7. from
8. with
9. with
10. to
11. in
12. at
13. for . . . at
14. at
15. A: with . . . about/over
    C: to
    A: to . . . about . . . with

☐ EXERCISE 9, p. 460. Preposition combinations. (Group E)

ANSWERS:

1. with
2. to
3. from
4. about
5. to
6. about/of
7. at
8. for
9. for
10. for
11. about
12. to
13. about

☐ **EXERCISE 10, p. 461. Preposition combinations. (Group F)**

ANSWERS:

1. to . . . for
2. for
3. of
4. for
5. on
6. for
7. on
8. to/with
9. from
10. on
11. of
12. to
13. from
14. of/from

☐ **EXERCISE 11, p. 462. Preposition combinations. (Group G)**

ANSWERS:

1. on
2. from
3. about
4. for
5. about
6. from
7. to . . . about
8. to
9. into
10. from
11. by
12. to
13. about
14. from

☐ **EXERCISE 12, p. 462. Review: preposition combinations. (Groups E, F, and G)**

ANSWERS:

1. on
2. about
3. with
4. from
5. from
6. to . . . for
7. of
8. to
9. from
10. to
11. for
12. of/from
13. from
14. on
15. on
16. of
17. about
18. for
19. to
20. to

CHART A2-2: PREPOSITION COMBINATIONS: A REFERENCE LIST
• This chart provides a list of the preposition combinations used throughout Appendix 2. It's designed as a quick and easy reference for students.

Index